Stories from the Old Testament
Volume I

THE CLASSIC BIBLE BOOKS SERIES

Forthcoming

++

STORIES FROM THE OLD TESTAMENT
VOLUME I
From Moses to King Saul

++

Partially abridged from the text of the Revised English Bible

INTRODUCED AND EDITED BY LAWRENCE BOADT
FOREWORD BY MONICA FURLONG

St. Martin's Griffin
New York

STORIES FROM THE OLD TESTAMENT: *VOLUME I*
FROM MOSES TO KING SAUL

Copyright © Lion Publishing, 1997. All rights reserved. Printed in the United States of America. No part of this book may be used or reproduced in any manner whatsoever without written permission except in the case of brief quotations embodied in critical articles or reviews. For information, address St. Martin's Press, 175 Fifth Avenue, New York, N.Y. 10010.

ISBN 0-312-22509-1 cloth
ISBN 0-312-22108-8 paperback

Library of Congress Cataloging-in-Publication Data

Stories from the Old Testament / introduction by Lawrence Boadt.
    p.   cm. -- (The Classic Bible series)
  "Partially abridged from the text of the Revised English Bible."
  Includes indexes.
  Contents: v. 1. From Moses to King Saul -- v. 2. From King David to the return from exile.
  ISBN 0-312-22108-8 (v. 1). -- ISBN 0-312-22110-X (v. 2)
  1. Bible stories, English--O.T. I. Boadt, Lawrence. II. Series.
BS550.2.S75 1999
221.9'505--dc21

99-28746
CIP

First published in Great Britain by Lion Publishing plc, 1997.
First St. Martin's Griffin edition: September 1999
10 9 8 7 6 5 4 3 2 1

Contents

ACKNOWLEDGMENTS

The Introduction has been taken from *Reading the Old Testament: An Introduction* by Lawrence Boadt, copyright © 1984 by permission of Paulist Press.

The text of 'Stories from the Old Testament in Literature' has been selected from *A Dictionary of Biblical Tradition in English Literature*, edited by David Lyle Jeffrey, copyright © 1992 by permission of Wm B. Eerdmans Publishing Co.

The abridged text of 'Stories from the Old Testament' (except Ruth, which is unabridged) has been taken from the Revised English Bible copyright © 1989 by permission of Oxford and Cambridge University Presses.

Foreword

My parents were not in the least religious and I learned first about the Bible and Christianity from what Winston Churchill called 'County Council religion', i.e. I was taught about it at my Mixed Infants and Junior state school from an early age. It turned out to be one of the best and most influential bits of my whole education. In those days Bible teaching was not kiddyfied, or not much, and at six or seven years old, we were expected to learn the 23rd and 121st Psalms by heart (the Authorised Version). I liked them and I found that they stuck in my memory.

At about the same time we were told the stories of Moses and his successors right through to Solomon. I was profoundly affected by the story of the burning bush and the great, mysterious reply: I AM. It has continued to haunt me all my life. A few years ago I camped with a party of friends in the Sinai desert, and starting from the Red Sea, moved across the desert to Mount Sinai which we climbed, partly on camel, partly by foot. We also visited the supposed site of the miracle of the burning bush, and there I recognized what I already partly knew, that this story of the revelation of God has become one of the roots of my being. To this day if I think about it, I can feel the hairs rising on the back of my neck, in a mixture of panic and awe. I know of no piece of spiritual literature in which the sense of the encounter with God is so strong as in that story, or in the account of Moses' subsequent partial glimpse of God 'in a cleft of the rock', or the time when the people of Israel witnessed 'the glory of the Lord... like a devouring fire on the top of the mountain.' To the small child that I was when I first learned about all this, it seemed both natural and entirely wonderful.

The story of Exodus is full of the space and silence and heat of the desert, and the wind, gentle or fierce, in which 'the still small voice' becomes terribly eloquent. That beautiful emptiness becomes the setting for plants and rocks, animals and birds, sun, moon, and stars which stand out like jewels. The simplicities of hunger and thirst, sunrise and sunset, make it possible for God, and the response to God, to take over. There, to this day, even for a postmodern person, the trivialities of our culture fall away before the naked momentary awareness of I AM.

The journey of the children of Israel from the slavery of Egypt to the Promised Land, with all its terrors, hopes, failures and its eventual success, is an archetypal account of what it is to escape from slavery, whether the slavery of race, institution, oppression, family, or the slavery of our own fears and addictions. The Hebrews, the noblest, most spiritually mature of peoples, were 'chosen' to make this pilgrimage on our behalf, and this makes some of us revere them for ever, but in another sense we are all chosen, and we all have our own Exodus to make in order to discover our identity and our 'place'. It is an immense, but absorbing effort, and the only sad people are the ones who never discover the need.

What is so encouraging about the biblical account is that the chosen people are not perfect. They are fearful, whingeing, sometimes faithless, and they are terrible worriers, convinced at every point that they are about to starve, die of thirst, be killed by the local inhabitants, as well as suffer various other dreadful fates. Yet somehow, because of Moses, or in spite of themselves, their remarkable, inescapable sense of God holds them to their course – they are intimate with this reality in a way that we have forgotten how to be – and in pain and terror and occasional ecstasy they make their way to the Promised Land.

What succeeds the epic journey is almost as fascinating as the journey itself since it describes the difficulty of building and maintaining a stable society, threatened as it is, as every society is, by greed, corruption, and lust for power, which damage the delicate networks of love and justice – caring for the poor, for the widows and orphans, in a way the Bible insists upon. As a child I was fascinated by the dynamic Saul, beloved of God, yet forfeiting his relationship by wrongdoing, and gradually being taken over by paranoid moods and a murderous hatred for David. The emotions are ones we can recognize in ourselves and in modern societies, and the Old Testament, so straightforward, so unmealy-mouthed, paints them for us in stark detail.

Detail, of another kind, is one of the most fascinating things about reading Bible texts closely for ourselves, and not just relying upon films or broad 'tellings' of the story. I love, for example, the way Moses tries to avoid any sort of exposure as a public speaker or spokesperson, and even when God assures him that he will help him, he still cannot quite find the courage to do it, and begs for Aaron's help. There is a Jewish tradition that Moses was a stammerer – pleading before Pharaoh must have seemed a formidable requirement.

Then there is the fascinating detail of the Ark of the Covenant – the travelling shrine or 'sanctuary' of divinity in the midst of all Israel's journeyings, where 'the bread of the Presence' and other sacred objects were kept. It was made of acacia wood – still the only wood that grows in the Sinai – together with gold, silver, 'blue and purple and scarlet stuff and fine twisted linen', tanned skins, fragrant incense, oil for the lamps, spices for the anointing oils, jewels and fine needlework. All this was fashioned into a curtained tabernacle in which veils separated 'the holy place from the most holy'. It was the forerunner of the static Temple in Jerusalem which succeeded it.

These early chapters of the Bible are primarily about mystery – the call or compulsion or attraction that invites people to seek, and find, God. There is much else besides – wonderful stories, like those of Ruth, or of Balaam, which reveal to us the choices and dilemmas of individuals – but the call is primary. We are invited, just as the Hebrews were, to make our Exodus in order to meet God, and it is in our response to the invitation that we discover our own identity.

Monica Furlong

INTRODUCTION

Egypt in the Period of the Exodus

The book of Genesis ends with the Hebrews settled prosperously in the land of Goshen, a fertile section of the Nile Delta nearest to Palestine. Egyptian records tell of Asiatic settlers there in almost every century. But in the 18th century BC, the flow of peoples from Asia Minor became more intense; possibly more war-like, they overwhelmed the weak Egyptian defences. Later Egyptian writings remembered bitterly the next 200 years of foreign rule by the Hyksos, literally, the 'foreign chiefs'.

But a new age dawned for Egypt when she finally overthrew the Hyksos under King Ahmose of Thebes about 1550BC. The princes of Thebes, far up the Nile from the Delta, had managed to stay nearly independent of the Hyksos, and gradually strengthened their position as the foreigners became weaker. Upon his final victory, Ahmose began a new dynasty, the 18th, which ushered in a glorious era of conquest in both Asia and Africa.

Under a skilled series of kings, all of them named either Thutmoses or Amenophis, Egypt expanded her empire to include the Sudan, Libya, Palestine and most of Syria. Wealth flowed to her from all over the known world, including Asiatic craftsmen, traders, ambassadors and prisoners in greater numbers than had been true under Hyksos rule. While Semites who had stayed on in the Delta area, and most newcomers, were no doubt subjected to rigorous supervision, and perhaps at times virtual slavery, there is no reason to believe that Egypt systematically tried to exclude foreigners from her soil. The evidence shows the opposite. Semitic influences in religion and culture increased enormously under the 18th dynasty (also called the *New Kingdom*).

Israel's time in Egypt

Exodus 1:8 says only, 'A new king came to power in Egypt who did not know Joseph.' The Israelites became persecuted and enslaved.

But when did this begin? One possibility is at the time when the foreign Hyksos were driven out in 1550BC. This could mean a long period of hardship. But Exodus 1 seems to indicate a fairly short period of actual persecution just before the actual escape. Since experts do not agree on the meaning of the dates and events mentioned in the exodus story, several quite different positions are argued for in books about the exodus. The two most common dates suggested are (1) between 1450–1350BC and (2) between 1300–1250BC. The latter is the more favoured today. Those who favour the earlier dates, however, point to the Amarna letters as evidence that groups of Apiru/Hebrews were already in Palestine by 1350. They also argue that the most likely time for a persecution of a Semitic tribe was shortly after the Egyptian defeat of the Hyksos and not much later. There is further evidence for Semitic slaves in the period between 1500 and 1400 at Serabit el Khadem, an Egyptian turquoise mine in the Sinai desert. The rocks nearby were covered with inscriptions written by Semitic workers in the mines. Finally, they point to the date suggested by 1 Kings 6:1 that Solomon dedicated the temple 480 years after Israel left Egypt. If the temple is to be placed about 950BC, this would mean an exodus date about 1430BC.

Those who maintain a date between 1300 and 1250 also point to specific evidence inside and outside the Bible. Exodus 1:11 clearly states that the Israelites were forced to build the store cities of Ramses and Pithom. Although archaeology has not yet definitely located these sites, Egyptian records reveal that they were building projects started by the founders of the 19th dynasty, Seti I and his son Rameses II, between 1310 and 1300. They moved the capital of Egypt from Thebes to the Delta's border with the Sinai desert in order to better direct military campaigns in Palestine and Syria. Moreover, proponents of the late date can point to the famous victory inscription of Pharaoh Merneptah, Rameses II's son, which dates to 1212 or so, mentioning his victory over Israel:

> The princes are prostrate, saying: 'Mercy!'
> Not one raises his head among the Nine Bows.
> Desolation is for Tehunu: Hatti is pacified;
> Plundered is the Canaan with every evil;

Carried off is Ashkelon; seized upon is Gezer;
Yanoam is made as that which does not exist;
Israel is laid waste, his seed is not;
Hurru has become a widow for Egypt![1]

Since Israel is marked with the sign for a tribe or clan, and not for a city or land, scholars argue that this means the Israelites had not yet settled down fully by 1225–1220BC.

A date for the exodus in the reign of Rameses II, sometime between 1300 and 1280, seems the most likely. It would fit the notice in Exodus 12:40 that Israel had been in Egypt 430 years, ie, since about 1700BC when the Hyksos took control of the country. But the biblical story does not depend on the certainty of the exact date. The drama of a people or clan escaping in the Sinai desert was probably a common occurrence, and several Egyptian documents actually mention attempts to stop such groups.[2] We do not expect to ever find mention of Moses or the exodus in Egyptian records of either the 15th or 14th centuries. What set this escape off from all others like it was the religious encounter with God that it involved *for Israel*. Egypt probably did not even realize this aspect at all. However, Egypt had a profound influence on Israel – even many of the names of Hebrews in the book of Exodus are Egyptian: Phineas, Hophni, Merari, and Moses himself (similar to Pharaohs Thut*moses* and Ah*moses*)! The Israel that took part in the exodus, whether a small group or large, whether early or late, always defined herself *in contrast* to the ways of Egypt.

The Book of Exodus

The book of Exodus is divided into several distinct episodes:
1. The childhood and call of Moses.
2. The struggle to free Israel by plagues, climaxing in the passover.
3. The escape and journey into the wilderness of Sinai.
4. The giving of the covenant and its laws.
5. The instructions for building the ark and the tent of meeting, and their execution.

There is a dramatic element to this story that cannot be overlooked. We are asked to see the hopelessness of the Hebrew situation, the almost impossible struggle to change the pharaoh's mind, the power of Yahweh and his total mastery of events at the show-down at the Red Sea, the bitter disappointment and forgetfulness of Israel in the desert, and the final, compelling show of divine majesty and offer of a covenant at Sinai. All of this is told from the viewpoint of Moses the leader. And yet, although Moses is certainly the hero of the story, he never claims the credit. He always appears instead as an instrument of God. The drama and tension of the story centre on whether God will act at this moment or not. We never doubt who runs the show, but only when he will choose to reveal his plan. At times we even despair over Moses and Aaron and the people for their hard-headed behaviour, their faults and lack of insight into what is happening.

In short, Israel narrates the story of the exodus to glorify God who saves. To modern readers, much of the biblical story seems harsh and primitive and too violent and warlike. But in a world where the weak had little protection and fewer rights, a God who can fight for his people and defend them is the God who receives worship. The Israelite story frankly praises God as a warrior, as *the* warrior. His military prowess is miraculous; he leads, he defeats enemies, he even marches triumphantly to his own holy mountain and receives his people's obedience and praise there. It is summed up in the victory hymn of Miriam at the Red Sea (Exodus 15:1–3):

> I shall sing to the Lord, for he has risen up in triumph,
> horse and rider he has hurled into the sea.
> The Lord is my refuge and my defence,
> he has shown himself my deliverer.
> He is my God, and I shall glorify him;
> my father's God, and I shall exalt him.
> The Lord is a warrior; the Lord is his name.

The Sinai Covenant

The Hebrew word *berit*, which is used most often to express the idea of a covenant, originally meant a 'shackle' or 'chain', but it came to be any form of binding agreement. It expresses the solemn *contract* between Jacob and Laban in Genesis 31:44, or the *alliance* of friendship between David and Jonathan in 1 Samuel 18:3. It describes the *peace pact* made by Abraham with a whole tribe of Amorites in Genesis 14:13, and the *bond of marriage* in Proverbs 2:17 or Malachi 2:14. And it can be a solemn *treaty* between kings, as is the case with Solomon and Hiram of Tyre in 1 Kings 5, or with Ahab and Benhadad of Syria in 1 Kings 20:34. But most often it is used of the special alliance between Yahweh and Israel.

Berit is a term so rich it captures the heart of Israel's religious beliefs: (1) they are bound to an unbreakable covenant-union with their God; (2) he has made known his love and his mercy to them; (3) he has given them commandments to guide their daily life; (4) they owe him worship, fidelity and obedience; (5) they are marked by the sign of that covenant-bond. The covenant created the unity of the nation Israel, based not on blood relationship but on submission to the divine will and the confession that he alone is God. In turn, God pledges himself to be Israel's personal protector and helper, not only against foreign enemies, but against sickness, disease, and chaos as well. Most of all, he will be present whether it is a time of prosperity or of failure, for he has laid claim to this people as his own. Yahweh is a personal God who demands personal loyalty. He gives no guarantee that his protective love and help always involves victory in battle, wealth in possessions, or increase of territory; it may at times include such gifts, but more often it describes the blessing that trust in the Lord will bring: freedom from fear in the promised land, the fruitfulness of children and crops, permanent peace and the joy of knowing God is near.

The Pentateuch as Law

Study of Israel's Laws reveals much about the daily life and customs of the people. Above all, we can distinguish between two large classes of law: *case law* and *apodictic law*. Case law (or casuistic law) follows the pattern of: *If* someone does this thing, *then* he receives this punishment.

Such laws are common everywhere in the ancient world, based on the problems of everyday conflicts. For each possible offence or case of dispute, a proper penalty or fine is worked out.

On the other hand, the ten commandments and the cult laws of Exodus 34 give no conditions and no suggested penalties. They are strong, dramatic demands made upon the believer with an unstated, but threatening, hint that disobedience will be severely dealt with. In ancient society, they may well reflect the commands of tribal leaders to all members of the clan. On the other hand, such direct proclamation of basic divine law is what would be expected during the celebration of the liturgy. In any case, the only expected answer is a firm 'Amen' said in trust. Although these laws are not found only in Israelite tradition, they do reflect *the special character of covenant obedience*. They are not open to compromise or discussion as is case law, but must be solemnly accepted. The ten commandments stand out among such apodictic laws both by their solemn form and by their precise number, easily counted and remembered on the fingers.

Both case law and apodictic law have very old roots in the Near East, but we can be quite sure that we are close indeed to the original directives of Moses himself in the first two commands of the ten, for they are so distinctively Israelite: Yahweh alone is God, no other gods are to be worshipped; and no images are to be made of him or of any other gods.

The Book of Deuteronomy

The final book of the Pentateuch[3] is Deuteronomy, which is written as the last speech and warning by Moses to the people on how to live in the land they are about to conquer. It was composed in the 7th century as a kind of commentary on the meaning of the Pentateuch and as a summary of its message. Looking back from the troubled times of the last kings of Judah, it offered hope to a discouraged 7th-century Israel, a new chance to obey the covenant and a lesson that God's punishment was not final. For these reasons, it stresses the divine word that never fails. It stands apart from the story structure of Genesis to Numbers in the form of a warning speech. It emphasizes how God tested Israel in the early days of its existence, yet did not destroy the people no matter how often they failed. The real meaning of the years in the desert can be found in the lesson God himself had taught there: 'A person does not live by bread alone, but by every word that proceeds from the mouth of Yahweh' (Deuteronomy 8:2–3).

The Book of Joshua

The book of Joshua falls naturally into two major sections. Chapters 2–12 describe the miraculous conquest of the land by the tribes under Joshua's leadership, and chapters 13–22 tell how Joshua divided the land among the tribes and settled all the boundary and territorial disputes. But the collectors of these traditions have added a preface in chapter 1 and an epilogue in chapters 23–24 which set the meaning of these events in a theological context. Both are done in the forms of speeches by Joshua himself. In chapter 1, he promises that God will make the victory possible if the people will obey the law given by Moses which they have accepted (see the details of this law in the book of Deuteronomy). In chapters 23–24, Joshua gives his final words, his last will and testament, in which he exhorts Israel to remain faithful after his death, and makes the people solemnly renew their covenant promise to God.

From the description in Joshua 2–12, we might easily get the impression that the conquest was swift and decisive, and that Israel's armies were able to defeat every opponent.

However, we must be cautious about the book of Joshua's account of Israel's invasion of the land. For one thing, the land area that Joshua captures is far less than the land he divides among the tribes. No mention is made in chapters 2–12 about taking Shechem or the central hill country, nor of capturing any cities on the coastal plains, nor of taking many major cities in the Jezreel Valley in the north. Despite his victories over the kings of some major strongholds such as Megiddo, Taanach and Gezer, short references in the second half of the book make it clear that Israel often failed to drive out the Canaanites because they had walled cities and chariot brigades (see

13:2–6; 15:63; 16:10; 17:11–13; 17:16–18). Many areas were only half conquered, and the biggest victories seemed to be in the mountain areas on the eastern part of the land. The book of Joshua idealizes the early victories but the reality at first fell far short of this account.

The reason for such an exalted telling of the story lies in the religious purpose of the book. Israel was not fighting on its own; it was God who gave the help and strength for this small band of tribes to overcome much more powerful enemies. Even if the battles gave Israel control over only a quarter of the land that the book describes, the victory was unbelievable unless God had helped. The city and town lists given for each tribe come from a later time when people were well established in the land and probably describe the settled conditions of the Israelites near the time of David about 1000BC. They reveal an Israel that claimed title to the whole land of Palestine because they had won it with the help of God who fought on their side. Just as the exodus story speaks about God as a warrior who fights on behalf of his people (Exodus 15), so the story of the conquest portrays God directing the battles needed to gain a foothold in the territory controlled by the Canaanites.

The people responsible for carrying on the ancient traditions of the conquest emphasized that the victories came from God and that Joshua and the tribes followed God's directions carefully and always dedicated their military victories as a sacrifice to God in thanksgiving for his aid. This is the terrible custom of the 'ban', called in Hebrew a *herem*, in which the Israelites were to slay everyone in the defeated towns. It was practised to show that Israel put all its trust in God alone during the war and sought nothing for itself.

The Book of Judges

The book of Judges continues the story of Israel's conquest and gradual occupation of the whole land. It tells the stories and legends of Israel's time of tribal life in Palestine which lasted about 200 years, from 1250 down to a little after 1050BC.

Altogether, the book follows the exploits of twelve judges during this period. Six are hardly more than names attached to a single incident only barely remembered: Shamgar, Tola, Jair, Ibzan, Elon and Abdon. As a result these are usually called the 'Minor Judges'. The other six are the 'Major Judges': Othniel, Ehud, Barak (with Deborah), Gideon, Jephthah and Samson. They were renowned for their brave exploits in battle and were really not legal judges primarily but warlords. They were leaders who arose in times of great need and led the tribes to victory in one or more battles. Because God had marked them out charismatically, they stayed on to guide the tribes during the rest of their lifetimes. Because of their recognized authority as war leaders, they also exercised power in legal disputes between tribes and in political squabbles.

The opening two chapters make clear what we have already suspected from the book of Joshua – that the tribes did indeed fail to conquer many of the cities and people who dwelt in Palestine. They settled down instead to a long period of co-existence and only very gradually gained control over the Canaanites. In fact, it was not until the days of Saul and David, after the book of Judges ends, that Israel began making really significant gains again as they had under Joshua.

The editors who recorded these traditions saw that the period of the judges represented a spirit of compromise with the pagan culture of the land. It was the greatest sin of the tribes and one which would be repeated again and again in Israel's later history. For this reason, the editors repeatedly used a pattern to describe the period: *the people sin, bring down Yahweh's wrath upon themselves, later repent, are delivered by a judge sent by God, and finally gain peace while the judge lives*. Naturally the real history of the times was much more complex, with many ups and downs that are not recorded in this book. It seems that most of the stories we do have involved only a few tribes and came from local memories rather than from wars waged by Israel as a whole. These were passed on orally at first among the tribes, and some have developed into full-blown hero legends in which the judge is bigger and more glorious than any normal person. Such is the case with the story of Gideon in Judges 6–8 and of Samson in Judges 13–16.

The picture that emerges shows an Israelite confederation of twelve tribes still struggling to find unity among themselves at the same time as they fought for footholds in different parts of the Canaanite territory. It was a time of small local wars and defensive fighting against desert nomads. The Song of Deborah in Judges 5 reveals that often one or more of the tribes would not come to the aid of others. The violent story of Abimelech in Judges 9 and the terrible incident of the Benjaminites in chapters 19–21 both picture tribes in open conflict with one another. Strife was the name of the game throughout the age of the judges. As one writer has remarked, it was like the wild west of American folklore.

The Book of Ruth

The book of Ruth appears in our Bible right after the book of Judges because its heroine is an ancestor of King David, whose story is told in the following books of 1 and 2 Samuel. It tells of an Israelite woman, Naomi, who marries a Moabite man and goes to live in his country. They have two sons who marry local Moabite women. But soon Naomi loses her husband and both sons in death, and she decides to return home to Israel. One daughter-in-law, Ruth, although a Moabitess, decides to follow Naomi and serve her needs, even though she would be far from her own people. In this way Ruth gives a charming example of filial respect and care that eventually leads to her fortunate marriage with Boaz, the leading citizen of Naomi's hometown of Bethlehem. From their marriage will come the house of David.

The one thing that is certain about this book is that the story comes from a time long after the period of the judges. Like many children's fairy tales, it begins, 'Once upon a time when there were judges...' It also has great interest in tracing the roots of David and ends with a little genealogy that goes from Boaz to David.

While the story is probably based on an old tale preserved in the folklore about King David and his family which goes back to the 9th or 10th century, it is written in its present form in the post-exilic period, although a more exact date cannot be decided upon. The conflicts with the foreign wives may reflect the struggles over marriage in the days of Ezra and Nehemiah. And like the book of Jonah, it has an outlook definitely favourable to foreigners. It prefers the pious person, no matter whether Jew or Gentile!

Ruth is a short story of very fine style. The characters all bear symbolic names that almost make it an allegory. Ruth means 'companion'. Boaz means 'strength', and Orpah, the daughter-in-law who did not follow Naomi, means 'disloyal'. The book has a simple message about true faith in Yahweh. It is not blood or marriage that most matters, but faith. Ruth, although a Moabitess, is a perfect example of Israelite faithfulness at its best.

The Life of Samuel

The First and Second books of Samuel form a transition from the loose tribal league in force since the time of Joshua to the strong, centralized state forged by David and Solomon. The major figure in this period of change was Samuel, a prophetic and religious leader as well as the most important political voice of the late 11th century BC.

1 Samuel opens at the shrine of Shiloh, where Eli the priest guards the ark of the covenant so that members of the twelve tribes can come to worship on the great feast days of the year. One mother, Hannah, whom God has blessed with a child after many years of barrenness, dedicates her child to serve at the shrine under Eli. There the boy Samuel receives a special call from God and develops into both a priest and a seer. In a desperate moment, Eli allows the tribes to take the ark into battle against overwhelming Philistine forces, and the Philistines destroy Israel's forces, capture the ark and kill Eli's sons. This terrible defeat leads to Eli's own sudden death on hearing the news, and Samuel emerges as the one religious force in the country. He not only presides at sacrifices, uses his powers of 'seeing' to find lost objects, and 'judges' disputes, but effectively controls political decisions for the stunned and desperate tribes as well.

Chapters 8 through to 15 then move on to describe how Israel got a king. The danger from the Philistines was so great that the tribes themselves realized they would not have a chance unless their forces were united more effectively under a single military leader. They even lacked iron weapons such as the Philistines had, having to fight with less effective bronze (1 Samuel 13:19–22). The people begged Samuel to give them a king 'as other nations have' (1 Samuel 8:5). Samuel warns them of the dangers of giving so much power to one person, but they insist, and God gives in, telling Samuel: 'At this time tomorrow I shall send you a man from the territory of Benjamin, and you are to anoint him prince over my people Israel. He will deliver my people from the Philistines; for I have seen the sufferings of my people, and their cry has reached my ears' (1 Samuel 9:16). Yet only a chapter later, Samuel says, 'Today you have rejected your God who saved you from all your misery and distress; you have said, "No! Set a king over us"' (1 Samuel 10:19). Thus even the early traditions show a mixed reaction to the decision to have a king.

Most scholars see at least two separate strands of tradition. One can be called the *pro-Saul* version. It is found in 1 Samuel 9:1–10:16 and 11:1–15. The other version is an *anti-Saul* source found in 1 Samuel 8: 1–22, 10: 17–26 and 12: 1–25. The book's editors have joined these two accounts and made them into a statement which gives both sides of the issue. It reveals that Samuel was reluctant to have a king, but accepted the people's demands when God made the choice evident in Saul, who stood 'head and shoulders above the rest of Israel' (1 Samuel 9:2).

Saul proves himself a valiant warrior and manages to rescue the Israelites of Jabesh-gilead from the Ammonite army, and to win a number of battles against the Philistines, but he never manages to gain that final victory he needs to unite Israel. Meanwhile his own moody, rash temperament and lack of organizational ability become his undoing. He turns Samuel against him by his arrogance, he almost executes his own son Jonathan because of a rash oath he took, and he persecutes his own most promising young follower, David.

Lawrence Boadt

Notes

1. *Ancient Near Eastern Texts* 378.
2. *Ancient Near Eastern Texts* 259.
3. The first five books of the Bible (Genesis, Exodus, Leviticus, Numbers and Deuteronomy), traditionally referred to as the Five Books of Moses.

STORIES FROM THE OLD TESTAMENT IN LITERATURE

Characters and Events

Characters and Events

Aaron

The older brother of Moses, Aaron stayed in Egypt after Moses' flight to avoid prosecution for murder. Later, when at his call to service Moses pleaded a lack of eloquence (Exodus 4:10), God said that Aaron would be his spokesman; Aaron came out to meet Moses in the desert 'at the mountain of God' as Moses was en route back to Egypt (4:27). In cooperation with his brother, Aaron was instrumental in the subjection of Pharaoh and the exodus of the children of Israel from bondage. In a later incident, he, with Hur, held up Moses' hands over the battle scene until the Israelites had defeated the forces of Amalek (17:10, 12). When Moses went up onto Mount Sinai to receive the commandments, Aaron's career sank to its low point as he yielded to the clamour of the people for a tangible material god and allowed the building of the golden calf idol, which so angered Moses on his return that he smashed the two tablets of the Law (Exodus 32).

Chosen for the official priesthood, Aaron was anointed with the holy oil (Leviticus 8:12), and with his sons served in the Tabernacle. Only he, however, could enter into the Holy of Holies, once a year on the Day of Atonement, there to make sacrifice for the sins of the people (Deuteronomy 16:12–14).

Two further events are prominently associated with Aaron: the revolt of Korah and his confederates against Moses and Aaron, which was ended by the rebels being swallowed up in an earthquake and 14,700 of their allies dying of the plague, a number which would have been far greater, it is said, had not Aaron rushed into the midst of the dying with his smoking censer, standing between the living and the dead to offer atoning intercession (Numbers 16). Immediately following, all dissent concerning the right to the priesthood was ended when God commanded that a 'rod' (or staff) from each of the eleven tribes be laid with that of Aaron, as representative of the Levites, overnight near the Ark of the Covenant in the sanctuary. In the morning Aaron's rod blossomed, and put forth as well both leaves and ripe almonds (Numbers 17).

Aaron's iconographic attributes from the Middle Ages through Renaissance and baroque art include his rod, censer, and priestly vestments, especially the twelve-jewelled breastplate – the latter of which is the subject of lapidarial symbology in writers from Ambrose (*De fide*, 2, introduction 1–10) to Pope Innocent III (in his famous letter to King John). Also depicted are his garment with bells on the lower fringe, Urim and Thummim, and, when he signifies the Christian priesthood, his mitre. Occasionally he has a tiara, in which case he represents the Pope. In Protestant art after Calvin, especially in the Netherlands, his typical headdress becomes a turban, partly in reaction to Catholic ecclesiology and vestments.

The development of Aaronic typology after the Reformation reflects divergent ecclesiological concerns. In England, where Anglicanism preserved much if not all of the typology of the medieval Church, George Herbert can make one of his most powerful reflections on his own priesthood a contrast between the rich inward significance of Aaron's vestments and the poverty of his own spirit in the moments before divine service:

> Holinesse on the head,
> Light and perfections on the breast,
> Harmonious bells below, raising the dead
> To lead them unto life and rest:
> Thus are true Aarons drest.

But only when he can say 'Christ is my onely head, / My alone onely heart and breast', is he able to put off the burdens of the 'old man' and, his 'doctrine tun'd by Christ', face his congregation: 'Come people; Aaron's drest' ('Aaron').

In a contrasting assessment, Calvin comments on Hebrews 5:4 that 'it was clear that Aaron's priesthood had been temporary, and was due to cease'. He continues, making it clear that he has in mind the traditional analogy between Aaron and his sons and the doctrine of apostolic succession in connection with the priesthood of Rome: 'What then is to be said of Aaron and the rest of his successors? This, that they had as much right as was given to them by God, but not as much as men have given them according to their own thinking.'

Aaron has thus little role in works by writers like Milton and

Bunyan, although in *Pilgrim's Progress* Christian is warned about the 'sins of Korah' by Hope. It may be coincidental, but Shakespeare's Aaron in *Titus Andronicus* is the agent and virtual personification of evil ministrations. In *Absalom and Achitophel*, Dryden calls the rebel Levites 'Aaron's race', though six years later, in his Catholic phase, *The Hind and the Panther* satirizes Calvin ('In Israel some believe him whelp'd long since') as actually descended from Korah:

> When Corah with his brethren did conspire,
> From Moyses hand the Sov'reign sway to wrest,
> And Aaron of his Ephod to divest:
> Till opening Earth made way for all to pass,
> And cou'd not bear the burden of a class. (185–89)

Most 18th-century allusions are casual, such as Pope's reference in the *Essay on Man* to the danger of obsession: 'And hence one master passion in the breast, / Like Aaron's serpent, swallows up the rest.'

Relatively rarely, despite Dryden's imagination, does Aaron obtain the affection of the Protestant typologist. One exception in American literature is Cotton Mather, who describes an old pastor welcoming his successor in terms drawn from the divesture of Aaron from his priestly garments just before his death so that his son Eleazar could be invested (Numbers 20:12–29): 'The good Old Man like Old Aaron, as it were disrobed himself, with an unspeakable Satisfaction, when he beheld his Garments put upon a Son so dear to him' ('The Life of John Eliot'). This passage may also be in Joyce's mind, less charitably, when 'Mulligan is stripped of his garments' in the 'Telemachus' section of *Ulysses*. Melville, perhaps reflecting his rebellion against Calvinism, also identifies the Hebrews with Korah in an allusion to the fate of ships and crews likewise 'swallowed up' by the elements (*Moby Dick*, chapter 58). In *Democratic Vistas* Walt Whitman seems to be thinking of Aaron's rod when, in reference to capitalistic opportunities, he says that 'the magician's serpent in the fable ate up all the other serpents; and money making is our magician's serpent, remaining sole master of the field'. The episode of the golden calf is the one which may most provide an opportunity for psychological development of Aaron's character: it is tantalizingly seized upon by Arnold Schoenberg in his opera *Moses und Aron* (1930–32); the work remains, however, unfinished.

Aaron's rod rather than Aaron himself seems most to have endured in modern literary allusions. In D.H. Lawrence's novel *Aaron's Rod* (1922) the image is applied, with typical syncretism, to the ambiguous artistic and sexual liberation of the central character, Aaron Sisson. David Jones, however, in his *Sleeping Lord* sequence, recurs to 'the budding rod' of Aaron in its larger christological context (64), the *historia humanae salvationis*.

David L. Jeffrey
University of Ottawa

Burning Bush

The burning bush was the shrub which burst into flame yet was not consumed at the theophany on Mount Horeb where Moses heard the call to take up his vocation as a deliverer of his people (Exodus 3:2–22; cf. Deuteronomy 33:16). After the voice called and Moses answered, he was commanded, 'put off thy shoes from off thy feet, for the place whereon thou standest is holy ground' (v. 5); the voice was that of God, who identified himself: 'I Am that I Am' (v. 14).

Of the saintly lady to whom he dedicated his 'Death' elegy, Donne wrote that 'Her heart was that strange bush, where, sacred fire, / Religion, did not consume, but inspire' (45–46). Elizabeth Barrett Browning, for whom in *Aurora Leigh,* 'Nature comes sometimes / And says, "I am ambassador for God"' (7.493), 'Earth's crammed with heaven, / And every common bush afire with God, / But only he who sees takes off his shoes' (*Aurora Leigh,* 7.499; cf. Whittier's 'Miracle of Autumn' for a similar sentiment). Ralph Waldo Emerson in his 'Good-Bye' laughs

...at the love and pride of man,
At the sophist schools and the learned clan;
For what are they all in their high conceit,
When man in the bush with God may meet.

Although Flannery O'Connor makes an amusing but biblically significant allusion to the incident in 'Parker's Back', naturalism continues to characterize most 20th-century allusions. Willa Cather's prairie in the August sun is like 'the bush that burned with fire and was not consumed' (*My Antonia*, chapter 1); for Aldous Huxley nature is 'proof of God's goodness', shining 'from every burning bush of incandescent blossom' (*Eyeless in Gaza*, 16). In the writing of D.H. Lawrence, where theophany is often reduced to sexual initiation, *The Lovely Lady* 'could not trust herself so near the Burning Bush, dared not go near for transfiguration, afraid of herself' ('The Overtone'). And in Joyce's *Portrait of the Artist*, Stephen recalls his near apprehension of vocation, and of communion with God, recalling how once 'he had lifted up his arms and spoken in ecstasy to the sombre nave of trees, knowing that he stood on holy ground and in a holy hour' (chapter 5).

David L. Jeffrey
University of Ottawa

Deborah, Song of Deborah

The victory ode in Judges 5, ascribed to Deborah, a prophetess, celebrates the northern Israelite triumph over a powerful Canaanite coalition as early as 1200–1150BC. Verses 1–11 praise the covenant God of Sinai for the deliverance when Deborah 'arose, a mother in Israel'. In vv. 12–18, Deborah summons the warriors whom Barak leads to battle; six loyal tribes are praised, and four absentees are taunted. In vv. 19–31, after the Canaanite defeat, the non-Israelite Jael harbours the escaping general, Sisera. Lulling him to sleep, she violates the hospitality code, hammering a tent peg through his skull. At the ironic conclusion, Sisera's mother, anxious about his delay, is silenced by the deluded princesses' dreams of booty. The poem contains many features of great antiquity, including archaic words, repetitious parallelism, paratactic syntax, conventions found in Near Eastern odes from 1300–1150BC, and motifs from Canaanite mythology.

Sidney judges the song to be one of the best antique imitations of 'the inconceivable excellencies of God' (*An Apologie for Poetrie*). Spenser makes Britomart more stout-hearted than '*Debora* [who] strake / Proud *Sisera*' (*Faerie Queene*, 3.4.2–3). In Shakespeare's *Henry VI (1)* (1.2.105), the Dauphin Charles cries out that his female victor fights 'with the sword of Deborah'. Donne's sermon of 15 September 1622, embroiders the medieval allegorical interpretation to defend

James I's religious settlement against Papists and Puritans (*Sermons*, ed. Potter and Simpson, 1959, 4.178–209). In Milton's *Samson Agonistes* (982–94), Dalila, failing to ensnare Samson anew, storms off with the prophecy that she, like Jael, will be praised for saving her country from a deadly enemy. Robert Lowth glosses over the Song's violence in favour of its 'striking picture of maternal solicitude' and praise of Israelite liberty (*Lectures on the Sacred Poetry of the Hebrews*, 1753, chapters 13, 28). In Browning's *The Ring and the Book* (10.663–64) the stars of Judges 5:20 condemn the drawing together of a priest and a married woman; Tennyson's *The Princess* (5.500–501) places Ida ominously 'Between a cymballed Miriam and a Jael'. Mark Twain, critical of violence in the Bible, sets Deborah and Jael in Satan's 'history of the progress of the human race' as it moves from the murder of Abel to the mass exterminations of modern warfare (*Mysterious Stranger*, chapter 8).

Victorian and Edwardian feminist pageants, such as Alfred Ford's *Jael and Sisera: A Woman's Rights Drama* (in his *Scenes and Sonnets*, 1872, 1–14), celebrate the Song's heroines uncritically. *Daughters of Dawn*, by Bliss Carman and Mary Perry King (1913), chooses Deborah, who rouses an oppressed nation, as one of a dozen characters 'typical chiefly of the liberal and beneficent power of woman's nature in her leadership and ascendancy in the life of the spirit and the destiny of the world' (vii).

Alexander Globe
University of British Columbia

Delilah

In Judges 16, Delilah (Vulgate and Milton 'Dalila'; Septuagint 'Dalida') is the last in a series of women amorously involved with Samson. She is not, explicitly, either his wife or a harlot, although in the 1st century both Josephus (*Antiquities*, 5.8.11) and Pseudo-Philo (43.5) view her as a harlot, and in Pseudo-Philo she becomes Samson's wife. At the instigation of the Philistine lords Delilah sets herself to find out from Samson the secret of his great strength. Three times he deceives her; finally he tells her the truth, that his strength is in his hair, uncut because of his Nazarite vow. She accepts money from the Philistines, lulls her lover to sleep in her lap, and calls for a man to shave off his 'seven locks'. The enfeebled Samson cannot resist capture by the Philistines and is blinded by them.

In literature and art Samson and Delilah are often associated with other biblical lovers (e.g., Solomon and Sheba, David and Bathsheba). St Philaster (*Liber de haeresibus* 8: *Patrologia Latina*, 12.1122) and St Augustine (*De civitate Dei*, 18.19: *Patrologia Latina*, 41.576) identified Samson with Hercules, and 19th-century scholarship connected the stories as solar myths and associated Delilah with Omphale, who humiliated Hercules, or (more frequently) with Dejanira, who caused his death. Some scholars argued that Delilah and Dejanira are actually the same name; Robert Graves compared Delilah's shearing of Samson with ritual shearing of the sun-god, associated with Hercules, by women (*The Greek Myths*, 1960, 145.4).

Delilah the betrayer was easily allegorized. Since Samson was viewed as a type of Christ (e.g., Augustine, *Sermo*, 364: *Patrologia Latina*, 39.1639), Delilah could be seen as the synagogue which connives at the Crucifixion (Rabanus Maurus, *De Universo*, 3.1: *Patrologia Latina*, 111.57). Isidore of Seville makes her an emblem of the (feminine) flesh betraying the (masculine) rational sense in mankind (*Quaestiones in Vetus Testamentum*, Judges 8, *Patrologia Latina*, 83.389–90), a reading reflected in Lydgate's *Pilgrimage of the Life of Man* (9533–58), which makes Delilah the flesh luring the pilgrim soul away from salvation.

But literal readings were also common. *Cursor Mundi* (7187–7262) stresses Samson's stupidity in succumbing to his wife Delilah after so much experience of women's wiles. It goes on to recount how she leaves him, engages to remarry, and then has Samson brought in to the wedding feast as 'entertainment', whereupon he pulls down the pillars; his revenge, in this version, is thus directed more at Delilah than Dagon. Abelard (*Planctus Israel super Samson*, *Patrologia Latina*, 178.1820–21), the *Roman de la Rose* (9165–76), Gower (*Confessio Amantis*, 8.2703) and Chaucer's *Monk's Tale* develop the theme of Delilah as a domestic traitor who brings about disaster through love. Chaucer has the Wife of Bath's husband read her the tales both of Samson and Delilah and Hercules and

Dejanira to illustrate how women ensnare brave men (*Wife of Bath's Tale*, Prologue 3.721–26).

By natural extension the name Dalila was given to an unruly daughter easily seduced by Iniquity in the Tudor interlude *Nice Wanton*. From the 16th to the 19th century, the name was used both in literature and homiletics of treacherous harlots, especially those luring men from religious or patriotic duty. Thackeray's Becky Sharp is dubbed Delilah in her ambivalent relations with her enormous soldier-husband (*Vanity Fair*, chapters 16, 45). Kipling's poem 'Delilah' concerns the betrayal of a Viceregal confidence imparted to a highly placed gossiping wife. In Browning's *The Ring and the Book* (11.2200) Guido calumniates his wife as being a Delilah to his Samson. Scott's references to beguiling books as 'Delilahs' (*Heart of Midlothian*, chapter 1; *Letters*, 8.127) are in the same tradition.

Only in the 16th and 17th centuries did the dramatic and erotic possibilities of the story attract close attention. Lost to us now are several English Samson plays, evidently following continental precedent, in which Delilah must have appeared. A famous painting by Rubens emphasizes Delilah's harlotry by incorporating a statuette of Venus and an aged procuress. Here, as in Milton's *Samson Agonistes* (711–22) and in Blake's 'Samson' (*Poetical Sketches 1769–1778*), she is voluptuously and immodestly dressed. In Titian's painting she wields the shears herself, as she does in Quarles' *Historie of Samson* (*Meditation*, 19.22) and in Milton, although in the biblical narrative she calls in a barber.

Milton's is the only sustained and imaginative treatment of the story and forms, in turn, the basis of Handel's oratorio *Samson*. In an episode original to the Miltonic version, Dalila, exotic, perfumed, and enticing, visits Samson in prison in Gaza seeking both to salve her conscience and to prove once again that she can dominate Samson by female guile. Dramatically, her visit allows Samson to demonstrate, before renouncing his role as God's champion, that despite past colourful sexual exploits he can now resist the lures of the flesh. Though Samson calls Dalila 'concubine' (537), Milton depicts her as his wife (227). This enables him to stress the traditional theme of domestic treachery while bringing in the hedonistic associations of the splendid courtesan.

The modern adventures of Delilah in opera (Saint-Saëns, opus 47, 1877), ballet (Ruth Page, 1946; Marcia Graham, 1961), and film (Cecil B. de Mille, 1949) seem to owe more to the sexual and dramatic interest of the story and its opulent visual dimension than to literary or exegetical tradition.

Brenda E. Richardson and Norman Vance
University of Sussex

Exodus

Exodus is the name given by the Vulgate and English translations of the Bible to the book which describes the bondage in Egypt of Jacob's and Joseph's descendants (1:1–6:27) and the subsequent departure from Egypt of the captive people under the leadership of Moses and Aaron (chapters 13–19); it narrates also the journey to Sinai, the giving of the Decalogue (20:1–17) and Covenant Law (20:22–23:33; 34:1–35), as well as directions for the erection of the Tabernacle. Its Hebrew name is taken from the opening words meaning 'and these are the names'. The events contained in this narrative are the most dramatic in the epic saga of the Jewish pilgrimage; from them spring fundamental biblical conceptions of law, justice, freedom, covenant, and worship, including the most important of Jewish feasts, the Passover. It is also the single most important biblical sourcebook for Jewish and Christian typology as well as hymnody. It provides plot and theme to countless narratives, a list of which would occupy a volume in itself.

Building on the typology of the prophets, Palestinian Judaism at the time of Christ saw Moses the deliverer as a type of the Messiah, and looked for their own messianic deliverance to come in the spring, at the time of Passover (Bonsirven, *Judaïsme palastinien*, 1.416). Jean Daniélou has shown that Matthew's gospel is permeated with allusions to Exodus, with Christ's life presented in the framework of the 'New Exodus, foretold by the Prophets' (157). Hence, immediately after his baptism, Jesus is 'led by the Spirit into the desert' (Matthew 4:1), where he spends forty days (cf. Israel's forty-year sojourn in the desert and Moses' forty-day fast). When Satan tempts Christ on the mountaintop he is rebuked with the first commandment given on Sinai, and in his Sermon on the Mount Jesus assumes the role of lawgiver of the New

Covenant. As Moses took the people over the waters into the 'land of promise', Jesus walks on the waters (Matthew 8:23–27); as through Moses' intercession manna was given to the twelve tribes, so Jesus gives bread miraculously to feed his twelve disciples and the multitude (Matthew 14:4). These parallels unfold not only in the first gospel but throughout the New Testament, a notable example coming in John 3:14, where the incident of Moses elevating the brazen serpent (Numbers 21) is seen as predictive of Jesus' Crucifixion.

Typology based upon Exodus became fundamental to Christian catechism from St Augustine through to Calvin and the American Puritans. The journey out of 'Egypt' through the 'waters of baptism' and through the desert towards the 'Promised Land' becomes a type of the Christian's pilgrimage out of a place of spiritual exile through testing in this world towards a life of faithful obedience to God's law and eventual entrance into the 'New Canaan'.

In early medieval allegorizations the essential features are largely consistent: Egypt is the world, Pharaoh the devil, and the Egyptian army 'besetting sins'. The desert sojourn is a figure for exile and pilgrimage, and the cloudy or fiery pillar a type of Christ who leads in the journey. The exodus motif itself becomes central to the development of the pilgrimage theme in medieval and Renaissance literature from *Piers Plowman* to *Pilgrim's Progress,* but it also generates models for a typologizing of history and future events which are of considerable importance for Protestant – especially Puritan – tradition. Calvinist typology and covenant theology were drawn to view this world from the perspective of 'a stranger in a strange land' (Exodus 2:22). Calvin (*Institutes,* 2.8.15) observes that:

> We again, instead of supposing that the matter has no reference to us, should reflect that the bondage of Israel in Egypt was a type of that spiritual bondage, in the fetters of which we are all bound, until the heavenly avenger delivers us by the power of his own arm, and transports us into his free kingdom. Therefore, as in old times, when he would gather together the scattered Israelites to the worship of his name, he rescued them from the intolerable tyranny of Pharaoh, so all who profess him now are delivered from the fatal tyranny of the devil, of which that of Egypt was only a type.

By a curious hermeneutical inversion, the 'spiritual' reading afforded by Calvin was often 'literalized' by subsequent writers, so that the Exodus story came to be seen as predictive of postbiblical national destinies. Thus, the type of national allegory found in Spenser's *Faerie Queene* is metamorphosed by the use of exodus typology in William Leigh's *Queen Elizabeth Paraleld* (1612) and *Israel and England Paralleled* (1648) by Paul Knell; it takes on particularly Calvinist flavouring in John Welles' *The Soules Progress to the Celestiall Canaan* (1639) and Faithfull Teate's *A Scripture Map of the Wilderness of Sin, and Way to Canaan* (1655). In New England Samuel Mather's *Figures and Types of the Old Testament* (1673), Cotton Mather's *Magnalia Christi Americana* (1702), and Jeremiah Romayne's *The American Israel* (1795) all illustrate the power of the Exodus story in the formation of American national identity. In this context a leader of the Plymouth pilgrims, William Bradford, is seen by Cotton Mather as Moses leading Israel away from the European 'fleshpots of Egypt' into the American wilderness (*Magnalia*, 1.104); John Winthrop is also a second Moses (1.109), and the expedition against Canada under Phips is described as a pushing out of Philistines from 'the skirts of Goshen' (1.167–68). In a later period, the experience of African slaves in America was often expressed in terms – borrowed, ironically, from their masters – of longing for release from Pharaoh's oppression and for access to the Promised Land. Nor has the exodus motif disappeared from contemporary American literature: Steinbeck's *The Grapes of Wrath* presents the Joads as modern Israelites fleeing through the desert from persecution toward the promised land of milk and honey in California, with Tom as their Moses. Leon Uris uses the re-establishment of Jews in Israel after the holocaust as the subject and theme of his modern *Exodus,* a novel which attempts to return the motif, without much of its attendant Western typology, to its original Canaan.

David L. Jeffrey
University of Ottawa

Gideon

Gideon, son of Joash, described himself as a lesser scion of an obscure family: 'poor in Manasseh and... least in [his] father's house' (Judges

34

6:15). His name means 'wood-cutter' or 'feller of trees'. Nevertheless, he became one of the great heroes of Israel and its fifth judge.

While Gideon was secretly threshing grain for his family to save it from the rapacious Midianites, a celestial visitor appeared to him and enjoined him to take up arms on behalf of his people: 'Go in this thy might and thou shalt save Israel... have I not sent thee?' (Judges 6:14). Gideon, wanting assurance that the origin of the call was divine, asked for a sign and was answered when the food he offered to the angel was consumed by fire at the touch of his staff (6:17–22). Gideon's mission was inaugurated later that night when the Lord commanded him to cut down the grove dedicated to the pagan deity Baal on his father's land and burn the wood on the altar. When the people discovered what Gideon had done, they demanded his death. His father, however, defended him, saying, 'If [Baal] be a god, let him plead for himself' (6:31). This incident earned Gideon the nickname 'Jerub-baal', indicating that he was a fighter against the pagan god.

Seeking further confirmation of his divine office, Gideon asked yet another sign – that God should cause the evening dew to fall upon a lamb's fleece while all the ground around it should remain dry. The next morning, discovering that this had indeed happened, he dared to ask for an alternate version of the miracle; the following morning the fleece was dry while all around the earth was soaked (Judges 6:36–40). Finally confident both of the origin and nature of his calling, he assembled his forces for battle. The Lord asked him to reduce his army by offering release from duty to any who were fearful. Twenty-two thousand gladly went home, leaving only 10,000. The Lord then commanded that all the would-be soldiers be sent by Gideon to the spring at Harod. Those who scooped up water to drink with one hand, still alert and able to hold their spears, were separated from those who knelt down on hands and knees to drink. A drastically reduced army of 300 men remained (7:1–9). Dividing his forces into three groups of 100 each, Gideon gave every soldier a trumpet and a pitcher to hold over a lamp. They surrounded the enemy and simultaneously blew their trumpets, shattered their pitchers, revealed the lamps, and cried, 'The sword of the Lord, and of Gideon.' At this the startled enemy forces were put to rout. The princes of Succoth and Penuel, both of whom had refused assistance to Gideon's men (8:5–17), were punished by Gideon; the first was beaten with thorns, and the second had his military tower destroyed.

When the delivered people wished to make him king (Judges 8:22–23), Gideon refused. He did, however, take the gold earrings captured from slain enemies and make an ephod – probably a surrogate for an 'ark' or sacral box – which he then placed in his own town of Ophrah. This became an object of idolatry and 'a snare unto Gideon and his house' (8:27).

In the New Testament Gideon appears in Hebrews 11, where, in recounting the exemplary Old Testament heroes of faith, the writer includes him with David, Samuel, and others among those 'who through faith subdued kingdoms, wrought righteousness, obtained promises... [and] out of weakness were made strong' (vv. 32–34).

Calvin's commentary on Hebrews 11, concerned to demonstrate that 'in every saint there is always to be found something reprehensible', concentrates on faults in the hero. Calvin argues that Gideon was 'slower than he need have been to take up arms'. George Herbert, seeing that 'the world grows old', looks back fondly upon the days when biblical characters could find themselves in the presence of God, times when God would directly 'struggle with Jacob, sit with Gideon' ('Decay'). In Milton's *Paradise Regained* Jesus rejects Satan's offer of wealth, declaring that without 'Virtue, Valour, Wisdom', they are empty: 'But men endu'd with these have oft attain'd / In lowest poverty to highest deeds.' Gideon is the first example Jesus gives of such a person (2.430–39). In *Samson Agonistes* the Chorus remembers 'the matchless Gideon' as Israel's 'great Deliverer' of his generation (277–81). In Bunyan's *Pilgrim's Progress*, when Christian reaches The House Beautiful, he is taken to the celestial Armory and shown some of the instruments by which the Lord's servants of yore 'had done wonderful things. They shewed him... the Pitchers, Trumpets and Lamps too, with which Gideon put to flight the Armies of Midian.' Cromwell in his fourth speech to Parliament (1655) bitterly denounced Anabaptists as 'levellers', referring to their fate with an allusion to the fate of the Midianite confederates Zebah and Zalmunna at Gideon's hand (Judges 8:20–22). Andrew Marvell's poem in praise of Cromwell of a year earlier alludes to the same score-settling events, 'when Gideon so did from the war retreat', but draws a further conclusion: 'No king might ever such a force have done, / Yet would not he be lord, nor yet his son' – a reference to Cromwell's refusal, on biblical principles drawn in part from the book of Judges, to perpetuate the English monarchy.

Characterization of Gideon in the 18th century reflects the tension between Calvin's rigorous qualification of his heroism and a strong affection in Independent and Calvinist preaching for the results of that heroism. Both elements are visible in the poetry of William Cowper. In 'Table Talk' he is at pains to ascribe all human achievement to the will of Providence: 'So Gideon earn'd a victr'y not his own; / Subserviency his praise, and that alone' (360–61), a point he returns to in describing a post-conversion letdown in 'The New Convert'. In *Olney Hymns* 4, 'Jehovah-Nissi', he ascribes Gideon's triumph to God yet laments his own 'unbelief, self will / Selfrighteousness and pride' which prevent him from spiritual victory, concluding with a hopeful assertion: 'Yet David's Lord, and Gideon's friend, / Will help his servant to the end.' The miracle of the fleece is adduced by Cowper as comfort to 'A Protestant Lady in France' (49–50), but according to the same premise, 'to give the creature her Creator's due / Were sin in me, and an offence to you' (3–4).

The 19th century tends to plant virtue more firmly in the human and to secularize or make humour of miraculous events. In one of his essays Charles Lamb compares two teachers, the more secure of whose 'thunders rolled innocuous for us; his storms came near, but never touched us; contrary to Gideon's miracle, while all around were drenched, our fleece was dry' ('Christ's Hospital Five and Thirty Years Ago'). A.H. Clough aspires 'to bleed for others' wrongs / In vindication of a cause, to draw / The sword of the Lord and of Gideon – oh, that seems / The flower and top of life.' Tennyson uses Gideon's chastisement of the men of Succoth as an analogue for the English victory over Napoleon at Trafalgar: 'late he learned humility / Perforce, like those whom Gideon school'd with briers' ('Napolean'). Carlyle's appropriation of the narrative in *Past and Present* makes the case that if one has courage, patience, and faith, one's work will be rewarded: 'Thy heart and life purpose shall be as a miraculous Gideon's fleece, spread out in silent appeal to heaven; and from the kind Immensities [will come] blessed dew-moisture.' 'Peace may be sought in two ways', declares Ruskin in *The Two Paths*; 'One way is as Gideon sought it, when he built his altar... naming it, "God send peace", yet sought this peace that he loved, as he was ordered to seek it, and the peace was sent in God's way.'

Hardy's uses of the story are, like those of Joyce, erudite but disaffirming. In *The Woodlanders* one of the characters declares that an abused tree will fall 'and cleave us, like the sword of the Lord and of Gideon' (chapter 14). A less apt borrowing is his favourable comparison of Tess ('despite her not inviolate past') with her still sexually innocent peers: 'Was not the gleaning of the grapes of Ephraim better than the vintage of Abi-ezer?' (*Tess of the D'Urbervilles*, chapter 49). In the 'Oxen of the Sun' passage in *Ulysses*, Joyce subverts the common medieval association between Gideon's fleece and virginity, especially that of Mary, when he makes sexual double entendre of the phrase 'thy fleece is drenched'.

Paddy Chayefsky's Broadway play *Gideon* (1961), adapted also for television, is a humorously ironic story of man's refusal to acknowledge God even after a series of miracles. Chayefsky's modern Gideon is a comic anti-hero but made so out of the playwright's poignant reflection that part of what it means to be resignedly 'modern' is the knowledge that heroism and faith are inextricable; when faith disappears, heroic self-transcendence disappears soon after.

David L. Jeffrey
University of Ottawa

Jephthah and his Daughter

The source of the story of Jephthah and his daughter is Judges 11:30–40. Jephthah, at war with the Ammonites, vowed that, if he was victorious, he would upon his return from battle offer up to the Lord whatever first came from his house to meet him. When he returned home triumphant, the first to emerge was his daughter, his only child. Regretting his vow but unable to go back on it, he allowed her, upon her request, two months to bewail her lot, and then he sacrificed her.

This tale of Jephthah's rash vow, regret, grief, and remorse and of his daughter's acceptance of her fate has inspired a variety of artistic treatments, including more than a hundred musical interpretations, and numerous paintings and etchings (including those by Lucas van Leyden, William Blake, Edgar Degas, Gustave Doré, J.E. Millais, and Benjamin West), and sculptures ranging from that of 15th-century Florentine Lorenzo Ghiberti to 20th-century Naum Aronson and Enrico Glicenstein.

Chaucer refers to the story of Jephthah's daughter in *The Physician's Tale* (*Canterbury Tales*, 6.238–44), and his contemporary John Gower, in the *Confessio Amantis* (4.505–1595), elaborates the narrative in great detail. English ballads about Jephthah survive from the 16th century. Shakespeare includes verses of the ballad 'Jephthah, Judge of Israel' in *Hamlet* (2.2.410–25), here referring satirically to Polonius as an old Jephthah who had 'one fair daughter and no more, / The which he loved passing well'.

The popularity of the theme in this period may owe largely to the Scottish humanist George Buchanan, who rendered the Jephthah story as a tragedy in the mid-16th century. His Latin drama *Jephthes,* written in 1540, and printed in 1554, was translated at least six times into English and exerted great influence throughout Europe, especially upon Christian Weise's German drama (1670) and Joost van den Vondel's Dutch play (1659). Humanists likened the Jephthah story to that of Iphigenia as treated by Euripides in his *Iphigenia in Aulis*. Erasmus translated the play in 1506, and his version influenced English humanist John Christopherson, who composed a Jephthah drama in Greek in 1544. Christopherson, who also rendered his play into Latin, explained that he had chosen the theme because of its similarity to the Euripidean play: Jephthah, like Agamemnon, father of Iphigenia, was caught in a conflict between his duty to God and his fatherly love. More than fifty dramas on this theme are recorded between the 16th and the 18th centuries throughout Europe. An English *Jephthah* drama was written by Thomas Dekker and Anthony Munday in 1602, but the text has not survived.

Among 17th-century poets, Francis Quarles includes a lyric of eighteen lines, 'On Jeptha's Vow', in his *Divine Fancies* (2.4). Robert Herrick's 'The Dirge of Jephthah's Daughter' (1647) recounts the annual lament of the young women of Israel over the plight of Jephthah's daughter.

In the 18th century the story was often treated in oratorios, the most popular being Handel's of 1751, for which Thomas Morell wrote the text. Though Iphis (Handel's name for Jephthah's daughter) is prepared, like Iphigenia, to go stoically to her death, Morell has an angel appear and announce that God is a loving, forgiving deity who does not want bloody sacrifice but rather that Iphis serve him as a priestess.

Byron's Jephthah poem of 1815, included in his *Hebrew Melodies,* emphasizes the daughter's nobility of soul, her filial obedience, her acquiescence in sacrificing herself for her country and her God. There follow poems by James Campbell, 'Jephtha's Rash Vow' (1826), and by Hartley Coleridge, 'On a Picture of Jephthah and His Daughter' (1851). Tennyson includes Jephthah's daughter in his long poem *A Dream of Fair Women* (1833) and in 'Aylmer's Field' and 'The Flight'. Among American poets, N.P. Willis includes 'Jephthah's Daughter' in his *Poetical Works* (1888), and Mark Van Doren has a poem of the same title in his *Collected New Poems* (1963).

Another noteworthy recasting of the tale is that by Lion Feuchtwanger in his last novel *Jephthah and his Daughter* (1957). Though the father fulfils his rash vow and sacrifices his pure and innocent daughter, his heart is a desert thereafter. Revered in Gilead and ruling his people justly, he nevertheless feels that his life's blood has been drained away. In the character of Jephthah, the novelist voices his own loss of faith in his earlier ideals and his disillusionment with his German countrymen, who drove him into exile and brought his Jewish kin as burnt-offerings to Auschwitz. The poem 'Jephthah's Daughter' by the British lyricist Karen Gershon appeared in the volume *Coming Back to Babylon* in 1979, after she had settled in Israel, and Naomi Ragen's novel *Jepthe's Daughter* appeared in 1989.

Sol Liptzin
Hebrew University of Jerusalem

Joshua

Joshua, son of Nun, is the military leader par excellence in the Old Testament. He appeared suddenly in Exodus 17:9 to lead the Hebrew people in their first armed struggle after the Exodus from Egypt, against the Amalekites, a prelude to the series of battles in which he commanded his forces in the conquest of the land of Canaan. This conquest is one of the major themes in the book of Joshua, the other being the subsequent division of land among the tribes of Israel.

In the Pentateuch, Joshua is associated closely with Moses, whose assistant, not equal, he is said to be (Exodus 24:13; 33:11, etc.). He won high praise after he and Caleb remained loyal to God when the other spies sent to reconnoitre the land of Canaan proved faithless (Numbers 13–14). For this act of faithfulness Joshua and Caleb, unlike Moses, were allowed to enter the Promised Land (Numbers 14; 26:65; 32:12). Joshua's piety and obedience are prime assets in military engagements as well, for the conquest of the land of Israel is portrayed as a holy war, in which Hebrew success is impossible apart from close adherence to the requirements of the covenant (e.g., Joshua 6–8).

When Joshua led the people in a ceremony of covenant renewal (Joshua 24), he once more demonstrated steadfastness of purpose and qualities of leadership appropriate to the individual whom Moses, at God's command, had appointed as his successor (Numbers 27:12–33; 34:17; Deuteronomy 1:38; 3:3–15, 23; 34:9).

As successor to Moses, the quintessential representative of the Law, and as conqueror of the Promised Land, Joshua was readily viewed by early Christian writers as a type of Christ. This identification was reinforced by the fact that *Iesous* is the Greek form of *Joshua*, leading the Septuagint translators to render *Joshua* as 'Jesus' throughout the saga of the conquest of Canaan (cf. Hebrews 4:8, where the King James Version transliterates Joshua's name as 'Jesus'). Joshua-Jesus typology was already well established in the early Church (cf. Hebrews 3) and elaborated extensively in the patristic period. (Centuries later, Milton, reflecting the ancient commonplace, can refer to 'Joshua, whom the Gentiles Jesus call', *Patrologia Latina*, 12.310.) In his working out of the typology, St Jerome is emphatic that Joshua remained chaste throughout his life, unlike Moses, 'the Law', who was married (*Adversus Jovinianum*).

Joshua's military prowess won for him a place among the nine worthies, as attested, among other places, in Shakespeare's *Love's Labour's Lost* (5.1.123). William Wordsworth speaks of 'righteous'

Joshua as warrior in *The Excursion* (7.813), and Joshua was pressed into service as a patriotic hero in such works as Thomas Morell's *Joshua, A Sacred Drama* (1748) and Timothy Dwight's epic poem *The Conqueror of Canaan* (1785). The violent nature of the conquest, pointedly described by Blake (in his annotations to *An Apology for the Bible* by R. Watson, 1796), is taken up in such works as the anonymous American ballad *The Battles of Joshua* (1843). Joshua is notably absent from both medieval and Renaissance drama – apart from one lost play by Samuel Rowley (1602).

Individual episodes in the life of Joshua merit occasional reference in English literature. The courage of Joshua and Caleb in the wilderness is alluded to in Blake's *Jerusalem* (43.37; 49.58–59), and the capture of Jericho recorded in Joshua 6 is recalled in such works as Patrick Dickinson's poem 'The Seven Days of Jericho' and the well-known spiritual 'Joshua Fit the Battle of Jericho'. The most popular single incident, however, is Joshua's stilling of the sun and moon at the valley of Ajalon (Joshua 10:12–13), which is remembered in various contexts by writers as diverse as Milton, Dryden, Tennyson, and Somerset Maugham. A witty allusion to Joshua's parentage is afforded in Emily Dickinson's 'Son of None'.

Leonard Greenspoon
Clemson University

Lex Talionis

For a number of specified offences the Mosaic law, like other Near Eastern codes (e.g., that of Hammurabi), provided for symmetrical retribution. The *lex talionis* or 'tit for tat' formula is amplified as 'life for life, eye for eye, tooth for tooth, hand for hand, foot for foot, burning for burning, wound for wound, stripe for stripe' (Exodus 21:23–25; cf. Leviticus 24:20; Deuteronomy 19:21). The intention of this law, as St Augustine among many others has observed, is actually to signify a measure of restraint in retribution, 'so that vengeance should not exceed the injury' (*De sermone Domini in Monte*, 1.19.56). Augustine's comments come in the context of discussion of Matthew 5:38, in which Jesus urges his hearers to go beyond this principle in extending mercy and to 'turn the other cheek'. He goes on to observe that the person 'who pays back just as much as he has received already forgives something: for the party who injures does not deserve merely just so much punishment as the one who was injured by him has innocently suffered' (1.19.57). Later commentators such as Matthew Poole argue that the 'Law of Retaliation', though it 'might sometimes be practised in the letter, yet it was not necessarily to be understood and executed so; as may appear... by the impossibility of just execution of it in many cases... Punishment may be less, but never should be greater than the Fault. And how could a Wound be made neither bigger nor less than that which he inflicted?' (*Annotations*, on Exodus 21:24).

This reflection, reminiscent of Portia's judgment concerning Shylock's bond in Shakespeare's *Merchant of Venice*, is directed against the 'civilized' barbarity of ruthless legalism. In Tennyson's *Beckett*, King Henry is impatient with the bishops for their failure to act with the cruder civil justice, having brought to their own ecclesiastical courts a cleric who had

> violated
> The daughter of his host and murdered him
> ...But since your canon will not let you take
> Life for a life, ye but degraded him
> When I had hang'd him.

From King Henry's point of view there is hypocrisy in the use of *lex talionis* for the one offence and not the other. In Emily Brontë's *Wuthering Heights*, Isabella says of Heathcliff that she will forgive him his ill-treatment of her only on the condition that she 'may take an eye for an eye, a tooth for a tooth; for every wrench of agony return a wrench: reduce him to my level'. Hardy's Bathsheba in *Far from the Madding Crowd* is driven by a similar confusion of justice with revenge: 'In Bathsheba's heated fancy the innocent white countenance expressed a dim triumphant consciousness of the pain she was retaliating for her pain with all the merciless rigour of the Mosaic law: "Burning for burning; wound for wound; strife for strife" [*sic*]' (chapter 43). Emerson, in 'Compensation', construes a symmetrical recension of both Old Testament and New Testament concepts, uniting allusions to Exodus 31:24 and the Sermon on the Mount when he observes: 'All things are double, one against the other – Tit for tat; an eye for an eye; a tooth for a tooth; blood for blood; measure for measure; love for love.'

David L. Jeffrey
University of Ottawa

Manna

Manna, the name given in the Septuagint to the food which was miraculously provided to the Hebrews during their forty-year sojourn in the desert, is described in Exodus 16:15–35, where it is said to look like white coriander seed and to taste like honey wafers; in Numbers 11:7–8 it is said to be the colour of bdellium and to taste like fresh oil. Found on the ground each morning, it was gathered and made into bread. Manna has been thought by some modern interpreters to be an excretion produced by two different insects on the tamarisk tree (thus now *Tamarix mannifera*); it is similar to the honeydew produced by many plant lice and is still used by the Sinai bedouins as a sweetener. The Old Testament account of manna, however, clearly emphasizes its miraculous nature, as do various other accounts. Josephus, e.g., several times notes that it had never been seen before and was provided by God for the special purpose of sustaining his people (*Antiquities* 3.26–32, 86; 4.45).

Moses ruled that manna was not to be kept overnight, and some who disobeyed found that the retained manna stank and bred worms; on the eve of the Sabbath, however, the people were instructed to gather twofold, for no manna was provided on the Sabbath. In this instance it remained fresh. Later, when the people complained about the manna and wanted flesh, God provided them with a surfeit of quails and a 'very great plague' (Numbers 11:33). They continued, therefore, to eat manna until they arrived in Jericho, where Joshua performed the circumcision covenant a second time (it had been neglected during the desert wanderings) and the people ate 'the old corn of the land' (Joshua 5:11), after which the manna disappeared.

Manna is allegorized by Moses, who says that God provided it to show that man does not live by bread alone but 'by every word that proceedeth out of the mouth of the Lord' (Deuteronomy 8:3). In the Psalms it is called 'angel's food' (78:25) and 'bread of heaven' (105:40). The latter term is used in the New Testament in John's account of the sequel to the feeding of the 5,000 (chapter 6), when Jesus calls himself the 'living bread'. Of the other New Testament uses of the word, one (Hebrews 9:4) refers to literal manna set aside in a special urn as a memorial of God's salvation of Israel (see Exodus 16:32–34), and the other (Revelation 2:17), in the message to the church at Pergamum, refers to the 'hidden manna' which will be given to 'him that overcometh' (the Wycliffite translation glosses 'manna hid' with 'angel's mete').

In George Herbert's 'The Sacrifice' the Psalm term 'angel's food' creates a two-layered metaphor in which manna is at once the Eucharist and Christ, the 'living bread', who is the speaker of the poem and the 'sacrifice'. Southwell's 'A Holy Hymn', also based on metaphorical treatment of the Eucharist, calls manna 'Angel's bread made *Pilgrimes* feeding'. In Milton's *Paradise Regained* Christ responds to Satan's temptation to turn stones into bread by referring to manna and quoting Moses' words from Deuteronomy 8:3. Marvell closes 'A Drop of Dew' with an image of manna and its property of melting in the sun, just as the dew, which is likened to the human soul, evaporates and 'returns' to heaven. Thoreau uses the property of melting metaphorically when, in *Walden*, he says he waited at evening for 'something, though I never caught much, and that, manna-wise would dissolve again in the sun'.

Malory's Lancelot, aboard a strange ship for a month, is fed by the grace of God as the Hebrews were fed by God's manna (*The Castle of Corbenic* in *Works*, ed. Vinaver, 3.1011.28). And when the Holy Grail at last enters the hall, 'every knight had such metes and drynken as he best loved in thys worlde' – a reference to the description of manna in Wisdom of Solomon 16:20 (*The Departure*, in *Works*, ed. Vinaver, 2.865.30–31). Defoe's Robinson Crusoe alludes to the manna when, having unwittingly discarded grain which later sprouted and produced fruit, he 'thought these the pure productions of Providence for my support'. In Blake's *Book of Thel* (1.23), 'morning manna' is a gratuitous gift of God. The idea of manna as a gratuitous gift, without particular religious significance, is developed relatively early in English; thus in Shakespeare's *Merchant of Venice* when Portia and Nerissa reveal their trick, Lorenzo says, 'Fair ladies, you drop manna in the way / Of starved people' (5.1). Donne contrasts the sweetness of manna with the bitter gall it may be transformed into by love in 'Twick'nam Garden', and Keats several times includes manna in lists of delicacies, simply as something sweet (*Endymion*, 'The Eve of St Agnes', 'La Belle Dame sans Merci').

In Otway's *The Atheist*, an allusion to manna concerns wishing for more than one already has (as the Israelites wanted flesh as well as manna) when the womanizing Courtine, who neglects his wife, is asked, 'Do you despise your own Manna indeed, and long after Quails?' Similarly, in *The Ring and the Book*, Browning's Count Guido Franceschini refers contemptuously to a hypothetical monk 'Who fancied Francis' manna meant roast quails'. The speaker of Hopkins' 'Soliloquy of One of the Spies Left in the Wilderness' grows tired of the manna and wishes for the comforts of Egypt.

C. Day Lewis' version of Virgil's fourth *Georgic* no doubt refers to European 'manna' (produced on different trees in the same way as Middle Eastern 'manna' and giving rise to the ancient belief that honey dropped like dew from heaven), appropriately if recondite ly: 'Next I come to the manna, the heavenly gift of honey' (1.1, translating *'aerii mellis celestia dona'*).

David L. Jeffrey
University of Ottawa

Moses

Moses is the chief prophet of Jewish tradition, the traditional author of the Pentateuch (also called 'The Five Books of Moses'), leader of the exodus of Israel from Egypt, a miracle-worker, and the 'lawgiver' who received from God the Ten Commandments. Moses may be regarded as the single most important personage in the Hebrew Scriptures and, after Jesus Christ and perhaps the Virgin Mary, the most important personage in the sacred text so far as Western art and literature are concerned. First among prophets and men of piety for the Jews, in the pre-modern Christian Church Moses was universally regarded as one of the signal Old Testament types of Christ.

Several events in the life of Moses receive frequent attention in Western arts and letters. Best known, perhaps, is the infancy narrative (Exodus 1:1–11). In order to circumvent Pharaoh's decree of death for male Hebrew children, Moses was left by his mother in a floating basket in the river where he was by chance found by Pharaoh's daughter, who saved the child and eventually brought him to the Egyptian court. Subsequently, as a young man, Moses slew an Egyptian persecutor of the Hebrew slaves, an incident which, when discovered, forced him to flee from Egypt to the land of Midian. It was here, while Moses was tending sheep, that he saw the famous theophany of the burning bush; as he approached the bush which burned without being consumed, God spoke to him, announcing that he was to rescue the children of Israel from slavery in Egypt (Exodus 3). The ineffective embassy of Moses and his brother Aaron before Pharaoh (Exodus 5) was the occasion (or prolegomena) of the ten plagues. Acting under God's instructions, Moses and Aaron coerced Pharaoh into liberating the Hebrews by inflicting upon him a series of pestilences: blood in the waters of Egypt, an epidemic of frogs, then of lice and flies, a murrain upon the cattle, boils in people and beasts, hail, locusts, and darkness over the whole land, and finally the death of all the eldest Egyptian children, 'from the firstborn of Pharaoh that sat on his throne unto the firstborn of the captive that was in the dungeon' (Exodus 7–11; 12:29–30). Moses then led the Hebrews out of Egypt, guided by a pillar of fire by night and a pillar of cloud by day (Exodus 13). Pursued by Pharaoh's army, he appealed to God, who miraculously parted the waters of the Red Sea to allow the children of Israel to pass through unharmed and drowned Pharaoh and his army when they tried to follow (Exodus 14). Moses was the instrument of various miracles of feeding in the wilderness, where the children of Israel sojourned for forty years (e.g., provision of quails and manna [Exodus 16] and of water miraculously springing from the hard rock [Exodus 17]). He received the Ten Commandments on Mount Sinai (Exodus 20) and then, coming down from the mountain, was enraged to discover that the Israelites had fallen into idolatry during his brief absence; in his anger he smashed the tablets of the Law. Finally, Moses was allowed to see – but not to enter – the promised land of Canaan from atop Mount Nebo, where he died at the age of 120, 'his eye... not dim, nor his natural force abated' (Deuteronomy 34). His body was hidden by God, and never found.

The dramatic richness of the narrative of Moses is exploited in the Haggadah and in such apocryphal texts as the Assumption of Moses. There is also in the history of the Exodus, however, a powerful literary delineation of character, and this aspect of the sacred text likewise inspired hagiographic veneration in many of its readers, even though Moses, biblically speaking, is not an unblemished hero. A murderer before he was called by God, he is presented as a reluctant saviour, an impatient prophet, and at times a dangerously irascible overlord. The children of Israel, for their part, are frequently ungrateful and unfaithful; their usual response to the miracles worked through Moses on their behalf is indifference followed by grumbling.

In patristic commentary the Pentateuch is followed somewhat more closely, if selectively, than in the Talmud, yet the range and variety is still considerable. The most famous patristic essay on Moses, St Gregory of Nyssa's *Vita Mosis*, takes the holy man of the Exodus to be the type of the ascetic life. Developing ideas current both in the Haggadah and in the Judaism of Alexandria, Gregory provides an essentially monastic portrait of Moses which greatly influenced medieval and Renaissance conceptions of him. Even in commentaries as late as those of Theodore Beza and Cornelius à Lapide (well known to Donne, Herbert, Andrewes, and Browne), or William Warburton's *The Divine Legation of Moses* (1738) (known to Blake), Gregory was cited to support the idea of Moses as an ideal type of the contemplative, who goes into the desert to hear the voice of God (see also St Gregory the Great, *Moralia in Iob*, 5.23.37). He is said to be, along with Samuel, a great exemplar of contemplative and intercessory prayer (cf. Jeremiah 7:16; 15:1), distinguished for praying for his enemies (Gregory, *Moralia*, 2.9.24) and for obtaining swift response from God. These ideas are still reflected in Richard Baxter's *Saints' Everlasting Rest* (1650), which concludes: 'As Moses, before he died, went up into Mount Nebo to take a survey of the land of Canaan; so the Christian ascends the mount of contemplation, and by faith surveys his rest.'

The association of Moses with mountain-top experience, hence mystical vision and transfiguration, was complicated by one of the most celebrated aspects of his medieval iconography, his 'horns'. The depiction of the 'horned Moses' was occasioned by a confusion in the Vulgate translation of the Hebrew expression used to convey the 'rays of light' which shone from his forehead after his sojourn with the Almighty on Sinai (Exodus 34:29). The Latin word chosen was *cornu*, or 'horn'; 'Moses wist not that the skin of his face shone' (King James Version) was thus rendered *ignorabat quod cornutaesset facies sua*. This confusion led to representations of Moses in prophetic or monastic dress with bovine horns protruding from just above his hairline. Notable examples are found in illustrations of the *Biblia Pauperum* and *Bible moralisée*, but the most famous is Michelangelo's statue of Moses (1513) for the tomb of Pope Julius III. In Guillaume de Guilville's *Pèlerinage de la vie humaine*, translated into English in the early 15th century by John Lydgate, Lady Reason counsels a character called Moses, who is sometimes represented with horns (Old Law), sometimes with a bishop's mitre (New Law). Moses, who tonsures servants who come for ordination, imagines that he must have been given horns to butt his 'sheep' into line; Reason urges that he temper this Old Law function with a New Law dispensation of humility and lovingkindness (MSS Douce 300 and Laud 740).

The other celebrated feature of Moses' iconography relates to the same biblical incident: when speaking to the people, Moses was obliged to shield his face so that their eyes might not be blinded by the reflected radiance of God's glory from whose presence he had come (Exodus 34:33–35). Gregory the Great offers the typical explanation for the 'veiled Moses' when he observes that Moses did this 'surely, in order to denote that the people of the Jews knew the words of the Law, but did not at all see the clearness of the Law' (*Moralia*, 4.18.60). 'Veiled Moses' is thus a type of the Word yet to be fulfilled in Christ, the letter of the Law without its fullness and clarifying spirit, yet a type revealed in such terms as strongly preserves the sense of Moses' own integrity and stature as a mediator of the divine word to mankind (cf. 2 Corinthians 3:12–18).

The rod Moses sometimes bears, along with the Decalogue (e.g., in the painting by Phillip de Champagne), is generally held to be a sign of the Incarnation. When Moses cast down his rod and it became a serpent which devoured the serpents of Egypt (Exodus

7:12), it signified, says Ambrose, 'that the Word should become flesh to destroy the poison of the dread serpent [Satan] by the forgiveness and pardon of sins' (*De officiis*, 3.15.94). The tablets and the rod, when featured together, are thus images of the Old Covenant and of the New Covenant prefigured in it (cf. Picinelli, *Mundus Symbolicus*, 3.83.245–52, under the words '*Moses ...auxiliante Deo*').

The 8th-century *Exodus* represents Moses as a wise leader, characterized by *sapientia et fortitudo* and a type of Christ. He is similarly cast in the medieval cycle dramas such as the York 'Departure' and N-Town 'Moses and the Two Tables'. At the end of Chaucer's *Pardoner's Tale,* the Pardoner invites his fellow pilgrims to avail themselves of his highly dubious spiritual ministrations. Referring to his written warrant of authority from the Pope, he says: '...offer nobles or sterlinges, / Or elles silver brooches, spoones, ringes. / Boweth your heed under this holy bulle!' – an allusion to the story of the golden calf. In *Piers Plowman,* Will angrily tears a 'pardon' to pieces in an action which imitates, physically and morally, Moses' angry destruction of the tables of the Law.

It was principally Moses' role as a lawgiver and prophet of the covenant which attracted attention in Reformation commentary and literature. Calvin sees the Mosaic miracles as 'so many sanctions of the law delivered, and the doctrine propounded, by him', a clear witness of God to Moses' authority (*Institutes* 1.8.5–8). Milton concurs, finding Moses 'the only lawgiver that we can believe to have been visibly taught of God' (*The Reason of Church Government,* preface). In Bunyan's *Pilgrim's Progress* Moses is a stern fellow: Faith relates to Christian how after his nearly succumbing to the attempt by the Old Man, 'Adam the first', to deflect him from his journey, he was chased and knocked to the ground by a man who refuses to stop hitting him, saying, 'I know not how to show mercy.' The character was Moses, and only Jesus could dissuade him from punishing Faith for his weakness. It is within this same nonconformist tradition that Moses still appears, as a judge, in Thornton Wilders' *The Skin of Our Teeth* (1942). Predictably, Moses' typological connections with Christ are also emphasized by a writer like Milton, who, in *Paradise Regained,* draws the parallel between the forty-day fast of Moses in the desert and the temptation of Christ (346–56) and has Satan tempt Christ to take for himself the rabbinical eminence of Moses' wisdom, 'on points and questions fitting Moses Chair'.

In Dryden's *Absalom and Achitophel* Corah, rebel against David, is given 'a Moses' face' (presumably shining), but in Longfellow's *Evangeline* the afterglow of the setting sun is described as Moses veiling his face on coming down from Sinai. Whittier has 'Rabbi Ishmael' see the face of the Lord in the Holy of Holies and then, 'Radiant as Moses from the Mount, he stood / And cried aloud unto the multitude: / "O Israel, hear! The Lord our God is good!"' According to William Blake, Moses delivered Israel from Egyptian bondage only to impose a more severe bondage to Law, which he had actually borrowed from the Egyptians, 'the forms of dark delusion' (*Africa*, 3.17) as Blake imagines, probably on the basis of reading Warburton. What happens in Blake's reworking of this idea in *Ahania* and 'The Song of Los', where the bondage of Mosaic law becomes as sinister as the bondage in Egypt, is that Israel has effectively absorbed much of Egyptian culture. The first chapter of *Ahania* parallels the commissioning of Moses as prophet of righteousness; the second covers the events in Exodus from the defeat of Pharaoh to the arrival on Sinai; the third deals with the establishment of the Law from the mountain; the fourth concerns the forty years wandering in the wilderness; and the fifth the coming into Canaan, Moses' farewell speeches (or songs), and the lament after his death.

The death of Moses became a major theme in Romantic and post-Romantic literature. The haggadic legend of 'Moses and the Worm', popularized by Johann Gottfried Herder in the 18th century, is central to American poet Richard Henry Stoddard's 'The Death of Moses', which ends with Moses reconciled to his demise, able to trust Israel's fortunes to his successor, Joshua. James Montgomery's 'Death of Moses' is less optimistic, as Moses looks into the future from atop Mount Nebo to find trans-Jordan bloodstained and abounding in pagan abominations. Thomas Moore's dirge on the death of Moses is also a less than hopeful lament. George Eliot's poetic narrative *The Death of Moses* is more elaborate, and based on haggadic Jewish sources. God himself comes to take Moses away, drawing forth his soul with a kiss and carrying it up to heaven (cf. Baba Batra 17a; Petirat Mosheh 129). Israel is comforted with the words: 'He has no tomb. He dwells not with you dead, but lives as Law.' Rilke's 'Der Tod Moses' (1922) draws on some of the same sources, in which the angels of death prove unable to interrupt Moses in his mountain task of making the final thirteen copies of the Torah, and only God himself can with a kiss steal away the soul of Moses, burying his body in a cleft of the mountain, then closed over with the very hands which, as Moses himself had only just written, fashioned the creation *ex nihilo*. One of the last poems of Dietrich Bonhoeffer to be smuggled out of prison before his execution was 'Der Tod des Mose', which takes its optimistic motto from Deuteronomy 34:1: 'And the Lord showed him all the land.'

The strong influence of the character of Moses upon German literature, which in turn has strengthened his presence in English and American literature, owes at least in part to Martin Luther, who once said that he 'had endeavoured to make Moses so German that no one would suspect he was a Jew'. His vivid image of the prophetic individual, a leader of his people from bondage into freedom, is the antithesis of Blake's Fuzon-Moses. It corresponds, however, to the later typology of Moses in American literature. Such an image of Moses, which stresses the individual, the spiritual, and the psychological at the expense of the national and the political, finds an acculturated secular continental expression in Friedrich Schiller's essay *Die Sendung Moses* (1790) and in Sigmund Freud's celebrated and controversial *Moses and Monotheism* (1937–39), in both of which it is suggested that Moses was in fact not representative of his people but an Egyptian all along – an old idea (cf. George Herbert, 'The Church Militant', 21–46), but one made yet more unsettling in its modern guise, even that of Karl Shapiro, 'The Murder of Moses', which takes up from Freud the theory that he was murdered by Hebrews in the wilderness.

The image of Moses as a political leader has also had great influence in the 19th and 20th centuries. The Jews' long experience of persecution has encouraged the parallel, common in all periods of Jewish messianic thought, between the historical Moses and the saviour to come who has, indeed, on occasion been described as a *Moses redivivus*. Similar modes of thinking have characterized various oppressed or marginal groups within the Christian world, including the religious community of African-Americans, whose self-identification with the children of Israel suffering beneath Pharaoh's yoke is powerfully suggested in many spirituals, including the well-known 'Go Down, Moses' (which was taken as the title of one of William Faulkner's novels). Many black American leaders of the 20th century, especially Martin Luther King, have phrased their contemporary agenda for political action in the metaphoric vocabulary of the Exodus story. Precisely parallel is the phenomenon of Irish nationalist identification with Israel vis-à-vis the 'Egypt' of imperial England recorded in the fictionalized version of an actual political speech in James Joyce's *Ulysses* ('Oxen of the Sun'). In Sholem Asch's postwar novel *Moses* (1951), allegorical connections are made throughout to the German persecutions and holocaust. Moses has in fact become the perennial symbol of the messianic leader who is despised in times of leisure and yearned for in times of crisis, as when H.G. Wells said of Europe after the war, 'Never before were the nations so eager to follow a Moses who would take them to the long promised land where wars are prohibited and blockades unknown' (*Short History of the World,* 'The Political and Social Reconstruction').

The Moses narrative, which has also inspired works as diverse as Handel's *Israel in Egypt* (1738), Alfred de Vigny's *Moise* (1822), Chateaubriand's somewhat cumbersome tragedy of the same title (1836), Lytton Strachey's *A Dialogue between Moses, Diogenes, and Mr Locke* (1922), and Schoenberg's opera *Moses und Aron* (1930–32, unfinished), continues to be one of the most enduring sources for serious writers in English literary tradition. Howard Nemerov observes, however, that Moses is an awkward character from the point of view of modern literature because he cannot be dispensed with according to merely aesthetic categories. Reflecting on critical displeasure with an exhibition of simple but powerful paintings, he writes:

> When Moses in Horeb struck the rock,
> And water came forth out of the rock,
> Some of the people were annoyed with Moses
> And said he should have used a fancier stick.
> ('On Certain Wits')

In complementary fashion, George Steiner has suggested (*In Bluebeard's Castle*) that the rod of Moses, like his 'pen', has always been a blunt instrument, culturally speaking. But it is there precisely, in its raw moral force, that its literary power also resides.

David L. Jeffrey
University of Ottawa
John V. Fleming
Princeton University

Pharaoh

The term *Pharaoh* originally came from an Egyptian word meaning 'great house'. By the 9th century BC the term was affixed to the royal name and thus became the title for the king of Egypt. The Old Testament specifically names five pharaohs and mentions six others by title. Some English writers use the term to suggest simply the pomp of pagan antiquity (Byron, 'The Age of Bronze', 142; Yeats, 'Vacillation', 84; Dylan Thomas, 'Altarwise by owl-light', 45, 123). Most references, though, deal with the pharaohs mentioned in Genesis 40–41 and Exodus 1–2 and 5–14.

By far the greatest number of references in English literature, however, are to the 'Pharaoh of the Oppression' who 'knew not Joseph' and enslaved the Hebrew residents of his kingdom (Exodus 1–2) and the 'Pharaoh of the Exodus' who, obdurate despite the embassy of Moses and Aaron and a subsequent series of divinely sent plagues, refused to liberate the Israelites (Exodus 5–14). These are often conflated into a single figure, invariably portrayed as a hard-hearted tyrant. Early Christian theologians – St Ambrose, St Augustine, Cassiodorus, St Gregory the Great, St Isidore of Seville, and the Venerable Bede among them – see Pharaoh as a type of devil; the Exodus becomes an allegory of the Christian's passing out of the power of the devil and sin into 'the Promised Land' of eternal life, generally by means of baptism. Hence the Old English *Exodus* refers to Pharaoh as *godes andsacan* (15) or 'God's adversary', a phrase normally reserved for Satan. Medieval drama portrays the king as a ranting tyrant, much like the devil himself. Other writers who employ this typology include Aelfric (homily 'For the Holy Day of Pentecost',

The Homilies of the Anglo-Saxon Church, ed. Thorpe, 1844, 1.312–13); St Thomas More ('A Treatise upon the Passion'); and Edward Taylor (*Preparatory Meditations*, 2nd series, no. 58). In *Paradise Lost*, Milton uses the same typology when he refers to the defeated Pharaoh as 'the river-dragon tamed' (12.191) and earlier when he compares the defeated devils lying in the burning lake to 'Busiris and his Memphian chivalry' (1.307) afloat in the Red Sea. In a more recent setting, John Updike revives the concept of Pharaoh as God's adversary in his short story 'From the Journal of a Leper', where the Satanic 'healing' of the narrator's disease of 'humiliation' is accomplished partly through 'Pharaonic pills'.

From at least the 17th century on, English authors use the figure of Pharaoh in political allegory and satire to represent an arrogant and oppressive monarch, often French. Milton compares Charles I's blindness in religious matters to Pharaoh's hard-heartedness ('Eikonoklastes', 5.231). Marvell uses him to represent Clarendon's greed and corruption ('Clarindon's House-Warming', 37–40) and elsewhere to suggest the corruption of the English court by the French ('Britannia and Rawleigh', 27–28). Dryden uses Pharaoh to represent the proud Louis XIV, whose oppression over his people is contrasted with the benevolence of David, i.e., Charles II (*Absalom and Achitophel*, 331–39; cf. *The Second Part of Absalom and Achitophel*, usually ascribed to Nahum Tate, 671–92). In *The Task*, Cowper sees the tyranny in France as deserving the punishment sent upon Egypt: 'Her house of bondage worse than that of old / Which God avenged on Pharaoh – the Bastille' (5.382–83). Wordsworth compares Napoleon's defeat in Russia to Pharaoh's in the Red Sea ('By Moscow self-devoted to a blaze', 12–13), and elsewhere he rails against political tyranny in England: '...has she no wand / From this curst Pharaoh-plague to rid the land?' ('Imitation of Juvenal – Satire 8', 15–16). In 'Red Leaves', Faulkner parallels the events of the Exodus by having the Indian chieftains, oppressive and decadent, enslave and harass their Negroes just as the pharaohs did the Hebrews.

Reflecting venerable Christian tradition (e.g., Adam the Scot, *Sermo 36, In Die Sanctorum Innocentium, Patrologia Latina*, 198.332), English writers frequently use the plagues visited on Egypt or the destruction of Pharaoh's army in the Red Sea as images of punishment for pride or the fall of prosperity and worldly glory (Herbert, 'Praise', 3.17; Wordsworth, 'To Enterprise', 104–18; Emily Dickinson, '"Red Sea," indeed! Talk not to me', 2; Tennyson, *Aylmer's Field*, 771).

Karl Tamburr
Sweet Briar College

Philistine

Philistine (*pelishtim*) refers to someone or something of Philistia, the nation of Canaan along the coast between Joppa and the Wadi Ghazzeh, just south of Gaza, in Old Testament times. The origin of the word, and the nation itself, is obscure. The people may have been from the Aegean or they may have been the Caphtorim from Caphtor (Crete) who expelled the Avim and took over their land (Deuteronomy 2:23), although in Genesis they are associated with the (otherwise unknown) Casluhim (Genesis 10:14). Of their early history in Canaan not much is known. Their prominent deities were Dagon, Ashtoreth, and Baal-zebub (2 Kings 1:2–6). They became prosperous farmers and had a strong army, equipped with weapons from iron foundries and smiths (1 Samuel 13:20; 17:5–6). During the Judges period of Israel's history the Philistines formed a confederation of five major cities: Gaza, Ashkelon, and Ashdod on the coast, and Gath and Ekron inland. They also carried on guerilla warfare with Israel and at a later date sold captured Israelites as slaves (Joel 3:6; Amos 1:6). When the Israelites united under a king, they fought the Philistines more intensively until David defeated them around 965BC. Solomon included all of Philistia in his kingdom.

Following the division of the kingdom of Judah, the Philistines once again grew in power and waged continuous war with their neighbours, even through the Babylonian captivity of the Jews, after which the Philistines were defeated by Nebuchadnezzar and intermarried with the people of Israel (1 Samuel 8:20; 10:5; 31:1–7; 1 Kings 4:21–24; 2 Kings 12:17; 1 Chronicles 28:1; 2 Chronicles 9:26; 18:18; 26:6; Nehemiah 13:23–24; Isaiah 9:11–12; Jeremiah 25:20; 47:1; Ezekiel 25:15–17).

An early story of victory over the Philistines centres around the hero Samson, who was enticed by Delilah and betrayed to the Philistines (Judges 16:17–30). Another famous victory over the Philistines was achieved by David when with a stone and sling he killed the huge Philistine soldier, Goliath (1 Samuel 17:1–51).

The Philistines are always represented in the Old Testament as ungodly, uncovenanted, and uncircumcised. They do not listen to God, are carnally obsessed, and worship false gods. Hence they persist as aliens and adversaries in exegetical tradition. In English literature the 'Philistine' appears most often as an enemy of the Jews, until the 17th century. Milton's blind hero Samson Agonistes is an example of one fighting the enemy who are outside God's covenant. The meaning 'enemy' later is broadened to refer not to a geographical nation, but to people from whom one must protect oneself: Dryden speaks of falling among the Philistines (*The Hind and the Panther*); Swift (*Polite Conversations*) says of one unfortunate that he went to court very drunk because he had been among Philistines; and Henry Fielding (*Amelia*, chapter 5) equates Philistines and bailiffs.

In the 19th century Carlyle uses the term *Philistines* to represent bores, dullards, and children of darkness (*Sterling*). The term thus enlarged came to mean a person who is so unenlightened that he thinks only the ordinary material things of life are of merit. Matthew Arnold gave the term general currency when speaking about the materialistic middle class, who are opposed to the enlightened and chosen few (e.g., in 'Sweetness and Light', from *Culture and Anarchy*). His first use of the term in this way comes in his essay on 'Heinrich Heine' (*Essays in Criticism*, 1), and conveys particularly Germanic overtones; 'Philistine' was a term applied to hostile townsmen by German university students in 'town / gown' controversy. The students Arnold took to be 'children of the light' (cf. Luke 1:8). In his *On the Study of Celtic Literature* he writes: 'We are imperilled by what I call the "Philistinism" of our middle class. On the side of beauty and taste, vulgarity; on the side of morals and feelings, coarseness; on the side of mind and spirit, unintelligence, – this is Philistinism.' For American essayist H.L. Mencken Mark Twain was a great artist unable to throw off his 'native Philistinism', so that in American letters of the 19th century 'the voice of Mark Twain was the voice of the Philistine'. Via Arnold the anti-cultural Philistine soon became a commonplace, as in Gilbert's lyrics for *Patience*: 'Though the Philistines may jostle, you will rank as an apostle / In the high aesthetic band.'

Linda Beamer
Ryerson Polytechnic Institute, Toronto, Ontario

Plagues of Egypt

After the unsuccessful attempt by Moses and Aaron to achieve the liberation of their people from slavery in Egypt, the Lord directed them to announce a series of plagues – each designed to induce Pharaoh's repentance and release of the people (Exodus 7:14–11:20). The ten plagues which ensued were: (1) the waters of the river turned to blood (7:14–24); (2) frogs (7:25–8:15); (3) lice (8:16–19); (4) flies (8:20–32); (5) murrain, an epidemic afflicting the Egyptians' livestock (9:1–7); (6) boils and blains (9:8–12); (7) hail (9:13–35); (8) locusts (10:1–20); (9) three days of palpable darkness (10:21–23); (10) slaying of the Egyptian firstborn (11:1–12:30). After each of the first nine plagues Pharaoh's heart was hardened, but in the wake of the tenth he granted the Israelite slaves their freedom. Almost immediately, however, he regretted his decision and pursued them into the wilderness where, with his entire army, he perished in the Red Sea.

In Milton's *Paradise Lost* Adam is given a vivid preview of the plagues to be visited upon 'Pharaoh, the lawless Tyrant' who, as a type of the 'River-dragon' or Leviathan opposing God, 'must be compelled by Signes and Judgments dire' (12.170–92). William Cowper takes his cue from Calvin (and perhaps from Reformation hymnody):

> Let Egypt's plagues, and Canaan's woes proclaim
> The favours pour'd upon the Jewish name –
> Their freedom, purchased for them at the cost
> Of all their hard oppressors valued most;
> Their title to a country not their own
> Made sure by prodigies till then unknown.
> ('Expostulation', 169–74)

But Cowper also anticipates the proverbial and clichéd use of the story. In his 'The Progress of Error' he chides the press for abusing its privileges, saying that because of its mendacity and flippancy in England 'worse plagues than Pharaoh's land befel' (460–64). Charles Lamb in 'Poor Relations' makes a trivializing allusion to 'the most irrelevant thing in nature, – a lion in your path, – a frog in your chamber, – a fly in your ointment' (cf. Proverbs 26:13; Ecclesiastes 10:1). Similarly, in Arnold Bennett's *The Matador of the Five Towns*, 'If you were a married man you'd know that the ten plagues of Egypts are simply nothing in comparison with your wife's relations' (chapter 1).

Some of the plagues have lent themselves to colourful invocation. Hardy is fond of the ninth plague, the 'palpable darkness' as Milton phrases it, which can describe anything from arboreal gloom (*Far from the Madding Crowd*, chapter 24) to winter ombré: 'On a moorland in wet weather it is thirty perceptible minutes to any fireside man, woman, or beast in Christendom – minutes that can be felt, like the Egyptian plague of darkness' (*The Hand of Ethelberta*, chapter 3). In Rose Macaulay's *Told by an Idiot*, 'American merchant princesses are descending on the land like locusts' (1.10). Occasionally, however, some of the moral or spiritual force of earlier interpretation attaches itself deliberately to such allusions. Charlotte Brontë's *Jane Eyre* draws forcibly on the biblical narrative in the memorable lines: 'My hopes were all dead – struck with a subtle doom, such as, in one night, fell on all the first-born in the land of Egypt' (chapter 26). And a voice of the reprobate in Sinclair Lewis' *The God-Seekers* is heard to say: 'My heart is literally harder than a millstone. My mind is as dark as the Egyptian darkness that could be felt. Can it be that Christ could die for one like me?' (chapter 34).

David L. Jeffrey
University of Ottawa

Ruth

The Old Testament story of Ruth the Moabitess is an idyllic romance built around the life of a domestic heroine. As a pastoral work, the story has a strong elemental quality in its references to home, family, religious devotion, earth, harvest, love, and nation.

The plot is a comic, U-shaped sequence. The four chapters are structured so as to accentuate the climactic night-time meeting between Ruth and Boaz: (1) the tragic background of the story, (2) the early stages of the romance, (3) the encounter at midnight on the threshing floor, and (4) the denouement. Underlying the story is a quest for a home (Ruth 1:9; 3:1), and there is a continuous tension between emptiness and fulness which is resolved happily in the last chapter. The story is noteworthy for its careful ordering of events; its use of the archetypes of harvest and the stranger or exile; its drama; its dramatic irony (Ruth and Boaz are oblivious to the likelihood of marriage); its controlling metaphor of ingathering; the use of allusion to salvation history (the domestic world of an obscure woman becomes linked with the mainstream of Old Testament history); and the intricate characterization of Ruth, Boaz, and Naomi.

Thematically the story celebrates the commonplace (nature, earth, harvest, family, home), domestic values, and wedded romantic love. It is also a story of divine providence. Late in the story (4:17) the writer suggests yet another interpretive framework when he places the child of Ruth in the Davidic/messianic line, thereby calling attention to the story as a chapter of salvation history. (The only other biblical reference to the story, Matthew 1:5, likewise places Obed and Boaz in the genealogy of Jesus.)

Poets' allusions to the story have covered its main phases. In Milton's Sonnet 9 ('Lady that in the prime of earliest youth') Ruth appears with Mary, sister of Martha, as a norm of true spiritual virtue, and if the speculation is accurate that the young woman of the sonnet is Milton's first wife Mary Powell, the allusion also includes Ruth's domestic identity as the idealized bride.

Blake, in *Jerusalem*, follows Dante, listing Ruth with Bathsheba and others as the 'Material Line' culminating in Mary (62.11), so emphasizing her sexuality. In a series of popular early 19th-century graphic illustrations on the theme of Ruth, four of eleven plates deal with sexual iconography in the narrative – notably the paintings of Laurens, Rembrandt, Delacroix, and Poussin, in the latter of which a harvest scene provides relevant background. Another iconic representation frequent in the 19th century shows Ruth gleaning, as in 'The Solitary Reaper'.

Byron compares himself and his readers searching after truth to Ruth and Boaz gathering grain (*Don Juan*, 13.96). Whittier remembers

Ruth at the feet of Boaz when he says regarding a mountain lake under the moon that it 'Sleeps dreaming of the mountains, fair as Ruth / In the old Hebrew pastoral, at the feet / Of Boaz' ('Among the Hills').

Ruth the exile prompts the most evocative of all the allusions to the story. In his 'Ode to a Nightingale', Keats elaborates his theme of the bird as a symbol of the immortality of nature by asserting that the song to which he is listening is 'the selfsame song that found a path / Through the sad heart of Ruth when, sick for home, / She stood in tears amid the alien corn' (65–67).

The book of Ruth has been the subject of a host of dramatic adaptations. While many of these have been intended for religious instruction, serious literary adaptations include *Ruth and Naomi* (1786) by the Comtesse de Genlis (Stephanie Felicite Ducrest du St Aubin), Andrew Young's dramatic poem *Boaz and Ruth* (1920), and William Ford Manley's *Ruth* (1928).

Leland Ryken
Wheaton College

Samson

The Hebrew name *Shimshon* (Septuagint *Samson*) may derive from *shemesh*, 'sun'; it has been suggested that the biblical stories associated with Samson may in fact have their origin in solar myth. The pericope of Samson in Judges 13–16 appears to have developed from the tradition of oral poetic sagas common in premonarchic Israel and, specifically, from a series of popular stories preserving accounts of a local hero from the district of Mahaneh-dan. Dating (probably) from the 10th century BC, the Samson saga was incorporated into the cyclic pattern of apostasy-faith-apostasy underpinning the Judges narrative (cf. Judges 2:16–19). It appears that at this time significant portions of the localized Samson legend were tailored to fit the paradigm of the charismatic 'judge', who, impelled by God, delivered the errant Israelites from subjugation to political freedom by bringing them back to the faith of their fathers.

The story of Samson falls into three clearly defined sections: (a) the distinctively religious birth narrative (chapter 13), in which Samson's birth is supernaturally foretold to a previously childless

Danite couple and in which Samson is dedicated from birth as a Nazarite (cf. Numbers 6); (b) the essentially nonreligious heroic exploits of Samson (chapters 14 and 15), in which the Danite strongman harasses the hostile Philistines by repeated attacks and stratagems; and (c) the religious conclusion (chapter 16), which moves from Samson's defeat and humiliation at the hands of Delilah to his final victory over the Philistines when he pulls down the pagan temple of Dagon on the heads of his enemies. The only other biblical reference to Samson occurs in Hebrews 11:32, where he is included in the roster of those who subdued kingdoms 'through faith'.

In English literature, the story receives its earliest detailed retelling in the 14th-century *Cursor Mundi* (7083–7262), where Samson is depicted as a noble hero brought low by feminine deceit. The narrator seems to delight in Samson's eventual revenge, when he is made (in an original twist) to pull down the temple at the marriage-feast celebrating Delilah's marriage to one of her fellow Philistines. Both Chaucer (*Monk's Tale*, 7.3205–84) and Lydgate (*Fall of Princes*, 2.6336–6510) set Samson in the *De casibus virorum illustrium* tradition (cf. Boccaccio, *De Casibus*, 1.17), emphasizing the tragedy of his fall from high to low estate and treating his ill-fated liaison with Delilah as a moral exemplum of domestic treachery. Gower (*Confessio Amantis*, 8.2703–04) also treats the Hebrew champion as a tragic lover, comparing him with Paris, Hercules, and Troilus. Typically, as these examples suggest, Middle English poets (unlike theologians) tended to eliminate – or at least downplay – the religious elements of the Samson story, preferring to shape it as a secular tragedy in which a noble hero, lacking discretion, was tumbled from high to low degree on Fortune's turning wheel because he fondly loved and foolishly confided in a treacherous woman.

In Renaissance literature, however, the spiritual significance of Samson's history re-emerges as a central preoccupation. Although the medieval view of Samson as a victim of unwise and ungoverned passion survived (e.g., Spenser, *Faerie Queene*, 5.8.2, and Shakespeare, *Love's Labour's Lost*, 1.2.70–88), Renaissance writers after 1600 almost invariably depicted him as a repentant sinner purified by trial and restored to God's favour. Francis Quarles devoted 3,468 lines of rhyming couplets in his *Historie of Sampson* (1631) to prolix retelling of the Old Testament story, interspersed with twenty-three versified 'meditations' explaining the prevailing theological interpretations of each episode. George Herbert, more economically, revived the allegorical interpretation of Samson as a prefiguration of Christ in his meditative lyric 'Sunday' (47–49). Milton, in *Areopagitica* (1644), casts his vision of a regenerate England in the simile of a reviving Samson: 'Methinks I see in my mind a noble and puissant nation rousing herself like a strong man after sleep, and shaking her invincible locks' (*Prose Works*, Yale ed., 2.552–53).

This focus owes a good deal to a series of German and Dutch Samson dramas composed during the 16th and 17th centuries. Basing their conception firmly on Hebrews 11:32 and dealing freely with the materials of the Judges account, such continental playwrights as Hieronymus Zieglerus (*Samson, Tragoedia Nova*, Basel, 1547), Marcus Andreas Wunstius (*Samson, Tragoedia Sacra*, Strassburg, circa 1600), and Joost van den Vondel (*Samson, of Heiligue Wraeck, Treurspel*, Amsterdam, 1660) transformed Samson from a quasi-chivalric hero of brute physical endowments into a divinely led instrument of faith. They made him, progressively, an exemplum of *mentis caecitas* (spiritual blindness) rather than love-blindness and transferred the dramatic interest away from his superficial relationship with Delilah, fixing it instead on Samson's own inner anguish and conflicts. The process of Samson's spiritual regeneration and eventual restoration as God's faithful champion became, thus, the dominant thematic concern.

The crowning glory of this Renaissance reformulation comes in Milton's *Samson Agonistes* (1671), a poetic drama synthesizing all the major literary and theological traditions which had grown up around the story. Introducing a Samson already betrayed, blinded, and slaving at the Philistine mill, Milton limits the action to the last few hours of his hero's life and centres attention on the process by which Samson is led, through a series of temptations, to repentance and spiritual renovation. The movement of the drama is focused on Samson's transformation from a hubristic Hebrew Hercules to a humble and obedient servant of God who becomes, in the closing semichorus (1687–1707), a prefiguration of Christ. Physical actions are reported rather than played out before the audience, and the Old Testament emphasis on Samson's strength and heroic exploits are largely parodied in the (nonbiblical) figure of Harapha, a vainglorious braggadocio who taunts Samson.

After *Samson Agonistes* there are no major treatments of the Samson saga in English literature. References after 1671 are confined largely to incidental allusions, and these – almost invariably miscellaneous metaphors of physical strength or of love betrayed – do nothing to enhance or develop the literary Samson tradition brought to a climax by Milton. Blake, e.g., has a fragment of a prose poem on Samson in his *Poetical Sketches,* and Browning includes an interesting typological exploration in book 8 of *The Ring and the Book* (632–49). The most original modern version of the story is D.H. Lawrence's short story 'Samson and Delilah', which, in the encounter between a voluptuous innkeeper and her estranged husband, reflects Lawrence's own stormy and passionate relationship with his wife, Frieda.

John Spencer Hill
University of Ottawa

Samuel

The last of the Old Testament judges and first of the prophets (after Moses), Samuel played a pivotal role in the establishment of kingship in Israel. He was born to Elkanah and Hannah, Elkanah's beloved but long-barren wife, after she vowed to consecrate to God any son he would give her. The etymology of his name, given in 1 Samuel 1:20 ('Because I have asked him of the Lord'), is based on puns on the verb *sha'al* (meaning both 'request' and 'dedicate'; cf. 1:28). Hannah was subsequently blessed with more children – three sons and two daughters – thus alleviating her misery at the hands of Peninnah, Elkanah's other wife, whose spitefulness and taunting had provoked her almost desperate plea for a child (1 Samuel 1:1–11).

As soon as he was weaned, Samuel was brought to the Temple at Shiloh by Hannah to serve Eli, the priest. As a boy he was called by God in the night, who revealed to him the imminent demise of the priestly line of Eli because of the wickedness of Eli's sons (1 Samuel 3). Samuel himself, it became clear, was to succeed Eli as priest.

In his role as priest and judge, Samuel was able both to rid Israel of the worship of Canaanite gods and to drive the Philistines out of Israel (1 Samuel 7:3–17). When his own sons, like those of Eli, proved faithless and unworthy to succeed him, the elders of Israel demanded 'a king to judge us like all the nations' – thus rejecting not only the temporal authority of Samuel and his family but also the unique kingship of God himself over Israel (1 Samuel 8:7). Warning the people of the consequences of their rejection of theocracy, Samuel nevertheless, with God's assent, bowed to their demands and appointed Saul. Twice Samuel confronted Saul about his disobedience, and with his own hands he killed Agag, whom Saul had spared against God's explicit directive (13:8–15; 15:1–35). Samuel's last important act was the anointing of David – a man after God's own heart – to succeed Saul as king (16:1–13). He later sheltered David from Saul's wrath (19:8–24). His death is mentioned very briefly (25:1; 28:3). At the behest of Saul, the Woman of Endor called up Samuel's ghost, which again foretold Saul's doom (28:3–20). This posthumous prophecy has appealed more to writers than any other event in Samuel's career.

Samuel is among the 'famous men' praised in the book of Ecclesiasticus, where his prophetic career is also rehearsed (46:13–20). Other biblical references to him are found in 2 Chronicles 35:18; Psalm 99:6; Jeremiah 15:1; Acts 3:24; 13:20. The author of Hebrews includes him among the great heroes of the faith (Hebrews 11:32).

Samuel's warning against the evils of kingship (8:10–18) became a key text in the constitutional controversies of the 17th century. Divine-right monarchists interpreted it as a statement of the prerogative of kings, while constitutional monarchists and republicans thought it to be merely a description of the way kings usually behave, with no implication of divine approval. Each party weighted God's reluctant acceptance of kingship (see also 8:7–9; 12:13–15) to suit its interests (e.g., R. Filmer, *Patriarcha,* 1680, section 23; Milton, *Defense of the English People,* chapter 2). In the following century Fielding accuses the Jacobites of supporting precisely the kind of king Samuel describes (*Jacobite's Journal,* nos. 25, 21 May 1748, and 46, 15 October 1748). Thomas Paine and the young Coleridge cite this passage as displaying the inherent evil of kingship and God's unambiguous disapproval of it (*Common Sense,* 'Of Monarchy and Hereditary Succession'; *Lectures on Revealed Religion,* 2).

In most of the many plays devoted to Saul and David and in Abraham Cowley's unfinished epic *Davideis* (1656), Samuel plays a minor role; indeed, he is often given less prominence than his ghost. D.H. Lawrence, however, gives him an eloquent and moving prayer in scene 2 of his *David* drama.

As the main character of Laurence Housman's *Samuel the Kingmaker,* Samuel is a scheming politician who identifies his own will with God's, engineers all his miracles, falsifies the historical record, and undermines and destroys Saul in order to satisfy his own lust for power and revenge. As the narrator of Robert Penn Warren's long monologue 'Saul at Gilboa', Samuel meditates on the meaning of Saul's tragic career. A vivid contemporary retelling of the story of Samuel's childhood call by God (1 Samuel 3) occurs in Rudy Wiebe's 'The Vietman Call of Samuel Reimer', chapter 12 of his *The Blue Mountains of China* (1970).

William Kinsley
Université de Montréal

Saul

Saul, the first king of Israel, is the principal figure of a considerable portion of the first book of Samuel (chapters 9–31). A member of the tribe of Benjamin, he was anointed king by the prophet Samuel, performed deeds of valour, and rescued Israel from many enemies. However, when he disobeyed God's commandment to exterminate the Amalekites by sparing their king, Agag, he was disowned by Samuel in favour of David, a 'man after God's own heart'. In repeated efforts to capture and to kill his young rival, who had gained fame and popularity through his extraordinary defeat of the Philistine giant Goliath (1 Samuel 17), he failed and succumbed to depression. Recognizing that God had turned against him, he consulted a medium in order to seek counsel from the ghost of Samuel, only to have judgment pronounced upon him again. Finally, wounded on the battlefield while fighting against the Philistines, he took his own life. A period of national mourning was led by David, who succeeded him and ushered in Israel's Golden Age.

As a tragic figure Saul has fascinated painters from Rembrandt to Joseph Israels, musicians from Handel to Honneger, and international writers such as Jean de la Taille, Grimmelshausen, Pierre du Ryer, Voltaire, Lamartine, Friedrich Ruckert, Karl Gutzkow, Karl Beck, André Gide, Richard Beer-Hofmann, Max Zweig, David Pinski, R.M. Rilke, and Karl Wolfskehl.

Among English authors, Milton refers to Saul frequently in his prose works as a bad and treacherous king, an example of unregenerate humanity. He sees Charles I as following Saul's course in fearing the people more than God while, like Saul, insisting on the righteousness of his acts. Charles' court and prelates are likened to the cattle of Amalek. For Milton, Charles is more blameworthy than Saul, however, because Saul 'was at length convinc'd', whereas Charles remained 'to the howr of death fix'd in his fals perswasion' (*Eikonoklastes*, 9). Saul plays a prominent role in Abraham Cowley's unfinished epic, *Davideis* (1656). In Dryden's political allegory *Absalom and Achitophel*, Saul is made to stand for Oliver Cromwell and Saul's son Ishbosheth for Cromwell's son Richard.

Byron devotes to Saul four of the twenty-three *Hebrew Melodies* (1816). In two of these lyrics the Romantic poet pours his own restless temperament into the soul of Israel's king; in a third he deals with Saul's invocation of the ghost of Samuel on the eve of battle; and in the fourth Saul sings his defiant song before entering into battle. For Byron, Saul represents the superior individual who walks to his doom with head unbowed before divine and human adversaries. Byron regarded Saul's encounter with the ghost of Samuel as the finest ghost scene ever written and refers to it in *Manfred*, 2.175–82, in the eleventh stanza of 'Dedication to Don Juan', and in *The Age of Bronze*, 2.380–83.

Browning's *Saul*, published in fragmentary form in 1845 and in completed form two years later, is a dramatic monologue spoken and sung by David, who recalls the memorable hour when Abner first brought him, the young shepherd, to comfort with his music the stricken king. The ageing monarch is gradually uplifted from despair by the talented harpist and singer. David, feeling love as well as sympathy for Saul, prophesies:

> O Saul, it shall be
> A Face like my face that receives thee; a Man like to me,
> Thou shalt love and be loved by, forever: a Hand like this
> hand,
> Shall throw open the gates of new life to thee! See the
> Christ stand!

This promise of Saul's forgiveness and ultimate salvation provides a new sense of closure for the Saul story. Nevertheless, Saul himself remains silent. The political future belongs to David.

D.H. Lawrence's play *David* (1926) begins with the conflict between Saul and Samuel after the defeat of the Amalekites and ends with David's flight to escape death by the envious Saul. The sixteen scenes focus on the decay of Saul's personality under the influence of jealousy at David's ever increasing popularity. J. M. Barrie's play *The Boy David* (1936) introduces Saul as a noble figure about whom the clouds of despondency have begun to gather. Browning's poem and Rembrandt's painting were Barrie's models for his characterization of Saul. The play ends, as does the final scene of Lawrence's play, with the covenant between David and Jonathan.

Sol Liptzin
Hebrew University of Jerusalem
Joseph McClatchey
Wheaton College

Ten Commandments

The Ten Commandments are presented initially in the Old Testament as the basic law of the covenant community formed at Mount Sinai (Exodus 20:2–17). Although the matter is debated, they would appear to date from the 13th century BC, the earliest period of Israel's history. The commandments are repeated, with minor differences, in Deuteronomy 5:6–21, in the context of an account of the renewal of Israel's covenant on the plains of Moab during the last days of Moses. In Hebrew, the commandments are called the 'Ten Words', from which title (via the Greek translation) comes the term *Decalogue*.

In their original context the commandments were the criminal law (or state law) of ancient Israel, a central part of the constitution of the nascent theocratic state established at Sinai. They were strictly apodictic laws in ancient Israel and passed into the religious and moral realms only with the demise of the Hebrew kingdoms. The commandments are said to have been inscribed on two stone tablets (Deuteronomy 5:22). Each tablet (contrary to later popular tradition) contained the full text of the commandments; one tablet belonged to each partner in the covenant relationship, symbolizing thereby the mutual recognition of responsibilities and authority. The first five commandments pertain primarily to the relationship between God and Israel and are thus essentially theological; the second five focus on interhuman relationships and regulate the social dimensions of life in the covenant community. According to many historians, the breach of any one of the commandments, upon a conviction being secured in the courts, could be followed by the sentence of death. In the reality of Israel's history, however, the commandments more often expressed the ideal of national life than the actuality. The fundamental presupposition of the commandments is *love,* God's electing love for Israel and the love required by God from Israel in return (Deuteronomy 6:5).

There is variation between different religious traditions as to the sequence and numbering of the commandments; the most commonly accepted sequence is employed in the following summary of their substance:

(1) *The prohibition of gods other than the Lord of Israel* (Exodus 20:3). The first commandment secures the integrity of Israel's faith and requires of the people total commitment to the single God. (2) *The prohibition of images* (Exodus 20:4–6). Specifically, images of the God of Israel are prohibited. Thereby the idolatry common in the religious practices of Israel's neighbours is eliminated, and the transcendence of the deity is safeguarded. (3) *The prohibition of the improper use of the divine name* (Exodus 20:7). The Law was not concerned with blasphemy or bad language, but with the protection of the sanctity of God's personal name (JHWH) from abuse in such practices as magic and incantation. (4) *The observation of the Sabbath* (Exodus 20:8–11). This positive commandment preserved the sanctity of the seventh day in commemoration both of creation

(Exodus 20:8–11) and of Israel's redemption from Egypt (Deuteronomy 5:15). (5) *The honour of parents* (Exodus 20:12). While having general familial implications, the primary thrust is the honour bestowed on parents by the children's acceptance of parental instruction in the faith (Deuteronomy 6:7). (6) *The prohibition of killing* (Exodus 20:13). The Law pertains specifically to culpable murder (other legislation deals with such matters as manslaughter and killing in warfare). (7) *The prohibition of adultery* (Exodus 20:14). (8) *The prohibition of theft* (Exodus 20:15). (9) *The prohibition of false witness* (Exodus 20:16). The Law specifically pertains to the giving of testimony in the courts of law, though it has general implications with respect to truthfulness. (10) *The prohibition of coveting* (Exodus 20:17). This is the most comprehensive of the commandments and is preventative in purpose, attempting to address those desires which might give rise to specific actions as anticipated in the first nine commandments. In his Sermon on the Mount Jesus develops the general principle of the tenth commandment in the understanding of such matters as murder (Matthew 5:21–23) and adultery (Matthew 5:27–28).

The Ten Commandments were from the beginning foundational to English law: King Alfred prefixed the Decalogue to his own legal code, and in a time when moral and civil law were not yet distinct Aelfric, in his *Catholic Homilies* (2.12), as also in his sermon *De Populo Israhel* (ed. Pope, 2.20), could apply the commandments readily to a civil context. Treatises on the Decalogue proliferated after the 13th century, partly in response to Archbishop Pecham's insistence in his Lambeth Constitutions (1273) on expanded catechetical instruction, an encouragement which led to popular Middle English lyrics on the subject (e.g., C. Brown, *English Lyrics of the XIIIth Century*, nos. 23, 70) and verse sermons (e.g., Brown, *Religious Lyrics of the XIVth Century*, no. 102). In the seventh play of the Towneley cycle (as in the sixth play of the *Ludus Coventriae*, or N-Town Corpus Christi cycle), Moses proclaims in epitome a typical pulpit exposition of the Decalogue, which is anachronistically followed later by the corresponding ten plagues upon Pharaoh's Egypt, said to be 'for brekinge of the X commaundementis'. The biblical order is retained by George Herbert's 'The Church Militant', where, in the redeemed life of God's chosen, 'The Ten Commandments there did flourish more / than the ten bitter plagues had done before.' A connection between transgression and natural judgment is reflected in hexaemeral literature from Bede to St Bonaventure (e.g., the *De Legibus* of William of Auvergne and the *De Legibus et Consuetudinibus Angliae* of the great 13th-century English jurist Henri de Bracton (or 'Bretton'). Matthew Tyndale's argument that the 'lawe of the kynge is Gods lawe' (*Obedience of a Christian Man*, 79) accords with basic English tradition from Alfred through Bracton to Blackstone.

Commentary on the second commandment in the 14th and 15th centuries was controversial, since it reflected directly on the use of images in churches, especially the propriety of their relation to meditation and catechism and the possibility that excessive veneration might constitute idolatry. This issue was strongly contested by the Lollards, who opposed images (see Owst, 134–43), and by members of the regular clergy such as John Mirk (*Festial*, 171ff.), who argued, against the Lollards, that simple people are not really led to believe that Matthew, Mark, Luke, and John were animals or that Moses really had 'two hornes' (261, 302); such images, they said, were not associated with the idolatry prohibited in the second commandment but were an invaluable instrument for teaching the gospel to illiterate or semiliterate persons.

Concerning the third commandment – which was thought to involve everything from blasphemous explication to false oath and perjury – there was less debate in the 14th century. Lollards and regular clergy agreed that breach of the commandment was out of hand among laity and clergy, young and old, male and female alike. 'Horible sweryinge, as the most parte of the pepull dose now-adaies' (MS Royal 18.B.23, fol. 86b) is a concern of many sermons, as it is in Chaucer's *Canterbury Tales,* whose Host is reproved for profanity and whose 'coy' Prioress is said to swear by 'St Loy', the patron saint of cart drivers (*General Prologue*, 1.120). Chaucer's Parson takes up the matter in his discussion of the sin of wrath ('*Sequitur de Ira*'): 'What seye we eke of hem that deliten hem in sweryng, and holden it a gentrie or a manly dede to swere grete othes, al be the caus not worth a straw? Certes, this is horrible synne' (*Parson's Tale*, 10.600–603). The early 15th-century dialogue sermon *Dives et Pauper* offers a dramatic exchange on the import of all the commandments, following typical patristic commentaries.

The Decalogue assumed fresh importance in the Reformation, in that many Reformers felt that a signal feature of corruption in the Church was a lax regard for rampant sin and insufficient attention to obedient living. Some of this laxity may have been occasioned theologically, arising from implications of the principle that 'the Old Law was good but imperfect' and that the Law ought to be seen as a means subservient to the end of inward grace (e.g., St Thomas Aquinas, *Summa Theologica* 1a–2ae.98.1; 106.1.2). For Matthew Tyndale, by contrast, though the Law is not our means of salvation, it is surely the standard of 'perfeccion and the marke where at all we oughte to shote' (*Obedience of a Christian Man*, 127). Calvin follows the main patristic tradition in most respects but gives more space to analysis of the Decalogue as basic to the Law by which the life of Christians is proscribed; for him a reading of the Decalogue is essential in regular worship, since it is effectively a statement of God's sovereign claim on the total obedience of his covenant people. 'Hence', he says, 'I make part of [worship] to consist in bringing our consciences into subjection to his Law.' He adds, amplifying Augustine, 'car c'est un hommage spirituel' (*Institutes* 2.8.13–59). Calvin departs from Augustine in enjoining strict observance of the fourth commandment, concerning the Sabbath, applying it to the Lord's Day, Sunday; in general he substantially elevates the role of the Decalogue in both liturgy and catechism. The official *Homilies Appointed to Be Read in Churches* (1562) in the time of Queen Elizabeth included homilies on the second (2.1.2), third (1.7), seventh (1.7), and eighth, ninth, and tenth commandments (1.12). Elizabeth also ordered that the Decalogue be painted over the communion table in English churches (over existing triptych altar paintings featuring the Crucifixion or Annunciation), or else on the tympanum. Later, under Archbishop Laud, much of the earlier type of painting and statuary was reintroduced, and some inscriptions of the Ten Commandments were then blotted out and replaced by crucifixes.

In England under the Puritans, differences of opinion concerning the degree to which Christians under the 'dispensation of grace' were obliged to literal observance of all precepts of the Law led to disagreements between the Puritans, who in general took the strong view of Calvin, and most Roman and some Anglican theologians, who took a less rigorous view, not only with respect to the fourth commandment but also, it was sometimes argued, with respect to the third, *de facto* winking at parishioners 'jurans par S. Jaques ou S. Antoine', as Calvin puts it (*Institutes* 2.8.25). The Puritans were strong on enforcement of the seventh comandment; their detractors wondered if in their mercantile practices they were as scrupulous concerning the eighth. In Shakespeare's *Measure for Measure*, in which excessive Puritan ardour in judgment concerning the seventh commandment is seen (in Angelo) as an index of spiritual pride, the devilish Lucio says to one of his bewildered interlocutors, 'Thou concludest like the sanctimonious pirate that went to sea with the Ten Commandments, but scraped one out of the table.' The gentleman replies, 'Thou shalt not steal?' – to which Lucio responds in the affirmative. Another then observes, 'Why, 'twas a commandment to command the captain and all the rest from their functions. They put forth to steal' (1.2.6–14).

In *King Lear*, when Edgar is feigning madness in the hut with Lear and Kent, he offers a crude summary of the commandments whose breach most affects the King's fortunes: 'Take heed o' the foul fiend. Obey thy parents, keep thy word justly, swear not, commit not with man's sworn spouse, set not thy sweet heart on proud array. Tom's a-cold' (3.4.82–85): the commandments ignored, anarchic passions reign instead.

The representation in Bunyan is, by contrast, that of the vindictive passion of the Mosaic law, when in *The Pilgrim's Progress* Moses overtakes Christian and trummels him, saying, 'I know not how to show mercy' for his breaches of the Law.

For the Calvinist poet William Cowper the Decalogue is as uncompromising as the occasion of its transmission was terrifying. Echoing the opening sentiments of Milton's *Paradise Lost,* he writes how God

> Marshalling all his terrors as he came;
> Thunder, and earthquake, and devouring flame;

> From Sinai's top Jehovah gave the law –
> Life for obedience – death for ev'ry flaw.
> When the great Sov'rein would his will express,
> He gives a perfect rule; what can he less? ('Truth', 547–52)

For Cowper the alternative to God's order is chaos, as the sinful world 'in scorn of God's commands' suggests, and inevitably judgment follows:

> Sad period to a pleasant course!
> Yet so will God repay
> Sabbaths profaned without remorse,
> And mercy cast away. ('Bill of Mortality, 1793')

The poems of Lord Byron, whose *Don Juan* ascribes to Malthus 'the eleventh commandment / Which says, "Thou shalt not marry", unless "well"' (15.297–99), are replete with rewritings of the Decalogue. In *The Deformed Transformed* the makings of Byron's demonic hero are already apparent: 'And thank your meanness, other God have you none' (2.3.318); the curse for dishonouring parents is alluded to in *Werner; or the Inheritance* (1.1.92–98; 3.4.597); the commandment against blasphemy is parodied in 'English Bards and Scotch Reviewers' (504–06), as also is the fourth commandment (320–21, 636–37), which is more gently treated in *Childe Harold* (1.684–97). '"Thou shalt not bear false witness" like "The Blues"' (*Don Juan*, 1.1643), rhyming with '"Thou shalt not covet" Mr Sotheby's Muse' (1641), introduces a pervasive theme in Byron's *Don Juan* (cf. 12.121–23) as in others of his poems ('Parisina', 65–66, 883). In his *Prophecy of Dante*, 'They who kneel to idols so divine / Break no commandment' (4.31–32); in short, as a creature of secular grace, the Romantic poet enjoys unlimited freedom *contra legem*.

The tendency to disparage or rewrite the Ten Commandments is unsurprisingly a common theme in modern literature. The 'eleventh commandment' of modern cynicism, as noted in the *Oxford English Dictionary*, is 'Thou shalt not be found out', since, as Somerset Maugham puts it in *Mrs Craddock*, 'in real life everyone [is] very virtuous and very dull' where 'the ten commandments' hedge one around 'with the menace of hell fire and eternal damnation' (chapter 27).

In fact, Byronic parody, though it takes a variety of forms, is but one strategy for deflecting the burden of the Decalogue. In Hardy's *Tess of the D'Urbervilles* 'to visit the sins of the fathers upon the children may be a morality good enough for divinities, [but] it is scorned by average human nature' (chapter 11), a stance Hardy generalizes upon not only with his satire on the evangelistic sign painter in that novel (who goes about painting the precepts of the Decalogue) but also in *Far from the Madding Crowd* (chapter 26), 'An Imaginative Woman', and elsewhere.

Thackeray finds little respect paid to the sixth and seventh commandments in French society, but rather the disavowal of them common among 'the politest people in the world' (*The Newcomes*, chapter 37). Carlyle's Teufelsdröckh pontificates, 'At a time when the Divine Commandment, Thou shalt not steal, wherein truly, if well understood, is comprised the whole Hebrew Decalogue... at a time, I say, when this Divine Commandment has all but faded away from the general remembrance; and, with a little disguise, a new opposite Commandment, Thou shalt steal, is everywhere promulgated – it perhaps behooves... the sound portion of mankind to bestir themselves and rally' (*Sartor Resartus*, 2.10). Some of the satire is more double-edged, such as Arthur Clough's 'The Latest Decalogue', in which are found the lines 'Thou shalt have but one God only; who / Would be at the expense of two', and 'No graven image may be / Worship'd, except the currency.' Carlyle's own position may be more clearly defined in his essay 'Characteristics', where he takes the view that 'The Duties of Man... to what is Highest in himself make but the First Table of the Law', a rationalization only too quickly seized upon by Sinclair Lewis' *Elmer Gantry* but bypassed in favour of gleeful antinomianism by Pilon in *Tortilla Flat*: '"I have been bad," Pilon continued ecstatically. He was enjoying himself thoroughly. "I have lied and stolen. I have been lecherous. I have committed adultery and taken God's name in vain"' (chapter 8). This is a popular form of John Stuart Mill's argument that Christian morality as reflected in use of the Decalogue is negative and passive rather than positive and vigorous: 'in its precepts "thou shalt not" predominates unduly over "thou shalt"' ('On Liberty'). Christina Rossetti, however, seems to have thought otherwise: her *Letter and Spirit* examines the Ten

Commandments positively, with a view to evincing their intention in constructive social terms. This was, however, even among Victorians, knowingly to go against the grain.

D.H. Lawrence regards American liberty as 'a liberty of THOU SHALT NOT... [in] the land of THOU SHALT NOT' *(Studies in Classic American Literature)*, whereas H.G. Wells, considering the opposite side of the coin, reflects that 'there are two distinct and contrasting methods of limiting liberty; the first is Prohibition, "thou shalt not," and the second Command, "thou shalt"' *(A Modern Utopia,* chapter 2).

As the need has arisen, modern writers have taken renewed interest in at least one of the commandments, as James Russell Lowell illustrates:

> In vain we call old notions fudge
> And bend our conscience to our dealing;
> The Ten Commandments will not budge,
> And stealing will continue stealing.
> ('International Copyright')

Peter C. Craigie
University of Calgary
David L. Jeffrey
University of Ottawa

STORIES FROM THE OLD TESTAMENT

Volume I

Part One: The Exodus

Part Two: Israel in the Wilderness

Part Three: The Last Words of Moses

Part Four: The Conquest of Canaan

Part Five: The Times of the Judges

Part Six: The Story of Ruth

Part Seven: Samuel the Prophet

The Exodus

ISRAEL IN EGYPT
Exodus 1:1 – 2:22

These are the names of the sons of Israel who, along with their households, accompanied Jacob to Egypt: Reuben, Simeon, Levi, and Judah; Issachar, Zebulun, and Benjamin; Dan and Naphtali, Gad and Asher. All told there were seventy direct descendants of Jacob. Joseph was already in Egypt.

In course of time Joseph and all his brothers and that entire generation died. The Israelites were prolific and increased greatly, becoming so numerous and strong that the land was full of them. When a new king ascended the throne of Egypt, one who did not know about Joseph, he said to his people, 'These Israelites have become too many and too strong for us. We must take steps to ensure that they increase no further; otherwise we shall find that, if war comes, they will side with the enemy, fight against us, and become masters of the country.' So taskmasters were appointed over them to oppress them with forced labour. This is how Pharaoh's store cities, Pithom and Rameses, were built. But the more oppressive the treatment of the Israelites, the more they increased and spread, until the Egyptians came to loathe them. They ground down their Israelite slaves, and made life bitter for them with their harsh demands, setting them to make mortar and bricks and to do all sorts of tasks in the fields. In every kind of labour they made ruthless use of them.

The king of Egypt issued instructions to the Hebrew midwives, of whom one was called Shiphrah, the other Puah. 'When you are attending the Hebrew women in childbirth,' he told them, 'check as the child is delivered: if it is a boy, kill him; if it is a girl, however, let her live.' But the midwives were godfearing women, and did not heed the king's words; they let the male children live. Pharaoh summoned the midwives and, when he asked them why they had done this and let the male children live, they answered, 'Hebrew women are not like Egyptian women; they go into labour and give birth before the midwife arrives.' God made the midwives prosper, and the people increased in numbers and strength; and because the midwives feared God he gave them families of their own. Pharaoh then issued an order to all the Egyptians that every new-born Hebrew boy was to be thrown into the Nile, but all the girls were to be allowed to live.

A certain man, a descendant of Levi, married a Levite woman. She conceived and bore a son, and when she saw what a fine child he was, she kept him hidden for three months. Unable to conceal him any longer, she got a rush basket for him, made it watertight with pitch and tar, laid him in it, and placed it among the reeds by the bank of the Nile. The child's sister stood some distance away to see what would happen to him.

Pharaoh's daughter came down to bathe in the river, while her ladies-in-waiting walked on the bank. She noticed the basket among the reeds and sent her slave-girl to bring it. When she opened it, there was the baby; it was crying, and she was moved with pity for it. 'This must be one of the Hebrew children,' she said. At this the sister approached Pharaoh's daughter: 'Shall I go and fetch you one of the Hebrew women to act as a wet-nurse for the child?' When Pharaoh's daughter told her to do so, she went and called the baby's mother. Pharaoh's daughter said to her, 'Take the child, nurse him for me, and I shall pay you for it.' She took the child and nursed him at her breast. Then, when he was old enough, she brought him to Pharaoh's daughter, who adopted him and called him Moses, 'because', said she, 'I drew him out of the water'.

One day after Moses was grown up, he went out to his own kinsmen and observed their labours. When he saw an Egyptian strike one of his fellow-Hebrews, he looked this way and that, and, seeing no one about, he struck the Egyptian down and hid his body in the sand. Next day when he went out, he came across two Hebrews fighting. He asked the one who was in the wrong, 'Why are you striking your fellow-countryman?' The man replied, 'Who set you up as an official and judge over us? Do you mean to murder me as you murdered the Egyptian?' Moses was alarmed and said to himself, 'The affair must have become known.' When it came to Pharaoh's ears, he tried to have Moses put to death, but Moses fled from his presence and went and settled in Midian.

As Moses sat by a well one day, the seven daughters of a priest of Midian came to draw water, and when they had filled the troughs to water their father's sheep, some shepherds came and drove them away. But Moses came to the help of the girls and watered the sheep. When they returned to Reuel, their father, he said, 'How is it that you are back so quickly today?' 'An Egyptian rescued us from the shepherds,' they answered; 'he even drew water for us and watered the sheep.' 'Then where is he?' their father asked. 'Why did you leave him there? Go and invite him to eat with us.' So it came about that Moses agreed to stay with the man, and he gave Moses his daughter Zipporah in marriage. She bore him a son, and Moses called him Gershom, 'because', he said, 'I have become an alien in a foreign land.'

THE BURNING BUSH
Exodus 2:23 – 3:15, 18–20; 4:1–16, 27–31

Years passed, during which time the king of Egypt died, but the Israelites still groaned in slavery. They cried out, and their plea for rescue from slavery ascended to God. He heard their groaning and called to mind his covenant with Abraham, Isaac, and Jacob; he observed the plight of Israel and took heed of it.

While tending the sheep of his father-in-law Jethro, priest of Midian, Moses led the flock along the west side of the wilderness and came to Horeb, the mountain of God. There an angel of the Lord appeared to him as a fire blazing out from a bush. Although the bush was on fire, it was not being burnt up, and Moses said to himself, 'I must go across and see this remarkable sight. Why ever does the bush not burn away?' When the Lord saw that Moses had turned aside to look, he called to him out of the bush, 'Moses, Moses!' He answered, 'Here I am!' God said, 'Do not come near! Take off your sandals, for the place where you are standing is holy ground.' Then he said, 'I am the God of your father, the God of Abraham, Isaac, and Jacob.' Moses hid his face, for he was afraid to look at God.

The Lord said, 'I have witnessed the misery of my people in Egypt and have heard them crying out because of their oppressors. I know what they are suffering and have come down to rescue them from the power of the Egyptians and to bring them up out of that country into a fine, broad land, a land flowing with milk and honey, the territory of Canaanites, Hittites, Amorites, Perizzites, Hivites, and Jebusites. Now the Israelites' cry has reached me, and I have also seen how hard the Egyptians oppress them. Come, I shall send you to Pharaoh, and you are to bring my people Israel out of Egypt.' 'But who am I', Moses said to God, 'that I should approach Pharaoh and that I should bring the Israelites out of Egypt?' God answered, 'I am with you. This will be your proof that it is I who have sent you: when you have brought the people out of Egypt, you will all worship God here at this mountain.'

Moses said to God, 'If I come to the Israelites and tell them that the God of their forefathers has sent me to them, and they ask me his name, what am I to say to them?' God answered, 'I AM that I am. Tell them that I AM has sent you to them.' He continued, 'You are to tell the Israelites that it is the Lord, the God of their forefathers, the God of Abraham, Isaac, and Jacob, who has sent you to them. This is my name for ever; this is my title in every generation...

'The elders will attend to what you say, and then you must go along with them to the king of Egypt and say to him, "The Lord the God of the Hebrews has encountered us. Now, we request you to give us leave to go a three days' journey into the wilderness to offer sacrifice to the Lord our God." I know well that the king of Egypt will not allow you to go unless he is compelled. I shall then stretch out my hand and assail the Egyptians with all the miracles I shall work among them. After that he will send you away...'

'But they will never believe me or listen to what I say,' Moses protested; 'they will say that it is untrue that the Lord appeared to me.' The Lord said, 'What is that in your hand?' 'A staff,' replied Moses. The Lord said, 'Throw it on the ground.' He did so, and it turned into a snake. Moses drew back hastily, but the Lord said, 'Put your hand out and seize it by the tail.' When he took hold of it, it turned back into a staff in his hand. 'This', said the Lord, 'is to convince the people that the Lord the God of their forefathers, the God of Abraham, of Isaac, and of Jacob, did appear to you.'

Then the Lord said to him, 'Put your hand inside the fold of your cloak.' He did so, and when he drew his hand out the skin was white as snow with disease. The Lord said, 'Put your hand in again'; he did so, and when he drew it out this time it was as healthy as the rest of his body. 'Now,' said the Lord, 'if they do not believe you and do not accept the evidence of the first sign, they may be persuaded by the second. But if they are not convinced even by these two signs and will not accept what you say, then fetch some water from the Nile and pour it out on the dry land, and the water from the Nile will turn to blood on the ground.'

'But, Lord,' Moses protested, 'I have never been a man of ready speech, never in my life, not even now that you have spoken to me; I am slow and hesitant.' The Lord said to him, 'Who is it that gives man speech? Who makes him dumb or deaf? Who makes him keen-sighted or blind? Is it not I, the Lord? Go now; I shall help you to speak and show you what to say.' Moses said, 'Lord, send anyone else you like.' At this the Lord became angry with Moses: 'Do you not have a brother, Aaron the Levite? He, I know, will do all the speaking. He is already on his way out to meet you, and he will be overjoyed when he sees you. You are to speak to him and put the words in his mouth; I shall help both of you to speak and tell you both what to do. He will do all the speaking to the people for you; he will be the mouthpiece, and you will be the god he speaks for...'

Meanwhile the Lord had ordered Aaron to go and meet Moses in the wilderness. Aaron did so; he met him at the mountain of God and kissed him. Moses told Aaron everything, the words the Lord had sent him to say and the signs he had commanded him to perform. Moses and Aaron then went and assembled all the elders of Israel. Aaron repeated to them everything that the Lord had said to Moses; he performed the signs before the people, and they were convinced. When they heard that the Lord had shown his concern for the Israelites and seen their misery, they bowed to the ground in worship.

'LET MY PEOPLE GO'
Exodus 5:1 – 6:1, 6–12; 7:8–13

After this, Moses and Aaron came to Pharaoh and told him, 'These are the words of the Lord the God of Israel: Let my people go so that they may keep a pilgrim-feast in my honour in the wilderness.' 'Who is the Lord,' said Pharaoh, 'that I should listen to him and let Israel go? I do not acknowledge the Lord: and I tell you I will not let Israel go.' They replied, 'The God of the Hebrews confronted us. Now we request leave to go three days' journey into the wilderness to offer sacrifice to the Lord our God, or else he may attack us with pestilence or sword.' But the Egyptian king answered, 'What do you mean, Moses and Aaron, by distracting the people from their work? Back to your labours! Your people already outnumber the native Egyptians; yet you would have them stop working!'

Pharaoh issued orders that same day to the people's slave-masters and their foremen not to supply the people with the straw used in making bricks, as they had done hitherto. 'Let them go and collect their own straw, but see that they produce the same tally of bricks as before; on no account reduce it. They are lazy, and that is why they are clamouring to go and offer sacrifice to their God. Keep these men hard at work; let them attend to that. Take no notice of their lies.' The slave-masters and foremen went out and said to the people, 'Pharaoh's orders are that no more straw is to be supplied. Go and get it for yourselves wherever you can find it; but there is to be no reduction in your daily task.' So the people scattered all over Egypt to gather stubble for the straw they needed, while the slave-masters kept urging them on, demanding that they should complete, day after day, the same quantity as when straw had been supplied. The Israelite foremen were flogged because they were held responsible by Pharaoh's slave-masters, who demanded, 'Why did you not complete the usual number of bricks yesterday or today?'

The foremen came and appealed to Pharaoh: 'Why does your majesty treat us like this?' they said. 'We are given no straw, yet they keep telling us to make bricks. Here are we being flogged, but the fault lies with your people.' The king replied, 'You are lazy, bone lazy! That is why you keep on about going to offer sacrifice to the Lord. Now get on with your work. You will not be given straw, but you must produce the full tally of bricks.' When they were told that they must not let the daily number of bricks fall short, the Israelite foremen realized the trouble they were in. As they came from Pharaoh's presence they found Moses and Aaron waiting to meet them, and said, 'May this bring the Lord's judgment down on you! You have made us stink in the nostrils of Pharaoh and his subjects; you have put a sword in their hands to slay us.'

Moses went back to the Lord and said, 'Lord, why have you brought trouble on this people? And why did you ever send me? Since I first went to Pharaoh to speak in your name he has treated your people cruelly, and you have done nothing at all to rescue them.' The Lord answered, 'Now you will see what I shall do to Pharaoh: he will be compelled to let them go, he will be forced to drive them from his country...'

'Therefore say to the Israelites, "I am the Lord. I shall free you from your labours in Egypt and deliver you from slavery. I shall rescue you with outstretched arm and with mighty acts of judgment. I shall adopt you as my people, and I shall be your God. You will know that I, the Lord, am your God, the God who frees you from your labours in Egypt. I shall lead you to the land which I swore with uplifted hand to give to Abraham, to Isaac, and to Jacob. I shall give it you for your possession. I am the Lord."' But when Moses repeated those words to the Israelites, they would not listen to him; because of their cruel slavery, they had reached the depths of despair.

Then the Lord said to Moses, 'Go and bid Pharaoh king of Egypt let the Israelites leave his country.' Moses protested to the Lord, 'If the Israelites do not listen to me, how will Pharaoh listen to such a halting speaker as me?'...

The Lord said to Moses, 'If Pharaoh demands some portent from you, then you, Moses, must say to Aaron, "Take your staff and throw it down in front of Pharaoh," and it will turn into a serpent.' When Moses and Aaron came to Pharaoh, they did as the Lord had told them; Aaron threw down his staff in front of Pharaoh and his courtiers, and it turned into a serpent. At this, Pharaoh summoned the wise men and the sorcerers, and the Egyptian magicians did the same thing by their spells: every man threw his staff down, and each staff turned into a serpent. But Aaron's staff swallowed up theirs. Pharaoh, however, was obstinate; as the Lord had foretold, he would not listen to Moses and Aaron.

THE TEN PLAGUES OF EGYPT
Exodus 7:14 – 11:10

The Lord said to Moses, 'Pharaoh has been obdurate: he has refused to let the people go. In the morning go to him on his way out to the river. Stand on the bank of the Nile to meet him, and take with you the staff that turned into a snake. Say to him: "The Lord the God of the Hebrews sent me with this message for you: Let my people go in order to worship me in the wilderness. So far you have not listened. Now the Lord says: By this you will know that I am the Lord. With this rod I hold in my hand, I shall strike the water of the Nile and it will be changed into blood. The fish will die and the river will stink, and the Egyptians will be unable to drink water from the Nile."'

The Lord told Moses to say to Aaron, 'Take your staff and stretch your hand out over the waters of Egypt, its rivers and its canals, and over every pool and cistern, to turn them into blood. There will be blood throughout the whole of Egypt, blood even in their wooden bowls and stone jars.' Moses and Aaron did as the Lord had commanded. In the sight of Pharaoh and his courtiers Aaron lifted his staff and struck the water of the Nile, and all the water was changed to blood. The fish died and the river stank, so that the Egyptians could not drink water from the Nile. There was blood everywhere in Egypt.

But the Egyptian magicians did the same thing by their spells. So Pharaoh still remained obstinate, as the Lord had foretold, and he did not listen to Moses and Aaron. He turned and went into his palace, dismissing the matter from his mind. The Egyptians all dug for drinking water round about the river, because they could not drink from the waters of the Nile itself. This lasted for seven days from the time when the Lord struck the Nile.

The Lord then told Moses to go to Pharaoh and say, 'These are the words of the Lord: Let my people go in order to worship me. If you refuse, I shall bring a plague of frogs over the whole of your territory. The Nile will swarm with them. They will come up from the river into your palace, into your bedroom and onto your bed, into the houses of your courtiers and your people, into your ovens and your kneading troughs. The frogs will clamber over you, your people, and all your courtiers.'

The Lord told Moses to say to Aaron, 'Take your staff in your hand and stretch it out over the rivers, canals, and pools, to bring up frogs on the land of Egypt.' When Aaron stretched his hand over the waters of Egypt, the frogs came up and covered the land. But the magicians did the same thing by their spells: they too brought up frogs on the land of Egypt.

Pharaoh summoned Moses and Aaron. 'Pray to the Lord', he said, 'to remove the frogs from me and my people, and I shall let the people go to sacrifice to the Lord.' Moses said, 'I give your majesty the choice of a time for me to intercede for you, your courtiers, and your people, to rid you and your houses of the frogs; none will be left except in the Nile.' 'Tomorrow,' said Pharaoh. 'It will be as you say,' replied Moses, 'so that you may know there is no one like our God, the Lord. The frogs will leave you, your houses, courtiers, and people: none will be left except in the Nile.' Moses and Aaron left Pharaoh's presence, and Moses asked the Lord to remove the frogs which he had brought on Pharaoh. The Lord granted the request, and in house, farmyard, and field all the frogs perished. They were piled into countless heaps and the land stank. But when Pharaoh found that he was given relief he became obdurate; as the Lord had foretold, he would not listen to Moses and Aaron.

The Lord told Moses to say to Aaron, 'Stretch out your staff and strike the dust on the ground, and it will turn into maggots throughout the whole of Egypt.' They obeyed, and when Aaron stretched out his hand with his staff in it and struck the dust, it turned into maggots on man and beast. Throughout Egypt all the dust turned into maggots. The magicians tried to produce maggots in the same way by their spells, but they failed. The maggots were everywhere, on man and beast. 'It is the hand of God,' said the magicians to Pharaoh, but Pharaoh remained obstinate; as the Lord had foretold, he would not listen.

The Lord told Moses to rise early in the morning and stand in Pharaoh's path as he went out to the river, and to say to him, 'These are the words of the Lord: Let my people go in order to worship me. If you refuse, I shall send swarms of flies on you, your courtiers, your people, and your houses; the houses of the Egyptians will be filled with the swarms and so will all the land they live in. But on that day I shall make an exception of Goshen, the land where my people live: there will be no swarms there. Thus you will know that I, the Lord, am here in the land. I shall make a distinction between my people and yours. Tomorrow this sign will appear.' The Lord did this; dense swarms of flies infested Pharaoh's palace and the houses of his courtiers; throughout Egypt the land was threatened with ruin by the swarms. Pharaoh summoned Moses and Aaron and said to them, 'Go and sacrifice to your God, but in this country.' 'That is impossible,' replied Moses, 'because the victim we are to sacrifice to the Lord our God is an abomination to the Egyptians. If the Egyptians see us offer such an animal, they will surely stone us to death. We must go a three days' journey into the wilderness to sacrifice to the Lord our God, as he commands us.' 'I shall let you go,' said Pharaoh, 'and you may sacrifice to your God in the wilderness; only do not go far. Now intercede for me.' Moses answered, 'As soon as I leave you I shall intercede with the Lord. Tomorrow the swarms will depart from Pharaoh, his courtiers, and his people. Only your majesty must not trifle any more with the people by preventing them from going to sacrifice to the Lord.'

Then Moses left Pharaoh and interceded with the Lord. The Lord did as Moses had promised; he removed the swarms from Pharaoh, his courtiers, and his people; not one was left. But once again Pharaoh became obdurate and would not let the people go.

The Lord said to Moses, 'Go in to Pharaoh and tell him, "The Lord the God of the Hebrews says: Let my people go in order to worship me. If you refuse to let them go, if you still keep them in subjection, the Lord will strike your livestock out in the country, the horses and donkeys, camels, cattle, and sheep with a devastating pestilence. But the Lord will make a distinction between Israel's livestock and the livestock of the Egyptians. Of all that belong to Israel not a single one will die."' The Lord fixed a time and said, 'Tomorrow

I shall do this throughout the land.' The next day the Lord struck. All the livestock of Egypt died, but from Israel's livestock not one single beast died. Pharaoh made enquiries and was told that from Israel's livestock not an animal had died; and yet he remained obdurate and would not let the people go.

The Lord said to Moses and Aaron, 'Take handfuls of soot from a kiln, and when Moses tosses it into the air in Pharaoh's sight, it will turn into a fine dust over the whole of Egypt. Throughout the land it will produce festering boils on man and beast.' They took the soot from the kiln and when they stood before Pharaoh, Moses tossed it into the air, and it produced festering boils on man and beast. The magicians were no match for Moses because of the boils, which attacked them and all the Egyptians. But the Lord made Pharaoh obstinate; as the Lord had foretold to Moses, he would not listen to Moses and Aaron.

The Lord then told Moses to rise early and confront Pharaoh, saying to him, 'The Lord the God of the Hebrews has said: Let my people go in order to worship me. This time I shall strike home with all my plagues against you yourself, your courtiers, and your people, so that you may know that there is none like me in all the world. By now I could have stretched out my hand, and struck you and your people with pestilence, and you would have vanished from the earth. I have let you live only to show you my power and to spread my fame all over the world. Since you still obstruct my people and will not let them go, tomorrow at this time I shall cause a violent hailstorm to come, such as has never been in Egypt from its first beginnings until now. Send now and bring your herds under cover, and everything you have out in the open field. Anything which happens to be left out in the open, whether man or beast, will die when the hail falls on it.' Those of Pharaoh's subjects who feared the warning of the Lord hurried their slaves and livestock into shelter; but those who did not take it to heart left them in the open.

The Lord said to Moses, 'Stretch your hand towards the sky to bring down hail on the whole land of Egypt, on man and beast and every growing thing throughout the land.' As Moses stretched his staff towards the sky, the Lord sent thunder and hail, with fire flashing to the ground. The Lord rained down hail on the land of Egypt, hail and fiery flashes through the hail, so heavy that there had been nothing like it in all Egypt from the time that Egypt became a nation. Throughout Egypt the hail struck down everything in the fields, both man and beast; it beat down every growing thing and shattered every tree. Only in the land of Goshen, where the Israelites lived, was there no hail.

Pharaoh summoned Moses and Aaron. 'This time I have sinned,' he said; 'the Lord is in the right; I and my people are in the wrong. Intercede with the Lord, for we can bear no more of this thunder and hail. I shall let you go; you need stay no longer.' Moses said, 'As soon as I leave the city I shall spread out my hands in prayer to the Lord. The thunder will cease, and there will be no more hail, so that you may know that the earth is the Lord's. But you and your subjects, I know, do not yet fear the Lord God.' (The flax and barley were destroyed because the barley was in the ear and the flax in bud, but the wheat and vetches were not destroyed because they come later.) Moses left Pharaoh's presence and went out of the city, where he lifted up his hands to the Lord in prayer: the thunder and hail ceased, and no more rain fell. When Pharaoh saw that the downpour, the hail, and the thunder had ceased, he went back to his sinful obduracy, he and his courtiers. Pharaoh remained obstinate; as the Lord had foretold through Moses, he would not let the people go.

The Lord said to Moses, 'Go in to Pharaoh. I have made him and his courtiers obdurate, so that I may show these signs among them, and so that you can tell your children and grandchildren the story: how I toyed with the Egyptians, and what signs I showed among them. Thus you will know that I am the Lord.'

Moses and Aaron went to Pharaoh and said to him, 'The Lord the God of the Hebrews has said: How long will you refuse to humble yourself before me? Let my people go in order to worship me. If you refuse to let them go, tomorrow I am going to bring locusts into your country. They will cover the face of the land so that it cannot be seen. They will eat up the last remnant left you by the hail. They will devour every tree that grows in your countryside. Your houses and your courtiers' houses, every house in Egypt, will be full of them; your fathers never saw the like, nor their fathers before them; such a thing has not happened from their time until now.' With that he turned and left Pharaoh's presence.

Pharaoh's courtiers said to him, 'How long must we be caught in this man's toils? Let their menfolk go and worship the Lord their God. Do you not know by now that Egypt is ruined?' So Moses and Aaron were brought back to Pharaoh, and he said to them, 'Go, worship the Lord your God; but who exactly is to go?' 'Everyone,' said Moses, 'young and old, boys and girls, sheep and cattle; for we have to keep the Lord's pilgrim-feast.' Pharaoh replied, 'The Lord be with you if I let you and your dependants go! You have some sinister purpose in mind. No, your menfolk may go and worship the Lord, for that is what you were asking for.' And they were driven from Pharaoh's presence.

The Lord said to Moses, 'Stretch out your hand over Egypt so that locusts may come and invade the land and devour all the vegetation in it, whatever the hail has left.' When Moses stretched out his staff over the land of Egypt, the Lord sent a wind roaring in from the east all that day and all that night; and when morning came the east wind had brought the locusts. They invaded the whole land of Egypt, and settled on all its territory in swarms so dense that the like of them had never been seen before, nor ever will be again. They covered the surface of the whole land till it was black with them; they devoured all the vegetation and all the fruit of the trees that the hail had spared; there was no green left on tree or plant throughout all Egypt.

Pharaoh hastily summoned Moses and Aaron. 'I have sinned against the Lord your God and against you,' he said. 'Forgive my sin, I pray, just this once, and intercede with the Lord your God to remove this deadly plague from me.' When Moses left Pharaoh and interceded with the Lord, the wind was changed by the Lord into a westerly gale, which carried the locusts away and swept them into the Red Sea. Not one locust was left within the borders of Egypt. But the Lord made Pharaoh obstinate, and he would not let the Israelites go.

Then the Lord said to Moses, 'Stretch out your hand towards the sky so that over the land of Egypt there may be a darkness so dense that it can be felt.' Moses stretched out his hand towards the sky, and for three days pitch darkness covered the whole land of

Egypt. People could not see one another, and for three days no one stirred from where he was. But where the Israelites were living there was no darkness.

Pharaoh summoned Moses. 'Go, worship the Lord,' he said. 'Your dependants may go with you; but your flocks and herds must remain here.' But Moses said, 'No, you yourself must supply us with animals for sacrifice and whole-offering to the Lord our God; and our own livestock must go with us too – not a hoof must be left behind. We may need animals from our own flocks to worship the Lord our God; we ourselves cannot tell until we are there how we are to worship the Lord.' The Lord made Pharaoh obstinate, and he refused to let them go. 'Be off! Leave me!' he said to Moses. 'Mind you do not see my face again, for on the day you do, you die.' 'You are right,' said Moses; 'I shall not see your face again.'

The Lord said to Moses, 'One last plague I shall bring on Pharaoh and Egypt. When he finally lets you go, he will drive you out forcibly as a man might dismiss a rejected bride. Tell the people that everyone, men and women, should ask their neighbours for silver and gold jewellery.' The Lord made the Egyptians well disposed towards them and, moreover, in Egypt Moses was a very great man in the eyes of Pharaoh's courtiers and of the people.

Moses said, 'The Lord said: At midnight I shall go out among the Egyptians. All the firstborn in Egypt shall die, from the firstborn of Pharaoh on his throne to the firstborn of the slave-girl at the handmill, besides the firstborn of the cattle. From all over Egypt there will go up a great cry, the like of which has never been heard before, nor ever will be again. But throughout all Israel no sound will be heard from man or beast, not even a dog's bark. Thus you will know that the Lord distinguishes between Egypt and Israel. All these courtiers of yours will come down to me, prostrate themselves, and cry, "Go away, you and all the people who follow at your heels." When that time comes I shall go.' In hot anger, Moses left Pharaoh's presence.

The Lord said to Moses, 'Pharaoh will not listen to you; I shall therefore show still more portents in the land of Egypt.' Moses and Aaron had shown all these portents in the presence of Pharaoh, and yet the Lord made him obstinate, and he would not let the Israelites leave his country.

THE PASSOVER
Exodus 12:1–14, 26–38

The Lord said to Moses and Aaron in Egypt: 'This month is to be for you the first of the months; you are to make it the first month of the year. Say to the whole community of Israel: On the tenth day of this month let each man procure a lamb or kid for his family, one for each household, but if a household is too small for one lamb or kid, then, taking into account the number of persons, the man and his nearest neighbour may take one between them. They are to share the cost according to the amount each person eats. Your animal, taken either from the sheep or the goats, must be without blemish, a yearling male. Have it in safe keeping until the fourteenth day of this month, and then all the assembled community of Israel must slaughter the victims between dusk and dark. They must take some of the blood and smear it on the two doorposts and on the lintel of the houses in which they eat the victims. On that night they must eat the flesh roasted on the fire; they must eat it with unleavened bread and bitter herbs. You are not to eat any of it raw or even boiled in water, but roasted: head, shins, and entrails. You are not to leave any of it till morning; anything left over until morning must be destroyed by fire.

'This is the way in which you are to eat it: have your belt fastened, sandals on your feet, and your staff in your hand, and you must eat in urgent haste. It is the Lord's Passover. On that night I shall pass through the land of Egypt and kill every firstborn of man and beast. Thus I shall execute judgment, I the Lord, against all the gods of Egypt. As for you, the blood will be a sign on the houses in which you are: when I see the blood I shall pass over you; when I strike Egypt, the mortal blow will not touch you.

'You are to keep this day as a day of remembrance, and make it a pilgrim-feast, a festival of the Lord; generation after generation you are to observe it as a statute for all time…

'When your children ask you, "What is the meaning of this rite?" you must say, "It is the Lord's Passover, for he passed over the houses of the Israelites in Egypt when he struck the Egyptians and spared our houses."' The people bowed low in worship.

The Israelites went and did exactly as the Lord had commanded

Moses and Aaron; and by midnight the Lord had struck down all the firstborn in Egypt, from the firstborn of Pharaoh on his throne to the firstborn of the prisoner in the dungeon, besides the firstborn of cattle. Before night was over Pharaoh rose, he and all his courtiers and all the Egyptians, and there was great wailing, for not a house in Egypt was without its dead.

Pharaoh summoned Moses and Aaron while it was still night and said, 'Up with you! Be off, and leave my people, you and the Israelites. Go and worship the Lord, as you request; take your sheep and cattle, and go; and ask God's blessing on me also.' The Egyptians urged on the people and hurried them out of the country, 'or else', they said, 'we shall all be dead'. The people picked up their dough before it was leavened, wrapped their kneading troughs in their cloaks, and slung them on their shoulders. Meanwhile, as Moses had told them, the Israelites had asked the Egyptians for silver and gold jewellery and for clothing. Because the Lord had made the Egyptians well disposed towards them, they let the Israelites have whatever they asked; in this way the Egyptians were plundered.

The Israelites set out from Rameses on the way to Succoth, about six hundred thousand men on foot, as well as women and children. With them too went a large company of others, and animals in great numbers, both flocks and herds.

ISRAEL CROSSES THE RED SEA
Exodus 13:17 – 15:21

When Pharaoh let the people go, God did not guide them by the road leading towards the Philistines, although that was the shortest way; for he said, 'The people may change their minds when war confronts them, and they may turn back to Egypt.' So God made them go round by way of the wilderness towards the Red Sea. Thus the fifth generation of Israelites departed from Egypt.

Moses took the bones of Joseph with him, because Joseph had exacted an oath from the Israelites: 'Some day', he said, 'God will show his care for you, and then, as you leave, you must take my bones with you.'

They set out from Succoth and encamped at Etham on the edge of the wilderness. And all the time the Lord went before them, by day a pillar of cloud to guide them on their journey, by night a pillar of fire to give them light; so they could travel both by day and by night. The pillar of cloud never left its place in front of the people by day, nor did the pillar of fire by night.

The Lord spoke to Moses. 'Tell the Israelites', he said, 'they are to turn back and encamp before Pi-hahiroth, between Migdol and the sea to the east of Baal-zephon; your camp shall be opposite, by the sea. Pharaoh will then think that the Israelites are finding themselves in difficult country, and are hemmed in by the wilderness. I shall make Pharaoh obstinate, and he will pursue them, so that I may win glory for myself at the expense of Pharaoh and all his army; and the Egyptians will know that I am the Lord.' The Israelites did as they were ordered.

When it was reported to the Egyptian king that the Israelites had gone, he and his courtiers had a change of heart and said, 'What is this we have done? We have let our Israelite slaves go free!' Pharaoh had his chariot yoked, and took his troops with him, six hundred picked chariots and all the other chariots of Egypt, with a commander in each. Then, made obstinate by the Lord, Pharaoh king of Egypt pursued the Israelites as they marched defiantly away. The Egyptians, all Pharaoh's chariots and horses, cavalry and infantry, went in pursuit, and overtook them encamped beside the sea by Pi-hahiroth to the east of Baal-zephon.

Pharaoh was almost upon them when the Israelites looked up and saw the Egyptians close behind, and in terror they clamoured to the Lord for help. They said to Moses, 'Were there no graves in Egypt, that you have brought us here to perish in the wilderness? See what you have done to us by bringing us out of Egypt! Is this not just what we meant when we said in Egypt, "Leave us alone; let us be slaves to the Egyptians"? Better for us to serve as slaves to the Egyptians than to perish in the wilderness.' But Moses answered, 'Have no fear; stand firm and see the deliverance that the Lord will bring you this day; for as sure as you see the Egyptians now, you will never see them again. The Lord will fight for you; so say no more.'

The Lord said to Moses, 'What is the meaning of this clamour?

Tell the Israelites to strike camp, and you are to raise high your staff and hold your hand out over the sea to divide it asunder, so that the Israelites can pass through the sea on dry ground. For my part I shall make the Egyptians obstinate and they will come after you; thus I shall win glory for myself at the expense of Pharaoh and his army, chariots and cavalry all together. The Egyptians will know that I am the Lord when I win glory for myself at the expense of their Pharaoh, his chariots and horsemen.'

The angel of God, who had travelled in front of the Israelites, now moved away to the rear. The pillar of cloud moved from the front and took up its position behind them, thus coming between the Egyptians and the Israelites. The cloud brought on darkness and early nightfall, so that contact was lost throughout the night.

Then Moses held out his hand over the sea, and the Lord drove the sea away with a strong east wind all night long, and turned the seabed into dry land. The waters were divided asunder, and the Israelites went through the sea on the dry ground, while the waters formed a wall to right and left of them. The Egyptians, all Pharaoh's horse, his chariots and cavalry, followed in pursuit into the sea. In the morning watch the Lord looked down on the Egyptian army through the pillar of fire and cloud, and he threw them into a panic. He clogged their chariot wheels and made them drag along heavily, so that the Egyptians said, 'It is the Lord fighting for Israel against Egypt; let us flee.'

Then the Lord said to Moses, 'Hold your hand out over the sea, so that the water may flow back on the Egyptians, their chariots and horsemen.' Moses held his hand out over the sea, and at daybreak the water returned to its usual place and the Egyptians fled before its advance, but the Lord swept them into the sea. As the water came back it covered all Pharaoh's army, the chariots and cavalry, which had pressed the pursuit into the sea. Not one survived. Meanwhile the Israelites had passed along the dry ground through the sea, with the water forming a wall for them to right and to left. That day the Lord saved Israel from the power of Egypt. When the Israelites saw the Egyptians lying dead on the seashore, and saw the great power which the Lord had put forth against Egypt, the people were in awe of the Lord and put their faith in him and in Moses his servant.

Then Moses and the Israelites sang this song to the Lord:

'I shall sing to the Lord, for he has risen up in triumph;
horse and rider he has hurled into the sea.
The Lord is my refuge and my defence;
he has shown himself my deliverer.
He is my God, and I shall glorify him;
my father's God, and I shall exalt him.
The Lord is a warrior; the Lord is his name.
Pharaoh's chariots and his army
he has cast into the sea;
the flower of his officers
are engulfed in the Red Sea.
The watery abyss has covered them;
they sank to the depths like a stone.
Your right hand, Lord, is majestic in strength;
your right hand, Lord, shattered the enemy.
In the fullness of your triumph
you overthrew those who opposed you:
you let loose your fury;
it consumed them like stubble.
At the blast of your anger the sea piled up;
the water stood up like a bank;
out at sea the great deep congealed.

'The enemy boasted, "I shall pursue, I shall overtake;
I shall divide the spoil,
I shall glut my appetite on them;
I shall draw my sword,
I shall rid myself of them."
You blew with your blast; the sea covered them;
they sank like lead in the swelling waves.

'Lord, who is like you among the gods?
Who is like you, majestic in holiness,
worthy of awe and praise, worker of wonders?
You stretched out your right hand;
the earth engulfed them.

'In your constant love you led the people
whom you had redeemed:
you guided them by your strength
to your holy dwelling-place.
Nations heard and trembled;
anguish seized the dwellers in Philistia.
The chieftains of Edom were then dismayed,
trembling seized the leaders of Moab,
the inhabitants of Canaan were all panic-stricken;
terror and dread fell upon them:
through the might of your arm
they stayed stone-still
while your people passed, Lord,
while the people whom you made your own passed by.
You will bring them in and plant them
in the mount that is your possession,
the dwelling-place, Lord, of your own making,
the sanctuary, Lord, which your own hands established.
The Lord will reign for ever and for ever.'

When Pharaoh's horse, both chariots and cavalry, went into the sea, the Lord brought back the waters over them; but Israel had passed through the sea on dry ground. The prophetess Miriam, Aaron's sister, took up her tambourine, and all the women followed her, dancing to the sound of tambourines; and Miriam sang them this refrain:

'Sing to the Lord, for he has risen up in triumph:
horse and rider he has hurled into the sea.'

THE PEOPLE COMPLAIN
Exodus 15:22 – 16:3, 11–32; 17:1–7

Moses led Israel from the Red Sea out into the wilderness of Shur, where for three days they travelled through the wilderness without finding water. When they came to Marah, they could not drink the water there because it was bitter; that is why the place was called Marah. The people complained to Moses, asking, 'What are we to drink?' Moses cried to the Lord, who showed him a log which, when thrown into the water, made the water sweet.

It was there that the Lord laid down a statute and rule of life; there he put the people to the test. He said, 'If only you will obey the Lord your God, if you will do what is right in his eyes, if you will listen to his commands and keep all his statutes, then I shall never bring on you any of the sufferings which I brought on the Egyptians; for I the Lord am your healer.'

They came to Elim, where there were twelve springs and seventy palm trees, and there they encamped beside the water.

The whole Israelite community, setting out from Elim, arrived at the wilderness of Sin, which lies between Elim and Sinai. This was on the fifteenth day of the second month after they left Egypt.

The Israelites all complained to Moses and Aaron in the wilderness. They said, 'If only we had died at the Lord's hand in Egypt, where we sat by the fleshpots and had plenty of bread! But you have brought us out into this wilderness to let this whole assembly starve to death...'

The Lord spoke to Moses: 'I have heard the complaints of the Israelites. Say to them: Between dusk and dark you will have flesh to eat and in the morning bread in plenty. You will know that I the Lord am your God.'

That evening a flock of quails flew in and settled over the whole camp; in the morning a fall of dew lay all around it. When the dew was gone, there over the surface of the wilderness fine flakes appeared, fine as hoar-frost on the ground. When the Israelites saw it, they said one to another, 'What is that?' because they did not know what it was. Moses said to them, 'That is the bread which the Lord has given you to eat. Here is the command the Lord has given: Each of you is to gather as much as he can eat: let every man take an omer apiece for every person in his tent.' The Israelites did this, and they gathered, some more, some less, but when they measured it by the omer, those who had gathered more had not too much, and those who had gathered less had not too little. Each had just as much as he could eat. Moses said, 'No one is to keep any of it till morning.' Some, however, did not listen to him; they kept part of it till morning, and it became full of maggots and stank, and Moses was angry with them.

Each morning every man gathered as much as he needed; it melted away when the sun grew hot. On the sixth day they gathered twice as much food, two omers each, and when the chiefs of the community all came and told Moses, 'This', he answered, 'is what the Lord has said: Tomorrow is a day of sacred rest, a sabbath holy to the Lord. So bake what you want to bake now, and boil what you want to boil; what remains over put aside to be kept till morning.' So they put it aside till morning as Moses had commanded, and it neither stank nor became infested with maggots. 'Eat it today,' said Moses, 'because today is a sabbath of the Lord. Today you will find none outside. For six days you may gather it, but on the seventh day, the sabbath, there will be none.'

Some of the people did go out to gather it on the seventh day, but they found nothing. The Lord said to Moses, 'How long will you Israelites refuse to obey my commands and instructions? You are aware the Lord has given you the sabbath, and so he gives you two days' food every sixth day. Let everyone stay where he is; no one may stir from his home on the seventh.' So the people kept the sabbath on the seventh day.

Israel called the food manna; it was like coriander seed, but white, and it tasted like a wafer made with honey.

'This', said Moses, 'is the command which the Lord has given: Take a full omer of it to be kept for future generations, so that they may see the bread with which I fed you in the wilderness when I brought you out of Egypt...'

The whole community of Israel set out from the wilderness of Sin and travelled by stages as the Lord directed. They encamped at Rephidim, but there was no water for the people to drink, and a dispute arose between them and Moses. When they said, 'Give us water to drink,' Moses said, 'Why do you dispute with me? Why do you challenge the Lord?' The people became so thirsty there that they raised an outcry against Moses: 'Why have you brought us out of Egypt with our children and our herds to let us die of thirst?' Moses appealed to the Lord, 'What shall I do with these people? In a moment they will be stoning me.' The Lord answered, 'Go forward ahead of the people; take with you some of the elders of Israel and bring along the staff with which you struck the Nile. Go, you will find me waiting for you there, by a rock in Horeb. Strike the rock; water will pour out of it for the people to drink.' Moses did this in the sight of the elders of Israel. He named the place Massah and Meribah, because the Israelites had disputed with him and put the Lord to the test with their question, 'Is the Lord in our midst or not?'

JOSHUA DEFEATS THE AMALEKITES
Exodus 17:8–16

The Amalekites came and attacked Israel at Rephidim. Moses said to Joshua, 'Pick men for us, and march out tomorrow to fight against Amalek; and I shall stand on the hilltop with the staff of God in my hand.' Joshua did as Moses commanded and fought against Amalek, while Moses, Aaron, and Hur climbed to the top of the hill. Whenever Moses raised his hands Israel had the advantage, and when he lowered his hands the advantage passed to Amalek. When his arms grew heavy they took a stone and put it under him and, as he sat, Aaron and Hur held up his hands, one on each side, so that his hands remained steady till sunset. Thus Joshua defeated Amalek and put its people to the sword.

The Lord said to Moses, 'Record this in writing, and tell it to Joshua in these words: I am resolved to blot out all memory of Amalek from under heaven.' Moses built an altar, and named it 'The Lord is my Banner' and said, 'My oath upon it: the Lord is at war with Amalek generation after generation.'

JETHRO ADVISES MOSES
Exodus 18

Jethro priest of Midian, father-in-law of Moses, heard all that God had done for Moses and for Israel his people, and how the Lord had brought Israel out of Egypt. When Moses had sent away his wife Zipporah, Jethro his father-in-law had received her and her two sons. The name of the one was Gershom, 'for', said Moses, 'I have become an alien living in a foreign land'; the other's name was Eliezer, 'for', he said, 'the God of my father was my help and saved me from Pharaoh's sword.'

Jethro, Moses' father-in-law, now came to him with his sons and his wife, to the wilderness where he was encamped at the mountain of God. Moses was told, 'Here is Jethro, your father-in-law, coming to you with your wife and her two sons.' Moses went out to meet his father-in-law, bowed low to him, and kissed him. After they had greeted one another and come into the tent, Moses told him all that the Lord had done to Pharaoh and to Egypt for Israel's sake, and about all their hardships on the journey, and how the Lord had saved them. Jethro rejoiced at all the good the Lord had done for Israel in saving them from the power of Egypt.

He said, 'Blessed be the Lord who has delivered you from the power of Egypt and of Pharaoh. Now I know that the Lord is the greatest of all gods, because he has delivered the people from the Egyptians who dealt so arrogantly with them.' Jethro, Moses' father-in-law, brought a whole-offering and sacrifices for God; and Aaron and all the elders of Israel came and shared the meal with Jethro in the presence of God.

The next day Moses took his seat to settle disputes among the people, and he was surrounded from morning till evening. At the sight of all that he was doing for the people, Jethro asked, 'What is this you are doing for the people? Why do you sit alone with all of them standing round you from morning till evening?' 'The people come to me to seek God's guidance,' Moses answered. 'Whenever there is a dispute among them, they come to me, and I decide between one party and the other. I make known the statutes and laws of God.' His father-in-law said to him, 'This is not the best way to do it. You will only wear yourself out and wear out the people who are here. The task is too heavy for you; you cannot do it alone. Now listen to me: take my advice, and God be with you. It is for you to be the people's representative before God, and bring their disputes to him, to instruct them in the statutes and laws, and teach them how they must behave and what they must do. But you should search for capable, godfearing men among all the people, honest and incorruptible men, and appoint them over the people as officers over units of a thousand, of a hundred, of fifty, or of ten. They can act as judges for the people at all times; difficult cases they should refer to you, but decide simple cases themselves. In this way your burden will be lightened, as they will be sharing it with you. If you do this, then God will direct you and you will be able to go on. And, moreover, this whole people will arrive at its destination in harmony.'

Moses heeded his father-in-law and did all he had suggested. He chose capable men from all Israel and appointed them leaders of the people, officers over units of a thousand, of a hundred, of fifty, or of ten. They sat as a permanent court, bringing the difficult cases to Moses but deciding simple cases themselves. When his father-in-law went back to his own country, Moses set him on his way.

THE TEN COMMANDMENTS
Exodus 19:1–12, 16–17; 20:1–21; 24:12–18

In the third month after Israel had left Egypt, they came to the wilderness of Sinai. They set out from Rephidim and, entering the wilderness of Sinai, they encamped there, pitching their tents in front of the mountain. Moses went up to God, and the Lord called to him from the mountain and said, 'This is what you are to say to the house of Jacob and tell the sons of Israel: You yourselves have seen what I did to Egypt, and how I have carried you on eagles' wings and brought you here to me. If only you will now listen to me and keep my covenant, then out of all peoples you will become my special possession; for the whole earth is mine. You will be to me a kingdom of priests, my holy nation. Those are the words you are to speak to the Israelites.'

Moses went down, and summoning the elders of the people he set before them all these commands which the Lord had laid on him. As one the people answered, 'Whatever the Lord has said we shall do.' When Moses brought this answer back to the Lord, the Lord said to him, 'I am coming to you in a thick cloud, so that I may speak to you in the hearing of the people, and so their faith in you may never fail.'

When Moses reported to the Lord the pledge given by the people, the Lord said to him, 'Go to the people and hallow them today and tomorrow and have them wash their clothes. They must be ready by the third day, because on that day the Lord will descend on Mount Sinai in the sight of all the people. You must set bounds for the people, saying, "Take care not to go up the mountain or even to touch its base." Anyone who touches the mountain shall be put to death...'

At dawn on the third day there were peals of thunder and flashes of lightning, dense cloud on the mountain, and a loud trumpet-blast; all the people in the camp trembled.

Moses brought the people out from the camp to meet God, and they took their stand at the foot of the mountain...

God spoke all these words:

I am the Lord your God who brought you out of Egypt, out of the land of slavery.

You must have no other god besides me.

You must not make a carved image for yourself, nor the likeness of anything in the heavens above, or on the earth below, or in the waters under the earth.

You must not bow down to them in worship; for I, the Lord your God, am a jealous God, punishing the children for the sins of the parents to the third and fourth generation of those who reject me. But I keep faith with thousands, those who love me and keep my commandments.

You must not make wrong use of the name of the Lord your God; the Lord will not leave unpunished anyone who misuses his name.

Remember to keep the sabbath day holy. You have six days to labour and do all your work; but the seventh day is a sabbath of the Lord your God; that day you must not do any work, neither you, nor your son or your daughter, your slave or your slave-girl, your cattle, or the alien residing among you; for in six days the Lord made the heavens and the earth, the sea, and all that is in them, and on the seventh day he rested. Therefore the Lord blessed the sabbath day and declared it holy.

Honour your father and your mother, so that you may enjoy long life in the land which the Lord your God is giving you.

Do not commit murder.

Do not commit adultery.

Do not steal.

Do not give false evidence against your neighbour.

Do not covet your neighbour's household: you must not covet your neighbour's wife, his slave, his slave-girl, his ox, his donkey, or anything that belongs to him.

When all the people saw how it thundered and the lightning flashed, when they heard the trumpet sound and saw the mountain in smoke, they were afraid and trembled. They stood at a distance and said to Moses, 'Speak to us yourself and we will listen; but do not let God speak to us or we shall die.' Moses answered, 'Do not be afraid. God has come only to test you, so that the fear of him may remain with you and preserve you from sinning.' So the people kept their distance, while Moses approached the dark cloud where God was...

The Lord said to Moses, 'Come up to me on the mountain, stay there, and let me give you the stone tablets with the law and commandment I have written down for their instruction.' Moses with Joshua his assistant set off up the mountain of God; he said to the elders, 'Wait for us here until we come back to you. You have Aaron and Hur; if anyone has a dispute, let him go to them.'

So Moses went up the mountain and a cloud covered it. The glory of the Lord rested on Mount Sinai, and the cloud covered the mountain for six days; on the seventh day he called to Moses out of the cloud. To the Israelites the glory of the Lord looked like a devouring fire on the mountaintop. Moses entered the cloud and went up the mountain; there he stayed forty days and forty nights.

THE GOLDEN CALF
Exodus 32:1–34

When the people saw that Moses was so long in coming down from the mountain, they congregated before Aaron and said, 'Come, make us gods to go before us. As for this Moses, who brought us up from Egypt, we do not know what has become of him.' Aaron answered, 'Take the gold rings from the ears of your wives and daughters, and bring them to me.' So all the people stripped themselves of their gold ear-rings and brought them to Aaron. He received them from their hands, cast the metal in a mould, and made it into the image of a bull-calf; then they said, 'Israel, these are your gods that brought you up from Egypt.' Seeing this, Aaron built an altar in front of it and announced, 'Tomorrow there is to be a feast to the Lord.' Next day the people rose early, offered whole-offerings, and brought shared-offerings. After this they sat down to eat and drink and then gave themselves up to revelry.

The Lord said to Moses, 'Go down at once, for your people, the people you brought up from Egypt, have committed a monstrous act. They have lost no time in turning aside from the way which I commanded them to follow, and cast for themselves a metal image of a bull-calf; they have prostrated themselves before it, sacrificed to it, and said, "Israel, these are your gods that brought you up from Egypt."' The Lord said to Moses, 'I have considered this people, and I see their stubbornness. Now, let me alone to pour out my anger on them, so that I may put an end to them and make a great nation spring from you.'

Moses set himself to placate the Lord his God: 'Lord,' he said, 'why pour out your anger on your people, whom you brought out of Egypt with great power and a strong hand? Why let the Egyptians say, "He meant evil when he took them out, to kill them in the mountains and wipe them off the face of the earth"? Turn from your anger, and think better of the evil you intend against your people. Remember Abraham, Isaac, and Israel, your servants, to whom you swore by your own self: "I shall make your descendants countless as the stars in the heavens, and all this land, of which I have spoken, I shall give to them, and they will possess it for ever."' So the Lord thought better of the evil with which he had threatened his people.

Moses went back down the mountain holding the two tablets of the Testimony, inscribed on both sides, on the front and on the back. The tablets were the handiwork of God, and the writing was God's writing, engraved on the tablets. Joshua, hearing the uproar the people were making, said to Moses, 'Listen! There is fighting in the camp.' Moses replied,

'This is not the sound of warriors,
nor the sound of a defeated people;
it is the sound of singing that I hear.'

As he approached the camp, Moses saw the bull-calf and the dancing, and in a burst of anger he flung down the tablets and shattered them at the foot of the mountain. He took the calf they had made and burnt it; he ground it to powder, sprinkled it on water, and made the Israelites drink it.

He demanded of Aaron, 'What did this people do to you that you should have brought such great guilt upon them?' Aaron replied, 'Please do not be angry, my lord. You know how wicked the people are. They said to me, "Make us gods to go ahead of us, because, as for this Moses, who brought us up from Egypt, we do not know what has become of him." So I said to them, "Those of you who have any gold, take it off." They gave it to me, I threw it in the fire, and out came this bull-calf.'

Moses saw that the people were out of control and that Aaron had laid them open to the secret malice of their enemies. He took his place at the gate of the camp and said, 'Who is on the Lord's side? Come here to me'; and the Levites all rallied to him. He said to them, 'The Lord the God of Israel has said: Arm yourselves, each of you, with his sword. Go through the camp from gate to gate and back again. Each of you kill brother, friend, neighbour.' The Levites obeyed, and about three thousand of the people died that day. Moses said, 'You have been installed as priests to the Lord today, because you have turned each against his own son and his own brother and so have brought a blessing this day upon yourselves.'

The next day Moses said to the people, 'You have committed a great sin. Now I shall go up to the Lord; perhaps I may be able to secure pardon for your sin.' When he went back to the Lord he said, 'Oh, what a great sin this people has committed: they have made themselves gods of gold.

'Now if you will forgive them, forgive; but if not, blot out my name, I pray, from your book which you have written.' The Lord answered Moses, 'Whoever has sinned against me, him I shall blot out from my book. Now go, lead the people to the place of which I have told you. My angel will go ahead of you, but a day will come when I shall punish them for their sin.'

GOD REVEALS HIS GLORY TO MOSES
Exodus 33:7 – 34:14, 27–35

Moses used to take the Tent and set it up outside the camp some distance away. He called it the Tent of Meeting, and everyone who sought the Lord would go outside the camp to the Tent of Meeting. Whenever Moses went out to the Tent, all the people would rise and stand, each at the door of his tent, and follow Moses with their eyes until he had entered the Tent. When Moses entered it, the pillar of cloud came down, and stayed at the entrance to the Tent while the Lord spoke with Moses. As soon as the people saw the pillar of cloud standing at the entrance to the Tent, they would all prostrate themselves, each at the door of his tent. The Lord used to speak with Moses face to face, as one man speaks to another, and Moses then returned to the camp, but his attendant, Joshua son of Nun, never moved from inside the Tent.

Moses said to the Lord, 'You tell me to lead up this people without letting me know whom you will send with me, even though you have said to me, "I know you by name, and, what is more, you have found favour with me." If I have indeed won your favour, then teach me to know your ways, so that I can know you and continue in favour with you, for this nation is your own people.' The Lord answered, 'I shall go myself and set your mind at rest.' Moses said to him, 'Indeed if you do not go yourself, do not send us up from here; for how can it ever be known that I and your people have found favour with you, except by your going with us? So we shall be distinct, I and your people, from all the peoples on earth.' The Lord said to Moses, 'I shall do what you have asked, because you have found favour with me, and I know you by name.'

But Moses prayed, 'Show me your glory.' The Lord answered, 'I shall make all my goodness pass before you, and I shall pronounce in your hearing the name "Lord". I shall be gracious to whom I shall be gracious, and I shall have compassion on whom I shall have compassion.' But he added, 'My face you cannot see, for no mortal may see me and live.' The Lord said, 'Here is a place beside me. Take your stand on the rock and, when my glory passes by, I shall put you in a crevice of the rock and cover you with my hand until I have passed by. Then I shall take away my hand, and you will see my back, but my face must not be seen.'

The Lord said to Moses, 'Cut for yourself two stone tablets like the former ones, and I shall write on them the words which were on the first tablets which you broke. Be ready by morning, and then go up Mount Sinai, and present yourself to me there on the top. No one is to go up with you, no one must even be seen anywhere on the mountain, nor must flocks or herds graze within sight of that mountain.' So Moses cut two stone tablets like the first, and early in the morning he went up Mount Sinai as the Lord had commanded him, taking the two stone tablets in his hands. The Lord came down in the cloud, and, as Moses stood there in his presence, he pronounced the name 'Lord'. He passed in front of Moses and proclaimed: 'The Lord, the Lord, a God compassionate and gracious, long-suffering, ever faithful and true, remaining faithful to thousands, forgiving iniquity, rebellion, and sin but without acquitting the guilty, one who punishes children and grandchildren to the third and fourth generation for the iniquity of their fathers!' At once Moses bowed to the ground in worship. He said, 'If I have indeed won your favour, Lord, then please go in our company. However stubborn a people they are, forgive our iniquity and our sin, and take us as your own possession.'

The Lord said: Here and now I am making a covenant. In full view of all your people I shall do such miracles as have never been performed in all the world or in any nation. All the peoples among whom you live shall see the work of the Lord, for it is an awesome thing that I shall do for you. Observe all I command you this day; and I for my part shall drive out before you the Amorites, Canaanites, Hittites, Perizzites, Hivites, and Jebusites. Beware of making an alliance with the inhabitants of the land against which you are going, or they will prove a snare in your midst. You must demolish their altars, smash their sacred pillars, and cut down their sacred poles. You are not to bow in worship to any other god, for the Lord's name is the Jealous God, and a jealous God he is...

The Lord said to Moses, 'Write these words down, because the covenant I make with you and with Israel is on those terms.' So Moses remained there with the Lord forty days and forty nights without food or drink. The Lord wrote down the words of the covenant, the Ten Commandments, on the tablets.

At length Moses came down from Mount Sinai with the two stone tablets of the Testimony in his hands, and when he came down, he did not know that the skin of his face shone because he had been talking with the Lord. When Aaron and the Israelites saw how the skin of Moses' face shone, they were afraid to approach him. He called out to them, and Aaron and all the chiefs in the community turned towards him. Moses spoke to them, and after that all the Israelites drew near. He gave them all the commands with which the Lord had charged him on Mount Sinai.

When Moses finished what he had to say, he put a veil over his face. But whenever he went in before the Lord to speak with him, he left the veil off until he came out. Then he would go out and tell the Israelites all the commands he had received. The Israelites would see how the skin of Moses' face shone, and he would put the veil back over his face until he went in again to speak with the Lord.

THE CONSECRATION OF THE TABERNACLE
Exodus 40:1–16, 34–38

The Lord said to Moses: On the first day of the first month you are to set up the Tabernacle of the Tent of Meeting. Put the Ark of the Testimony in it and screen the Ark with the curtain. Bring in the table and lay it; then bring in the lampstand and mount its lamps. Then set the gold altar of incense in front of the Ark of the Testimony and put the screen of the entrance of the Tabernacle in place. Place the altar of whole-offering in front of the entrance of the Tabernacle of the Tent of Meeting, and the basin between the Tent of Meeting and the altar, and put water in it. Set up the court all round, and put in place the screen at the entrance of the court.

With the anointing oil anoint the Tabernacle and everything in it, thus consecrating it and all its furnishings; it will then be holy.

Anoint the altar of whole-offering and all its vessels, thus consecrating it; it will be most holy. Anoint the basin and its stand and consecrate it.

Bring Aaron and his sons to the entrance of the Tent of Meeting and wash them with the water. Then clothe Aaron with the sacred vestments, anoint him, and consecrate him to be my priest. Then bring forward his sons, clothe them in tunics, and anoint them as you anointed their father; and they will be my priests. Their anointing inaugurates a hereditary priesthood for all time.

Moses did everything exactly as the Lord had commanded him... And the cloud covered the Tent of Meeting, and the glory of the Lord filled the Tabernacle. Moses was unable to enter the Tent of Meeting, because the cloud had settled on it and the glory of the Lord filled the Tabernacle. At every stage of their journey, when the cloud lifted from the Tabernacle, the Israelites used to break camp; but if the cloud did not lift from the Tabernacle, they used not to break camp until such time as it did lift. For the cloud of the Lord was over the Tabernacle by day, and there was fire in the cloud by night, and all the Israelites could see it at every stage of their journey.

ANIMAL SACRIFICES
Leviticus 1:1–3; 4:27–31

The Lord summoned Moses and spoke to him from the Tent of Meeting. He told him to say to the Israelites: When anyone among you presents an animal as an offering to the Lord, it may be chosen either from the herd or from the flock.

If his offering is a whole-offering from the herd, he must present a male without blemish; he must present it at the entrance to the Tent of Meeting so as to secure acceptance before the Lord...

If anyone among the ordinary lay people sins inadvertently and does what is forbidden in any of the Lord's commandments, thereby incurring guilt, and the sin he has committed is made known to him, he must bring as his offering for the sin which he has committed a she-goat without blemish. He must lay his hand on the head of the victim and slaughter it at the place where the whole-offering is slaughtered. The priest must then take some of its blood with his finger and smear it on the horns of the altar of whole-offering; the rest of the blood he is to pour out at the base of the altar. He must remove all its fat as the fat is removed from the shared offering, and burn it on the altar as a soothing odour to the Lord. Thus the priest is to make expiation for that person's guilt, and it will be forgiven him.

CLEAN AND UNCLEAN ANIMALS
Leviticus 11:1–8, 43–44

The Lord told Moses and Aaron to say to the Israelites: These are the creatures you may eat: Of all the larger land animals you may eat any hoofed animal which has cloven hoofs and also chews the cud; those which only have cloven hoofs or only chew the cud you must not eat. These are: the camel, because though it chews the cud it does not have cloven hoofs, and is unclean for you; the rock-badger, because though it chews the cud it does not have cloven hoofs, and is unclean for you; the hare, because though it chews the cud it does not have a parted foot; it is unclean for you; the pig, because although it is a hoofed animal with cloven hoofs it does not chew the cud, and is unclean for you. You are not to eat the flesh of these or even touch their dead carcasses; they are unclean for you...

You must not contaminate yourselves through any creatures that swarm; you must not defile yourselves with them and make yourselves unclean by them. For I am the Lord your God; you are to make yourselves holy and keep yourselves holy, because I am holy.

THE DAY OF ATONEMENT
Leviticus 16:1–9, 20–22, 29–30

The Lord spoke to Moses after the death of Aaron's two sons, who died when they offered illicit fire before the Lord. He said to him: Tell your brother Aaron that on pain of death he must not enter the sanctuary behind the curtain, which is in front of the cover over the Ark, except at the appointed time; for I appear in the cloud above the cover. When Aaron enters the sanctuary, this is what he must do. He must bring a young bull for a purification-offering and a ram for a whole-offering; he is to wear a sacred linen tunic and linen shorts to cover himself, and he is to put a linen sash round his waist and wind a linen turban round his head; all these are sacred vestments, and he must bathe in water before putting them on. He is to receive from the community of the Israelites two he-goats for a purification-offering and a ram for a whole-offering.

He must offer the bull reserved for his purification-offering and make expiation for himself and his household. Then he must take the two he-goats and set them before the Lord at the entrance to the Tent of Meeting. He must cast lots over the two goats, one to be for the Lord and the other for Azazel. He must present the goat on which the lot for the Lord has fallen and deal with it as a purification-offering...

When Aaron has finished the purification of the sanctuary, the Tent of Meeting, and the altar, he is to bring forward the live goat. Laying both his hands on its head he must confess over it all the iniquities of the Israelites and all their acts of rebellion, that is all their sins; he is to lay his hands on the head of the goat and send it away into the wilderness in the charge of a man who is waiting ready. The goat will carry all their iniquities upon itself into some barren waste, where the man will release it, there in the wilderness...

This is to be a rule binding on you for all time: on the tenth day of the seventh month you must fast; you, whether native Israelite or alien settler among you, must do no work, because on this day expiation will be made on your behalf to cleanse you, and so make you clean before the Lord from all your sins.

'LOVE YOUR NEIGHBOUR'
Leviticus 19:1–4, 9–18

The Lord told Moses to say to the whole Israelite community: You must be holy, because I, the Lord your God, am holy. Each one of you must revere his mother and father. You must keep my sabbaths. I am the Lord your God. Do not resort to idols or make for yourselves gods of cast metal. I am the Lord your God...

When you reap the harvest in your land, do not reap right up to the edges of your field, or gather the gleanings of your crop. Do not completely strip your vineyard, or pick up the fallen grapes; leave them for the poor and for the alien. I am the Lord your God.

You must not steal; you must not cheat or deceive a fellow-countryman. You must not swear in my name with intent to deceive and thus profane the name of your God. I am the Lord. You are not to oppress your neighbour or rob him. Do not keep back a hired man's wages till next morning. Do not treat the deaf with contempt, or put an obstacle in the way of the blind; you are to fear your God. I am the Lord.

You are not to pervert justice, either by favouring the poor or by subservience to the great. You are to administer justice to your fellow-countryman with strict fairness. Do not go about spreading slander among your father's kin; do not take sides against your neighbour on a capital charge. I am the Lord. You are not to nurse hatred towards your brother. Reprove your fellow-countryman frankly, and so you will have no share in his guilt. Never seek revenge or cherish a grudge towards your kinsfolk; you must love your neighbour as yourself. I am the Lord.

THE YEAR OF JUBILEE
Leviticus 25:1–2, 8–19

When the Lord spoke to Moses on Mount Sinai he told him to say to the Israelites: When you enter the land which I am giving you, the land must keep sabbaths to the Lord...

You are to count off seven sabbaths of years, that is seven times seven years, forty-nine years, and in the seventh month on the tenth day of the month, on the Day of Atonement, you are to send the ram's horn throughout your land to sound a blast. Hallow the fiftieth year and proclaim liberation in the land for all its inhabitants. It is to be a jubilee year for you: each of you is to return to his holding, everyone to his family. The fiftieth year is to be a jubilee for you: you are not to sow, and you are not to harvest the self-sown crop, or gather in the grapes from the unpruned vines, for it is a jubilee, to be kept holy by you. You are to eat the produce direct from the land.

In this year of jubilee every one of you is to return to his holding. When you sell or buy land amongst yourselves, neither party must exploit the other. You must pay your fellow-countryman according to the number of years since the jubilee, and he must sell to you according to the remaining number of annual crops. The more years there are to run, the higher the price; the fewer the years, the lower, because what he is selling you is a series of crops. You must not victimize one another, but fear your God, because I am the Lord your God. Observe my statutes, keep my judgments, and carry them out; and you will live without any fear in the land. The land will yield its harvest; you will eat your fill and live there secure.

Part Two

Israel in the Wilderness

THE PRIESTLY BLESSING
Numbers 1:1; 6:22–27

On the first day of the second month in the second year after the Israelites came out of Egypt, the Lord spoke to Moses in the Tent of Meeting in the wilderness of Sinai...

The Lord said to Moses, 'Say this to Aaron and his sons: These are the words with which you are to bless the Israelites:

May the Lord bless you and guard you;
may the Lord make his face shine on you and be gracious
to you;
may the Lord look kindly on you and give you peace.

'So they are to invoke my name on the Israelites, and I shall bless them.'

THE ARK OF THE COVENANT
Numbers 10:11, 33–36

In the second year, on the twentieth day of the second month, the cloud lifted from the Tabernacle of the Testimony...

Then they moved off from the mountain of the Lord and journeyed for three days, and the Ark of the Covenant of the Lord kept three days' journey ahead of them to find them a place to rest. The cloud of the Lord was over them by day when they moved camp. Whenever the Ark set out, Moses said,

'Arise, Lord, and may your enemies be scattered;
may those hostile to you flee at your approach.'

Whenever it halted, he said,

'Rest, Lord of the countless thousands of Israel.'

THE PEOPLE ASK FOR MEAT
Numbers 11:4–6, 10–34

A mixed company of strangers had joined the Israelites, and these people began to be greedy for better things. Even the Israelites themselves with renewed weeping cried out, 'If only we had meat! Remember how in Egypt we had fish for the asking, cucumbers and water-melons, leeks and onions and garlic. Now our appetite is gone; wherever we look there is nothing except this manna.'... Moses heard all the people lamenting in their families at the opening of their tents. The Lord became very angry, and Moses was troubled, and said to the Lord, 'Why have you brought trouble on your servant? How have I displeased the Lord that I am burdened with all this people? Am I their mother? Have I brought them into the world, and am I called on to carry them in my arms, like a nurse with a baby, to the land promised by you on oath to their fathers? Where am I to find meat to give them all? They pester me with their wailing and their "Give us meat to eat." This whole people is a burden too heavy for me; I cannot carry it alone. If that is your purpose for me, then kill me outright: if I have found favour with you, spare me this trouble afflicting me.'

The Lord answered Moses, 'Assemble for me seventy of Israel's elders, men known to you as elders and officers in the community; bring them to the Tent of Meeting, and there let them take their place with you. I shall come down and speak with you there. I shall withdraw part of the spirit which is conferred on you and bestow it on them, and they will share with you the burden of the people; then you will not have to bear it alone. And say to the people: Sanctify yourselves in readiness for tomorrow; you will have meat to eat. You wailed in the Lord's hearing; you said, "If only we had meat! In Egypt we lived well." The Lord will give you meat and you will eat it. Not for one day only, nor for two days, nor five, nor ten, nor twenty, but for a whole month you will eat it until it comes out at your nostrils and makes you sick; because you have rejected the Lord who is in your midst, wailing in his presence and saying, "Why did we ever come out of Egypt?"'

Moses said, 'Here am I with six hundred thousand men on the march around me, and you promise them meat to eat for a whole month! How can the sheep and oxen be slaughtered that would be enough for them? If all the fish in the sea could be caught, would they be enough?' The Lord replied, 'Is there a limit to the power of the Lord? You will now see whether or not my words come true.'

Moses went out and told the people what the Lord had said. He assembled seventy men from the elders of the people and stationed them round the Tent. Then the Lord descended in the cloud and spoke to him. He withdrew part of the spirit which had been conferred on Moses and bestowed it on the seventy elders; as the spirit alighted on them, they were seized by a prophetic ecstasy, for the first and only time.

Two men, one named Eldad and the other Medad, who had been enrolled with the seventy, were left behind in the camp. Though they had not gone out to the Tent, the spirit alighted on them none the less, and they were seized by prophetic ecstasy there in the camp. A young man ran and told Moses that Eldad and Medad were in an ecstasy in the camp, whereupon Joshua son of Nun, who had served since boyhood with Moses, broke in, 'Moses my lord, stop them!' But Moses said to him, 'Are you jealous on my account? I wish that all the Lord's people were prophets and that the Lord would bestow his spirit on them all!' Moses then rejoined the camp with the elders of Israel.

There sprang up a wind from the Lord, which drove quails in from the west, and they were flying all round the camp for the distance of a day's journey, three feet above the ground. The people were busy gathering quails all that day and night, and all next day, and even those who got least gathered ten homers of them. They spread them out to dry all about the camp. But the meat was scarcely between their teeth, and they had not so much as bitten it, when the Lord's anger flared up against the people and he struck them with a severe plague. That place came to be called Kibroth-hattaavah, because there they buried the people who had been greedy for meat.

MIRIAM AND AARON SPEAK AGAINST MOSES
Numbers 11:35 – 12:15

From Kibroth-hattaavah the Israelites went on to Hazeroth, and while they were there, Miriam and Aaron began to find fault with Moses. They criticized him for his Cushite wife (for he had married a Cushite woman), and they complained, 'Is Moses the only one by whom the Lord has spoken? Has he not spoken by us as well?' – though Moses was a man of great humility, the most humble man on earth. But the Lord heard them and at once said to Moses, Aaron, and Miriam, 'Go out all three of you to the Tent of Meeting.' When they went out, the Lord descended in a pillar of cloud and, standing at the entrance to the tent, he summoned Aaron and Miriam. The two of them came forward, and the Lord said,

> 'Listen to my words.
> If he were your prophet and nothing more,
> I would make myself known to him in a vision,
> I would speak with him in a dream.
> But my servant Moses is not such a prophet;
> of all my household he alone is faithful.
> With him I speak face to face,
> openly and not in riddles.
> He sees the very form of the Lord.
> How dare you speak against my servant Moses?'

With his anger still hot against them, the Lord left them; and as the cloud moved from the tent, there was Miriam, her skin diseased and white as snow. When Aaron, turning towards her, saw her skin diseased, he said to Moses, 'My lord, do not make us pay the penalty of sin, foolish and wicked though we have been. Let her not be like something stillborn, whose flesh is half eaten away when it comes from the womb.' So Moses cried, 'Lord, not this! Heal her, I pray.' The Lord answered, 'Suppose her father had spat in her face, would she not have to remain in disgrace for seven days? Let her be confined outside the camp for seven days and then be brought back.' So Miriam was shut outside for seven days, and the people did not strike camp until she was brought back.

MOSES SENDS SPIES INTO CANAAN
Numbers 12:16 – 13:3, 17 – 14:24, 35–38

After that they moved on from Hazeroth and pitched camp in the wilderness of Paran. The Lord said to Moses, 'Send men out to explore Canaan, the land which I am going to give to the Israelites; from each ancestral tribe send one man, a man of high rank.' So at the Lord's command Moses sent them out from the wilderness of Paran, all of them leading men among the Israelites...

When Moses sent them to explore Canaan, he said, 'Make your way up by the Negeb, up into the hill-country, and see what the land is like, and whether the people who live there are strong or weak, few or many. See whether the country in which they live is easy or difficult, and whether their towns are open or fortified. Is the land fertile or barren, and is it wooded or not? Go boldly in and bring some of its fruit.' It was the season when the first grapes were ripe.

They went up and explored the country from the wilderness of Zin as far as Rehob by Lebo-hamath. Going up by the Negeb they came to Hebron, where Ahiman, Sheshai, and Talmai, the descendants of Anak, were living. (Hebron was built seven years before Zoan in Egypt.) They came to the wadi Eshcol, and there they cut a branch with a single bunch of grapes, which they carried on a pole between two of them; they also picked pomegranates and figs. That place was named the wadi Eshcol from the bunch of grapes the Israelites cut there.

After forty days they returned from exploring the country and, coming back to Moses and Aaron and the whole community of Israelites at Kadesh in the wilderness of Paran, they made their report, and showed them the fruit of the country. They gave Moses this account: 'We made our way into the land to which you sent us. It is flowing with milk and honey, and here is the fruit it grows; but its inhabitants are formidable, and the towns are fortified and very large; indeed, we saw there the descendants of Anak. We also saw the Amalekites who live in the Negeb, Hittites, Jebusites, and Amorites who live in the hill-country, and the Canaanites who live by the sea and along the Jordan.'

Caleb silenced the people for Moses. 'Let us go up at once and occupy the country,' he said; 'we are well able to conquer it.' But the men who had gone with him said, 'No, we cannot attack these people; they are too strong for us.' Their report to the Israelites about the land which they had explored was discouraging: 'The country we explored', they said, 'will swallow up any who go to live in it. All the people we saw there are men of gigantic stature. When we set eyes on the Nephilim (the sons of Anak belong to the Nephilim) we felt no bigger than grasshoppers; and that is how we must have been in their eyes.'

At this the whole Israelite community cried out in dismay and the people wept all night long. Everyone complained against Moses and Aaron: 'If only we had died in Egypt or in the wilderness!' they said. 'Why should the Lord bring us to this land, to die in battle and leave our wives and our dependants to become the spoils of war? It would be better for us to go back to Egypt.' And they spoke of choosing someone to lead them back there.

Then Moses and Aaron flung themselves on the ground before the assembled community of the Israelites, and two of those who had explored the land, Joshua son of Nun and Caleb son of Jephunneh, tore their clothes, and encouraged the whole community: 'The country we travelled through and explored', they said, 'is a very good land indeed. If the Lord is pleased with us, he will bring us into this land, a land flowing with milk and honey, and give it to us. But you must not act in defiance of the Lord. You need not fear the people of the country, for we shall devour them. They have lost the protection that they had: the Lord is with us. You have nothing to fear from them.' As the whole assembly threatened to stone them, the glory of the Lord appeared in the Tent of Meeting to all the Israelites.

The Lord said to Moses, 'How much longer will this people set me at naught? How much longer will they refuse to trust me in spite of all the signs I have shown among them? I shall strike them with pestilence. I shall deny them their heritage, and you and your descendants I shall make into a nation greater and more numerous than they.' But Moses answered the Lord, 'What if the Egyptians hear of it? You brought this people out of Egypt by your might. What if they tell the inhabitants of this land? They too have heard of you, Lord, that you are with this people and are seen face to face, that your cloud stays over them, and that you go before them in a pillar of cloud by day and in a pillar of fire by night. If then you do put them all to death at one blow, the nations who have heard these reports about you will say, "The Lord could not bring this people into the land which he promised them by oath; and so he destroyed them in the wilderness."

'Now let the Lord's might be shown in its greatness, true to your proclamation of yourself – "The Lord, long-suffering, ever faithful, who forgives iniquity and rebellion, and punishes children to the third and fourth generation for the iniquity of their fathers, though he does not sweep them clean away." You have borne with this people from Egypt all the way here; forgive their iniquity, I beseech you, as befits your great and constant love.'

The Lord said, 'Your prayer is answered, and I pardon them. But as I live, and as the glory of the Lord fills the whole earth, not one of all those who have seen my glory and the signs which I wrought in Egypt and in the wilderness shall see the country which I promised on oath to their fathers. Ten times they have challenged me and not obeyed my voice. None of those who have set me at naught shall see this land. But my servant Caleb showed a different spirit and remained loyal to me. Because of this, I shall bring him into the land in which he has already set foot, the territory of the Amalekites and the Canaanites who dwell in the Vale, and I shall put his descendants in possession of it...

'I, the Lord, have spoken. This I swear to do to all this wicked community who have combined against me. There will be an end of them here in this wilderness; here they will die.'

The men whom Moses had sent to explore the land, and who came back and by their report set all the community complaining against him, died of a plague before the Lord; they died of plague because they had made a bad report. Of those who went to explore the land, Joshua son of Nun and Caleb son of Jephunneh alone survived.

THE REBELLION OF KORAH, DATHAN AND ABIRAM
Numbers 16

Korah son of Izhar, son of Kohath, son of Levi, along with the Reubenites Dathan and Abiram sons of Eliab and On son of Peleth, challenged the authority of Moses. Siding with them in their revolt were two hundred and fifty Israelites, all chiefs of the community, conveners of assembly and men of good standing. They confronted Moses and Aaron and said, 'You take too much on yourselves. Each and every member of the community is holy and the Lord is among them. Why do you set yourselves up above the assembly of the Lord?' When Moses heard this, he prostrated himself, and he said to Korah and all his company, 'Tomorrow morning the Lord will declare who is his, who is holy and who may present offerings to him. The man whom the Lord chooses may present them. This is what you must do, you, Korah, and all your company: you must take censers, and put fire in them and place incense on them before the Lord tomorrow. The man whom the Lord then chooses is the man who is holy. You take too much on yourselves, you Levites.'

Moses said to Korah, 'Listen, you Levites. Is it not enough for you that the God of Israel has set you apart from the community of Israel, bringing you near him to maintain the service of the Tabernacle of the Lord and to stand before the community as their ministers? He has had you come near him, and all your brother Levites with you; now do you seek the priesthood as well? That is why you and all your company have combined together against the Lord. What is Aaron that you should make these complaints against him?'

Moses sent to fetch Dathan and Abiram sons of Eliab, but they answered, 'We will not come. Is it not enough that you have brought us away from a land flowing with milk and honey to let us die in the wilderness? Must you also set yourself up as prince over us? What is more, you have not brought us into a land flowing with milk and honey, nor have you given us fields and vineyards to inherit. Do you think you can hoodwink men like us? We are not coming.' Moses became very angry, and said to the Lord, 'Take no notice of their murmuring. I have not taken from them so much as a single donkey; I have not wronged any of them.'

Moses said to Korah, 'Present yourselves before the Lord tomorrow, you and all your company, you and they and Aaron. Each man of you is to take his censer and put incense on it. Then you shall present them before the Lord with their two hundred and fifty censers, and you and Aaron shall also bring your censers.' So each man took his censer, put fire in it, and placed incense on it. Moses and Aaron took their stand at the entrance to the Tent of Meeting, and Korah gathered his whole company together and faced them at the entrance to the Tent of Meeting.

Then the glory of the Lord appeared to the whole community, and the Lord said to Moses and Aaron, 'Stand apart from them, so that I may make an end of them in a single moment.' But Moses and Aaron prostrated themselves and said, 'God, you God of the spirits of all mankind, if one man sins, will you be angry with the whole community?' But the Lord said to Moses, 'Tell them all to stand back from the dwellings of Korah, Dathan, and Abiram.'

Moses rose and went to Dathan and Abiram, and the elders of Israel followed him. He said to the whole community, 'Stand well away from the tents of these wicked men; touch nothing of theirs, or you will be swept away because of all their sins.' So they moved away from the dwellings of Korah, Dathan, and Abiram. Dathan and Abiram had come out and were standing at the entrance of their tents with their wives, their children, and their dependants. Moses said, 'By this you shall know that it is the Lord who sent me to do all I have done, and it was not my own heart that prompted me. If these men die a natural death, merely sharing the common fate of man, then the Lord has not sent me; but if the Lord works a miracle, and the ground opens its mouth and swallows them and all that is theirs, and they go down alive to Sheol, then you will know that these men have set the Lord at naught.'

Hardly had Moses spoken when the ground beneath them split apart; the earth opened its mouth and swallowed them and their homes – all the followers of Korah and all their property. They went down alive into Sheol with all that they had; the earth closed over them, and they vanished from the assembly. At their cries all the Israelites around them fled. 'Look out!' they shouted. 'The earth might swallow us.' Fire came out from the Lord and consumed the two hundred and fifty men presenting the incense.

Then the Lord said to Moses, 'Order Eleazar son of Aaron the priest to set aside the censers from the burnt remains, and scatter the fire from them a long way off, because they are holy. The censers of these men who sinned at the cost of their lives you shall make into beaten plates to overlay the altar; they are holy, because they have been presented before the Lord. Let them be a sign to the Israelites.' Eleazar the priest took the bronze censers which the victims of the fire had presented, and they were beaten into plates to cover the altar, to be a reminder to the Israelites that no lay person, no one not descended from Aaron, should come forward to burn incense before the Lord, or his fate would be that of Korah and his company. All this was done as the Lord commanded Eleazar through Moses.

Next day the whole Israelite community raised complaints against Moses and Aaron and taxed them with causing the death of some of the Lord's people. As they gathered against Moses and Aaron, they turned towards the Tent of Meeting and saw that the cloud covered it, and the glory of the Lord appeared. When Moses and Aaron came to the front of the Tent of Meeting, the Lord said to them, 'Stand well clear of this community, so that in a single moment I may make an end of them.' They prostrated themselves, and then Moses said to Aaron, 'Take your censer, put fire from the altar in it, set incense on it, and go with it quickly to the assembled community to make expiation for them. Wrath has gone forth already from the presence of the Lord; the plague has begun.' As Moses had directed him, Aaron took his censer, ran into the midst of the assembly, and found that the plague had indeed begun among the people. He put incense on the censer and made expiation for the people, standing between the dead and the living, and the plague was stopped. Fourteen thousand seven hundred died of it, in addition to those who had died for Korah's offence. When Aaron came back to Moses at the entrance to the Tent of Meeting, the plague had stopped.

AARON'S STAFF
Numbers 17:1–11

The Lord said to Moses, 'Speak to the Israelites and get from them a staff for each tribe, one from every tribal chief, twelve in all, and write each man's name on his staff. On Levi's staff write Aaron's name, for there must be one staff for each head of a tribe. Put them all in the Tent of Meeting before the Testimony, where I meet you, and the staff of the man whom I choose will put forth buds. I shall rid myself of the complaints of these Israelites, who keep on complaining against you.'

Moses gave those instructions to the Israelites, and each of their chiefs handed him a staff for his tribe, twelve in all, and Aaron's staff among them. Moses laid them before the Lord in the Tent of the Testimony, and next day when he entered the tent, he found that Aaron's staff, the staff for the tribe of Levi, had budded. Indeed, it had put forth buds, blossomed, and produced ripe almonds. Moses then brought out the staffs from before the Lord and showed them to all the Israelites; they saw for themselves, and each man took his own staff. The Lord said to Moses, 'Put back Aaron's staff in front of the Testimony to be kept as a warning to rebels, so that you may rid me of their complaints, and then they will not die.' Moses did this, doing exactly as the Lord had commanded him.

WATER FROM THE ROCK
Numbers 20:1–13

In the first month the whole community of Israel arrived in the wilderness of Zin and stayed some time at Kadesh. Miriam died and was buried there.

As the community was without water, the people gathered against Moses and Aaron. They disputed with Moses. 'If only we had perished when our brothers perished before the Lord!' they said. 'Why have you brought the Lord's assembly into this wilderness for us and our livestock to die here? Why did you make us come up from Egypt to land us in this terrible place, where nothing will grow, neither grain nor figs nor vines nor pomegranates? There is not even water to drink.'

Moses and Aaron went from the assembly to the entrance of the Tent of Meeting, where they prostrated themselves, and the glory of the Lord appeared to them. The Lord said to Moses, 'Take your staff, and then with Aaron your brother assemble the community, and in front of them all command the rock to yield its waters. Thus you will produce water for the community out of the rock, for them and their livestock to drink.' Moses took his staff from before the Lord, as he had been ordered. He with Aaron assembled the people in front of the rock, and said to them, 'Listen, you rebels. Must we get water for you out of this rock?' Moses raised his hand and struck the rock twice with his staff. Water gushed out in abundance and they all drank, men and animals. But the Lord said to Moses and Aaron, 'You did not trust me so far as to uphold my holiness in the sight of the Israelites; therefore you will not lead this assembly into the land I am giving them.' Such were the waters of Meribah, where the people disputed with the Lord and through which his holiness was upheld.

THE DEATH OF AARON
Numbers 20:22–29

The whole community of Israel set out from Kadesh and came to Mount Hor. There, near the frontier of Edom, the Lord said to Moses and Aaron, 'Aaron is now to be gathered to his father's kin. He will not enter the land which I am giving to the Israelites, because over the waters of Meribah you both rebelled against my command. Take Aaron and his son Eleazar, and go up Mount Hor. Strip Aaron of his robes and invest Eleazar his son with them, for Aaron is to be taken from you: he will die there.' Moses did as the Lord had commanded: in full view of the whole community they went up Mount Hor, where Moses stripped Aaron of his robes and invested his son Eleazar with them. Aaron died there on the mountaintop. When Moses and Eleazar came down from the mountain, the whole Israelite community saw that Aaron had died, and all the people mourned for thirty days.

THE BRONZE SERPENT
Numbers 21:4–9

From Mount Hor they left by way of the Red Sea to march round the flank of Edom. But on the way the people grew impatient and spoke against God and Moses. 'Why have you brought us up from Egypt', they said, 'to die in the desert where there is neither food nor water?

We are heartily sick of this miserable fare.' Then the Lord sent venomous snakes among them, and they bit the Israelites so that many of them died.The people came to Moses and said, 'We sinned when we spoke against the Lord and you. Plead with the Lord to rid us of the snakes.' Moses interceded for the people, and the Lord told him to make a serpent and erect it as a standard, so that anyone who had been bitten could look at it and recover. So Moses made a bronze serpent and erected it as a standard, in order that anyone bitten by a snake could look at the bronze serpent and recover.

BALAAM AND THE DONKEY
Numbers 22:1, 3 – 24:19, 25

The Israelites moved on and encamped in the lowlands of Moab on the farther side of the Jordan opposite Jericho... and Moab was in terror of the people because there were so many of them. The Moabites were overcome with fear at the sight of them; and they said to the elders of Midian, 'This horde will soon eat up everything round us as an ox eats up the new grass in the field.' Balak son of Zippor, who was at that time king of Moab, sent a deputation to summon Balaam son of Beor, who was at Pethor by the Euphrates in the land of the Amavites, with this message, 'A whole nation has just arrived from Egypt: they cover the face of the country and are settling at my very door. Come at once and lay a curse on them, because they are too many for me. I may then be able to defeat them and drive them out of the country. I know that those whom you bless are blessed, and those whom you curse are cursed.'

The elders of Moab and Midian took the fees for augury with them, and coming to Balaam they gave him Balak's message. 'Spend this night here,' he replied, 'and I shall give you whatever answer the Lord gives me.' So the Moabite chiefs stayed with Balaam. God came to Balaam and asked him, 'Who are these men with you?' Balaam replied, 'Balak son of Zippor king of Moab has sent them to me and he says, "A people which has just come out of Egypt is covering the face of the country. Come at once and put a curse on them for me; then I may be able to give battle and drive them away."' God said to

Balaam, 'You are not to go with them or curse the people, because they are to be blessed.' So when Balaam rose in the morning he said to Balak's chiefs, 'Go back to your own country; the Lord has refused to let me go with you.' The Moabite chiefs took their leave and went back to Balak, and reported to him that Balaam had refused to come with them.

Balak sent a second embassy, larger and more high-powered than the first. When they came to Balaam they said, 'This is the message from Balak son of Zippor: "Let nothing stand in the way of your coming to me. I shall confer great honour upon you and do whatever you ask me. But you must come and put a curse on this people for me."' Balaam gave this answer to Balak's messengers: 'Even if Balak were to give me all the silver and gold in his palace, I could not disobey the command of the Lord my God in anything, small or great. But stay here for this night, as the others did, that I may learn what more the Lord may have to say to me.' During the night God came to Balaam and said to him, 'If these men have come to summon you, then rise and go with them, but do only what I tell you.' When morning came Balaam rose, saddled his donkey, and went with the Moabite chiefs.

But God was angry because Balaam was going, and as he came riding on his donkey, accompanied by his two servants, the angel of the Lord took his stand in the road to bar his way. When the donkey saw the angel standing in the road with his sword drawn, she turned off the road into the fields, and Balaam beat her to bring her back on to the road. The angel of the Lord then stood where the road ran through a hollow, with enclosed vineyards on either side. The donkey saw the angel and, squeezing herself against the wall, she crushed Balaam's foot against it, and again he beat her. The angel of the Lord moved on farther and stood in a narrow place where there was no room to turn to either right or left. When the donkey saw the angel, she lay down under Balaam. At that Balaam lost his temper and beat the donkey with his staff.

The Lord then made the donkey speak, and she said to Balaam, 'What have I done? This is the third time you have beaten me.' Balaam answered, 'You have been making a fool of me. If I had had a sword with me, I should have killed you on the spot.' But the donkey answered, 'Am I not still the donkey which you have ridden all your life? Have I ever taken such a liberty with you before?' He said, 'No.' Then the Lord opened Balaam's eyes: he saw the angel of the Lord standing in the road with his sword drawn, and he bowed down and prostrated himself. The angel said to him, 'What do you mean by beating your donkey three times like this? I came out to bar your way, but you made straight for me, and three times your donkey saw me and turned aside. If she had not turned aside, I should by now have killed you, while sparing her.' 'I have done wrong,' Balaam replied to the angel of the Lord. 'I did not know that you stood confronting me in the road. But now, if my journey displeases you, I shall turn back.' The angel of the Lord said to Balaam, 'Go with the men; but say only what I tell you.' So Balaam went on with Balak's chiefs.

When Balak heard that Balaam was coming, he went out to meet him as far as Ar of Moab by the Arnon on his frontier. Balak said to Balaam, 'Did I not send time and again to summon you? Why did you not come? Did you think that I could not do you honour?' Balaam replied, 'I have come, as you see. But now that I am here, what power have I of myself to say anything? It is only whatever word God puts into my mouth that I can speak.' So Balaam went with Balak till they came to Kiriath-huzoth, and Balak slaughtered cattle and sheep and sent portions to Balaam and to the chiefs who were with him.

In the morning Balak took Balaam and led him up to Bamoth-baal, from where he could see the full extent of the Israelite host. Then Balaam said to Balak, 'Build me here seven altars and prepare for me seven bulls and seven rams.' Balak followed Balaam's instructions; after offering a bull and a ram on each altar, he said to him, 'I have prepared the seven altars, and I have offered the bull and the ram on each altar.' Balaam answered, 'You stand here beside your sacrifice, and let me go off by myself. It may be that the Lord will meet me. Whatever he reveals to me, I shall tell you.' He went off to a height, where God met him. The Lord put words into Balaam's mouth and said, 'Go back to Balak, and speak as I tell you.' He went back, and found Balak standing by his sacrifice, and with him all the Moabite chiefs. Then Balaam uttered his oracle:

> 'From Aram, from the mountains of the east,
> Balak king of Moab has brought me:
> "Come, lay a curse on Jacob for me," he said.
> "Come, denounce Israel."
> How can I curse someone God has not cursed,
> how denounce someone the Lord has not denounced?
> From the rocky heights I see them,
> I watch them from the rounded hills.
> I see a people that dwells apart,
> that has not made itself one with the nations.
> Who can count the host of Jacob
> or number the myriads of Israel?
> Let me die as those who are righteous die;
> grant that my end may be as theirs!'

Balak said, 'What is this you have done? I sent for you to put a curse on my enemies, and what you have done is to bless them.' Balaam replied, 'I can but keep to the words which the Lord puts into my mouth.'

Balak then said to him, 'Come with me now to another place from which you will see them, though not the full extent of them; you will not see them all. Curse them for me from there.' So he took him to the Field of the Watchers on the summit of Pisgah, where he built seven altars and offered a bull and a ram on each altar. Balaam said to Balak, 'You stand beside your sacrifice; I shall meet the Lord over there.' The Lord met Balaam and put words into his mouth, and said, 'Go back to Balak, and speak as I tell you.' He went, and found him standing beside his sacrifice with the Moabite chiefs. Balak asked what the Lord had said, and Balaam uttered his oracle:

> 'Up, Balak, and listen:
> hear what I am charged to say, son of Zippor.
> God is not a mortal that he should lie,
> not a man that he should change his mind.
> Would he speak, and not make it good?
> What he proclaims, will he not fulfil?
> I have received a command to bless;
> I shall bless, and I cannot gainsay it.

He has discovered no iniquity in Jacob
and has seen no mischief in Israel.
The Lord their God is with them,
acclaimed among them as King.
What its curving horns are to the wild ox,
God is to them, who brought them out of Egypt.
Surely there is no divination in Jacob,
and no augury in Israel;
now it is said to Jacob
and to Israel, "See what God has wrought!"
Behold a people rearing up like a lioness,
rampant like a lion;
he will not couch till he has devoured the prey
and drunk the blood of the slain.'

Then Balak said to Balaam, 'You will not put a curse on them; then at least do not bless them.' He answered, 'Did I not warn you that I must do whatever the Lord tells me?'

Balak said, 'Come, let me take you to another place; perhaps God will be pleased to let you curse them for me there.' So he took Balaam to the summit of Peor overlooking Jeshimon, and Balaam told him to build seven altars for him there and prepare seven bulls and seven rams. Balak did as Balaam had said, and he offered a bull and a ram on each altar.

But now that Balaam knew that the Lord wished him to bless Israel, he did not go and resort to divination as before. He turned towards the desert, and before his eyes he saw Israel encamped tribe by tribe; and, the spirit of God coming on him, he uttered his oracle:

'The word of Balaam son of Beor,
the word of the man whose sight is clear,
the word of him who hears the words of God,
who with opened eyes sees in a trance
the vision from the Almighty:
Jacob, how fair are your tents,
Israel, your encampments,
like long palm groves,
like gardens by a river,

like aloe trees planted by the Lord,
like cedars beside the waters!
The water in his vessels shall overflow,
and his seed shall be like great waters
so that his king may be taller than Agag,
and his kingdom lifted high.
What its curving horns are to the wild ox,
God is to him, who brought him out of Egypt;
he will devour hostile nations,
crunch their bones, and break their backs.
When he reclines he couches like a lion
or like a lioness; who dares to rouse him?
Blessed be those who bless you,
and let them who curse you be accursed!'

At that Balak's anger was aroused against Balaam; beating his hands together, he cried, 'It was to curse my enemies that I summoned you, and three times you have persisted in blessing them. Off with you at once to your own place! I promised to confer great honour upon you, but now the Lord has kept this honour from you.' Balaam answered, 'But I said to your messengers: "Were Balak to give me all the silver and gold in his palace, I could not disobey the command of the Lord by doing anything of my own will, good or bad. What the Lord says to me, that is what I must say." Now I am going to my own people; but first, let me warn you what this people will do to yours in the days to come.' Then he uttered his oracle:

'The word of Balaam son of Beor,
the word of the man whose sight is clear,
the word of him who hears the words of God,
who shares the knowledge of the Most High,
who with opened eyes sees in a trance
the vision from the Almighty:
I see him, but not now;
I behold him, but not near:
a star will come forth out of Jacob,
a comet will arise from Israel.
He will smite the warriors of Moab,

and beat down all the sons of Sheth.
Edom will be his by conquest
and Seir, his enemy, will become his.
Israel will do valiant deeds;
Jacob will trample them down,
the last survivor from Ar will he destroy.'...

Then Balaam arose and returned home, and Balak also went on his way.

THE ZEAL OF PHINEHAS
Numbers 25:1–13

When the Israelites were in Shittim, the men began to have intercourse with Moabite women, who invited them to the sacrifices offered to their gods. The Israelites ate the sacrificial food and prostrated themselves before the gods of Moab; they joined in the worship of the Baal of Peor. This aroused the anger of the Lord, who said to Moses, 'Take all the leaders of the people and hurl them down to their death before the Lord in the full light of day, that the fury of my anger may turn away from Israel.' Moses gave this order to the judges of Israel: 'Each of you put to death those of his tribe who have joined in the worship of the Baal of Peor.'

One of the Israelites brought a Midianite woman into his family in open defiance of Moses and all the community of Israel, while they were weeping by the entrance of the Tent of Meeting. When Phinehas son of Eleazar, son of Aaron the priest, saw him, he got up from the assembly and took a spear, and went into the nuptial tent after the Israelite, where he transfixed the two of them, the Israelite and the woman, pinning them together. Then the plague which had attacked the Israelites was brought to a stop; but twenty-four thousand had already died.

The Lord said to Moses, 'Phinehas son of Eleazar, son of Aaron the priest, has turned my wrath away from the Israelites; he displayed among them the same jealous anger that moved me, and therefore I did not exterminate the Israelites in my jealous anger. Make known that I hereby grant him my covenant pledge of prosperity: he and his descendants after him shall enjoy the priesthood under a covenant for all time, because he showed his zeal for his God and made expiation for the Israelites.'

HOLY WAR AGAINST THE MIDIANITES
Numbers 31:1–31

The Lord said to Moses, 'You are to exact vengeance for Israel on the Midianites. After that you will be gathered to your father's kin.'

Moses addressed the people: 'Let men among you be drafted for active service; they are to fall on Midian and exact vengeance in the Lord's name. Send out a thousand men from each of the tribes of Israel.' So men were called up from the clans of Israel, a thousand from each tribe, twelve thousand in all, drafted for active service. Moses sent out this force, a thousand from each tribe, with Phinehas son of Eleazar the priest, who was in charge of the sacred equipment and of the trumpets to give the signal for the battle cry. They made war on Midian as the Lord had commanded Moses, and slew every male. In addition to those slain in battle they killed the five kings of Midian – Evi, Rekem, Zur, Hur, and Reba – and they put to death also Balaam son of Beor. The Israelites took the Midianites' women and dependants captive, and carried off all their herds, flocks, and property. They set fire to all the towns in which they lived, and all their encampments. They collected the spoil and plunder, both man and beast, and brought it all – captives, plunder, and spoil – to Moses and Eleazar the priest and to the whole Israelite community at the camp in the lowlands of Moab by the Jordan over against Jericho.

Moses and Eleazar the priest and all the chiefs of the community went to meet them outside the camp. Moses spoke angrily to the officers of the army, the commanders of units of a thousand and of a hundred, who were returning from the campaign: 'Have you spared all the women?' he said. 'Remember, it was they who, on Balaam's departure, set about seducing the Israelites into disloyalty to the Lord in the affair at Peor, so that the plague struck the community of the Lord. Now kill every male child, and kill every woman who has had intercourse with a man, but you may spare for yourselves every woman among them who has not had intercourse. You yourselves, every one of you who has taken life and every one who has touched the dead, must remain outside the camp for seven days. Purify yourselves and your captives on the third day and on the seventh day, and purify also every piece of clothing, every article made of hide, everything woven of goats' hair, and everything made of wood.'

Eleazar the priest said to the soldiers returning from battle, 'This is a statute of the law which the Lord has ordained through Moses. Anything which will stand fire, whether gold, silver, copper, iron, tin, or lead, you must pass through fire and then it will be clean. Other things must be purified by the water of ritual purification; whatever cannot stand fire is to be passed through the water. On the seventh day wash your clothes and be clean; after that you may re-enter the camp.'

The Lord said to Moses, 'You and Eleazar the priest and the heads of families in the community must count everything that has been captured, whether human beings or animals, and divide them equally between the fighting men who went on the campaign and the rest of the community. Levy a tribute for the Lord: from the combatants it is to be one out of every five hundred, whether human beings, cattle, donkeys, or sheep, to be taken out of their share and given to Eleazar the priest as a contribution for the Lord. Out of the Israelites' share it is to be one out of every fifty taken, whether human beings or cattle, donkeys, or sheep, all the animals, to be given to the Levites who are in charge of the Lord's Tabernacle.' Moses and Eleazar the priest did as the Lord had commanded Moses.

Part Three

The Last Words of Moses

GOD'S CHOSEN PEOPLE
Deuteronomy 1:1; 4:5–13, 32–36

These are the words that Moses addressed to all Israel in the wilderness beyond the Jordan...

I have taught you statutes and laws, as the Lord my God commanded me; see that you keep them when you go into and occupy the land. Observe them carefully, for thereby you will display your wisdom and understanding to other peoples. When they hear about all these statutes, they will say, 'What a wise and understanding people this great nation is!' What great nation has a god close at hand as the Lord our God is close to us whenever we call to him? What great nation is there whose statutes and laws are so just, as is all this code of laws which I am setting before you today?

But take care: keep careful watch on yourselves so that you do not forget the things that you have seen with your own eyes; do not let them pass from your minds as long as you live, but teach them to your children and to your children's children. You must never forget the day when you stood before the Lord your God at Horeb, and the Lord said to me, 'Assemble the people for me; I shall make them hear my words and they will learn to fear me all their lives in the land, and they will teach their children to do so.' Then you came near and stood at the foot of the mountain, which was ablaze with fire to the very skies, and there was dark cloud and thick mist. When the Lord spoke to you from the heart of the fire you heard a voice speaking, but you saw no form; there was only a voice. He announced to you the terms of his covenant, bidding you observe the Ten Commandments, which he wrote on two stone tablets...

Search into days gone by, long before your time, beginning at the day when God created man on earth; search from one end of heaven to the other, and ask if any deed as mighty as this has been seen or heard. Did any people ever hear the voice of a god speaking from the heart of the fire, as you heard it, and remain alive? Or did a god ever attempt to come and take a nation for himself away from another nation, with a challenge, and with signs, portents, and wars, with a strong hand and an outstretched arm, and with great deeds of terror, like all you saw the Lord your God do for you in Egypt? You have had sure proof that the Lord is God; there is none other. From heaven he let you hear his voice for your instruction, and on earth he let you see his great fire, and from the heart of the fire you heard his words.

THE SHEMA
Deuteronomy 6:4–11; 7:1–10

Hear, Israel: the Lord is our God, the Lord our one God; and you must love the Lord your God with all your heart and with all your soul and with all your strength. These commandments which I give you this day are to be remembered and taken to heart; repeat them to your children, and speak of them both indoors and out of doors, when you lie down and when you get up. Bind them as a sign on your hand and wear them as a pendant on your forehead; write them on the doorposts of your houses and on your gates.

The Lord your God will bring you into the land which he swore to your forefathers Abraham, Isaac, and Jacob that he would give you, a land of large, fine towns which you did not build, houses full of good things which you did not provide, cisterns hewn from the rock but not by you, and vineyards and olive groves which you did not plant...

When the Lord your God brings you into the land which you are about to enter to occupy it, when he drives out many nations before you – Hittites, Girgashites, Amorites, Canaanites, Perizzites, Hivites, and Jebusites, seven nations more numerous and powerful than you – and when the Lord your God delivers them into your power for you to defeat, you must exterminate them. You must not make an alliance with them or spare them. You must not intermarry with them, giving your daughters to their sons or taking their daughters for your sons, because if you do, they will draw your children away from the Lord to serve other gods. Then the anger of the Lord will be roused against you and he will soon destroy you. But this is what you must do to them: pull down their altars, break their sacred pillars, hack down their sacred poles, and burn their idols, for you are a people holy to the Lord your God, and he has chosen you out of all peoples on earth to be his special possession.

It was not because you were more numerous than any other nation that the Lord cared for you and chose you, for you were the smallest of all nations; it was because the Lord loved you and stood by his oath to your forefathers, that he brought you out with his strong hand and redeemed you from the place of slavery, from the power of Pharaoh king of Egypt. Know then that the Lord your God is God, the faithful God; with those who love him and keep his commandments he keeps covenant and faith for a thousand generations, but those who defy and reject him he repays with destruction: he will not be slow to requite any who reject him.

JUSTICE AND MERCY
Deuteronomy 16:18–20; 24:14–22

In every settlement which the Lord your God is giving you, you must appoint for yourselves judges and officers, tribe by tribe, and they will dispense true justice to the people. You must not pervert the course of justice or show favour or accept a bribe; for bribery makes the wise person blind and the just person give a crooked answer. Justice, and justice alone, must be your aim, so that you may live and occupy the land which the Lord your God is giving you...

You must not keep back the wages of a man who is poor and needy, whether a fellow-countryman or an alien living in your country in one of your settlements. Pay him his wages on the same day before sunset, for he is poor and he relies on them: otherwise he may appeal to the Lord against you, and you will be guilty of sin.

Parents are not to be put to death for their children, nor children for their parents; each one may be put to death only for his own sin.

You must not deprive aliens and the fatherless of justice or take a widow's cloak in pledge. Bear in mind that you were slaves in Egypt and the Lord your God redeemed you from there; that is why I command you to do this.

When you reap the harvest in your field and overlook a sheaf, do not go back to pick it up; it is to be left for the alien, the fatherless, and the widow, so that the Lord your God may bless you in all that you undertake.

When you beat your olive trees, do not strip them afterwards; what is left is for the alien, the fatherless, and the widow.

When you gather the grapes from your vineyard, do not glean afterwards; what is left is for the alien, the fatherless, and the widow. Keep in mind that you were slaves in Egypt; that is why I command you to do this.

THE FIRSTFRUITS
Deuteronomy 26:1–11

After you come into the land which the Lord your God is giving you to occupy as your holding and settle in it, you are to take some of the firstfruits of all the produce of the soil, which you harvest from the land which the Lord your God is giving you, and, having put them in a basket, go to the place which the Lord your God will choose as a dwelling for his name. When you come to the priest, whoever he is at that time, say to him, 'I acknowledge this day to the Lord your God that I have entered the land which the Lord swore to our forefathers to give us.' The priest will receive the basket from your hand and set it down before the altar of the Lord your God. Then you must solemnly recite before the Lord your God: 'My father was a homeless Aramaean who went down to Egypt and lived there with a small band of people, but there it became a great, powerful, and large nation. The Egyptians treated us harshly and humiliated us; they imposed cruel slavery on us. We cried to the Lord the God of our fathers for help, and he listened to us, and, when he saw our misery and hardship and oppression, the Lord led us out of Egypt with a strong hand and outstretched arm, with terrifying deeds, and with signs and portents.

He brought us to this place and gave us this land, a land flowing with milk and honey. Now I have brought here the firstfruits of the soil which you, Lord, have given me.' You are then to set the basket before the Lord your God and bow in worship before him. You are to rejoice, you and the Levites and the aliens living among you, in all the good things which the Lord your God has bestowed on you and your household.

BLESSINGS AND CURSES
Deuteronomy 27:1 – 28:20, 62–68

Moses, with the elders of Israel, gave the people this charge: Keep all the commandments that I now lay upon you. On the day you cross the Jordan to the land which the Lord your God is giving you, you are to set up great stones. Coat them with plaster, and inscribe on them all the words of this law, when you have crossed over to enter the land which the Lord your God is giving you, a land flowing with milk and honey, as the Lord the God of your forefathers promised you.

When you have crossed the Jordan you are to set up these stones on Mount Ebal, as I instruct you this day, and coat them with plaster. Build an altar there to the Lord your God, an altar of stones on which no iron tool is to be used. Build the altar of the Lord your God with blocks of undressed stone, and offer whole-offerings on it to the Lord your God. Slaughter shared-offerings and eat them there, and rejoice before the Lord your God. Inscribe on the stones all the words of this law, engraving them clearly and carefully.

Moses and the levitical priests said to all Israel: Be silent, Israel, and listen; this day you have become a people belonging to the Lord your God. Obey the Lord your God, and observe his commandments and statutes that I now lay upon you.

That day Moses gave the people this command: When you have crossed the Jordan those who are to stand on Mount Gerizim to bless the people are: Simeon, Levi, Judah, Issachar, Joseph, and Benjamin. Those who are to stand on Mount Ebal to pronounce the curse are: Reuben, Gad, Asher, Zebulun, Dan, and Naphtali.

The Levites, in the hearing of all Israel, are to intone these words: 'A curse on anyone who carves an image or casts an idol, anything abominable to the Lord, a craftsman's handiwork, and sets it up in secret': the people must all respond, 'Amen.'

'A curse on anyone who slights his father or his mother': the people must all say, 'Amen.'

'A curse on anyone who moves his neighbour's boundary stone': the people must all say, 'Amen.'

'A curse on anyone who misdirects a blind man': the people must all say, 'Amen.'

'A curse on anyone who withholds justice from the alien, the fatherless, and the widow': the people must all say, 'Amen.'

'A curse on anyone who lies with his father's wife, for he brings shame upon his father': the people must all say, 'Amen.'

'A curse on anyone who lies with any animal': the people must all say, 'Amen.'

'A curse on anyone who lies with his sister, whether his father's daughter or his mother's daughter': the people must all say, 'Amen.'

'A curse on anyone who lies with his wife's mother': the people must all say, 'Amen.'

'A curse on anyone who strikes another in secret': the people must all say, 'Amen.'

'A curse on anyone who accepts payment for killing an innocent person': the people must all say, 'Amen.'

'A curse on anyone who does not fulfil this law by doing all that it prescribes': the people must all say, 'Amen.'

If you faithfully obey the Lord your God by diligently observing all his commandments which I lay on you this day, then the Lord your God will raise you high above all nations of the earth, and the following blessings will all come and light on you, because you obey the Lord your God.

A blessing on you in the town; a blessing on you in the country.

A blessing on the fruit of your body, the fruit of your land and cattle, the offspring of your herds and lambing flocks.

A blessing on your basket and your kneading trough.

A blessing on you as you come in, and a blessing on you as you go out.

May the Lord deliver up to you the enemies who attack you,

and let them be put to rout before you. Though they come out against you by one way, they will flee before you by seven.

May the Lord grant you a blessing in your granaries and on all your labours; may the Lord your God bless you in the land which he is giving you.

The Lord will establish you as his own holy people, as he swore to you, provided you keep the commandments of the Lord your God and conform to his ways. All people on earth seeing that the Lord has named you as his very own will go in fear of you. The Lord will make you prosper greatly in the fruit of your body and of your cattle, and in the fruit of the soil in the land which he swore to your forefathers to give you. May the Lord open the heavens for you, his rich storehouse, to give your land rain at the proper time and bless everything to which you turn your hand. You may lend to many nations, but borrow from none; the Lord will make you the head and not the tail: you will always be at the top and never at the bottom, if you listen to the commandments of the Lord your God, which I give you this day to keep and to fulfil. Deviate neither to right nor to left from all the things which I command you this day, and do not go after other gods to serve them.

But if you will not obey the Lord your God by diligently observing all his commandments and statutes which I lay upon you this day, then all the following curses will come and light upon you.

A curse on you in the town, a curse in the country.

A curse on your basket and your kneading trough.

A curse on the fruit of your body, the fruit of your land, the offspring of your herds and your lambing flocks.

A curse on you as you come in, and a curse on you as you go out.

May the Lord send on you cursing, confusion, and rebuke in whatever you are doing, until you are destroyed and soon perish for the evil you have done in forsaking him...

Then you who were countless as the stars in the heavens will be left few in number, because you did not obey the Lord your God. Just as the Lord took delight in you, prospering you and increasing your numbers, so now it will be his delight to ruin and exterminate you, and you will be uprooted from the land which you are entering to occupy.

The Lord will disperse you among all peoples from one end of the earth to the other, and there you will serve other gods of whom neither you nor your forefathers have had experience, gods of wood and stone. Among those nations you will find no peace, no resting-place for the sole of your foot. Then the Lord will give you an unquiet mind, dim eyes, and failing appetite. Your life will hang continually in suspense, fear will beset you night and day, and you will find no security all your life long. Every morning you will say, 'Would God it were evening!' and every evening, 'Would God it were morning!' because of the terror that fills your heart and because of the sights you see. The Lord will bring you back sorrowing to Egypt by that very road of which I said to you, 'You shall not see that road again'; there you will offer yourselves for sale as slaves to your enemies, but there will be no buyer.

THE SONG OF MOSES
Deuteronomy 31:14–19, 21–22; 32:1–22, 44–47

The Lord said to Moses, 'The time of your death is drawing near. Summon Joshua, and present yourselves in the Tent of Meeting so that I may give him his commission.' When Moses and Joshua went and presented themselves in the Tent of Meeting, the Lord appeared in a pillar of cloud, which stood over the entrance of the Tent.

The Lord said to Moses, 'You are about to die and join your forefathers, and then this people, when they come into the land and live among foreigners, will wantonly worship their gods; they will abandon me and break the covenant which I have made with them. My anger will be roused against them on that day, and I shall abandon them and hide my face from them. They will be an easy prey, and many terrible disasters will come upon them. On that day they will say, "These disasters have come because our God is not among us." On that day I shall hide my face because of all the evil they have done in turning to other gods.

'Now write down this song and teach it to the Israelites; make them repeat it, so that it may be a witness for me against them. ...For even before I bring them into the land which I swore to give them, I already know which way their thoughts incline.'...

That day Moses wrote down this song and taught it to the Israelites...

Give ear, you heavens, to what I say;
listen, earth, to the words I speak.
May my teaching fall like raindrops,
my words distil like dew,
like fine rain on tender grass,
like lavish showers on growing plants.

When I proclaim the name of the Lord,
you will respond: 'Great is our God,
the Creator, whose work is perfect,
for all his ways are just,
a faithful God who does no wrong;
how righteous and true is he!'

Perverted and crooked generation
whose faults have proved you no children of his,
is this how you repay the Lord,
you senseless, stupid people?
Is he not your father who formed you?
Did he not make you and establish you?
Remember the days of old,
think of the years, age upon age;
ask your father to inform you,
the elders to tell you.

When the Most High gave each nation its heritage,
when he divided all mankind,
he laid down the boundaries for peoples
according to the number of the sons of God;
but the Lord's share was his own people,
Jacob was his allotted portion.

He found his people in a desert land,
in a barren, howling waste.

He protected and trained them,
he guarded them as the apple of his eye.
As an eagle watches over its nest,
hovers above its young,
spreads its pinions and takes them up,
and bears them on its wings,
the Lord alone led his people, no alien god at his side.

He made them ride over the heights of the earth
and fed them on the harvest of the fields;
he satisfied them with honey from the crags
and oil from the flinty rock,
curds from the cattle, milk from the herd,
the fat of lambs' kidneys,
of Bashan rams, and of goats,
with the finest flour of wheat;
and you, his people, drank red wine from the juice of the grape.

Jacob ate and was well fed,
Jeshurun grew fat and unruly,
they grew fat and bloated and sleek.
They forsook God their Maker
and dishonoured the Rock of their salvation.
They roused his jealousy with alien gods
and provoked him to anger with abominable practices.
They sacrificed to demons that are no gods,
to gods who were strangers to them;
they consorted with upstart gods from their neighbours,
gods whom your fathers did not acknowledge.
You forsook the Creator who begot you
and ceased to care for God who brought you to birth.

The Lord saw and spurned them;
his own sons and daughters provoked his anger.
'I shall hide my face from them,' he said;
'let me see what their end will be,
for they are a subversive generation,

children not to be trusted.
They roused my jealousy with a god of no account,
with their worthless idols they provoked me to anger;
so I shall rouse their jealousy with a people of no account,
with a foolish nation I shall provoke them.
For fire is set ablaze by my anger,
it burns to the depths of Sheol;
it devours earth and its harvest
and the flames reach the very roots of the mountains...

These are the words of the song that Moses, when he came with Joshua son of Nun, recited in full in the hearing of the people.

When Moses had finished reciting all these words to Israel he said: Take to heart all the warnings which I give you this day: command your children to be careful to observe all the words of this law. For you they are no empty words; they are your very life, and by them you will enjoy long life in the land which you are to occupy after crossing the Jordan.

THE DEATH OF MOSES
Deuteronomy 32:48–52; 34:1–7, 10

That same day the Lord said to Moses, 'Go up the mountain of the Abarim, Mount Nebo in Moab, to the east of Jericho, and view the land of Canaan that I am giving to the Israelites for their possession. On this mountain you will die and be gathered to your father's kin, just as Aaron your brother died on Mount Hor and was gathered to his father's kin. This is because both of you broke faith with me at the waters of Meribah-kadesh in the wilderness of Zin, when you did not uphold my holiness among the Israelites. You may see the land from a distance, but you may not enter the land I am giving to the Israelites.'...

Moses went up from the lowlands of Moab to Mount Nebo, to the top of Pisgah eastwards from Jericho, and the Lord showed him the whole land, from Gilead to Dan; the whole of Naphtali; the territory of Ephraim and Manasseh, and all Judah as far as the western sea; the

Negeb and the plain; the valley of Jericho, city of palm trees, as far as Zoar. The Lord said to him, 'This is the land which I swore to Abraham, Isaac, and Jacob that I would give to their descendants. I have let you see it with your own eyes, but you will not cross over into it.'

There in the Moabite country Moses the servant of the Lord died, as the Lord had said. He was buried in a valley in Moab opposite Beth-peor; but to this day no one knows his burial-place. Moses was a hundred and twenty years old when he died, his sight undimmed, his vigour unimpaired...

There has never yet risen in Israel a prophet like Moses, whom the Lord knew face to face...

Part Four

The Conquest of Canaan

GOD COMMISSIONS JOSHUA
Joshua 1:1–4, 9–11

After the death of Moses the Lord's servant, the Lord said to Joshua son of Nun, Moses' assistant, 'Now that my servant Moses is dead, get ready to cross the Jordan, you and all this people, to the land which I am giving to the Israelites. Every place where you set foot is yours: I have given it to you, as I promised Moses. From the desert and this Lebanon to the great river, the Euphrates, and across all the Hittite country westwards to the Great Sea, all of it is to be your territory... This is my command: be strong, be resolute; do not be fearful or discouraged, for wherever you go the Lord your God is with you.'

Then Joshua instructed the officers to pass through the camp and give this order to the people: 'Get food ready to take with you, for within three days you will be crossing this Jordan to occupy the country which the Lord your God is giving you to possess.'

RAHAB AND THE SPIES
Joshua 2

Joshua son of Nun sent out two spies secretly from Shittim with orders to reconnoitre the land and especially Jericho. The two men set off and came to the house of a prostitute named Rahab to spend the night there. When it was reported to the king of Jericho that some Israelites had arrived that night to explore the country, he sent word to Rahab: 'Bring out the men who have come to you and are now in your house, for they have come to spy out the whole country.' The woman, who had taken the two men and hidden them, replied, 'True, the men did come to me, but I did not know where they came from; and at nightfall when it was time to shut the gate, they had gone. I do not know where they were going, but if you hurry after them you may overtake them.' In fact, she had brought them up on to the roof and concealed them among the stalks of flax which she had laid out there in rows. The messengers went in pursuit of them in the direction of the fords of the Jordan, and as soon as they had gone out the gate was closed.

The men had not yet settled down, when Rahab came up to them on the roof, and said, 'I know that the Lord has given the land to you; terror of you has fallen upon us, and the whole country is panic-stricken. We have heard how the Lord dried up the waters of the Red Sea before you when you came out of Egypt, and what you did to Sihon and Og, the two Amorite kings beyond the Jordan, for you destroyed them. When we heard this, our courage failed; your coming has left no spirit in any of us; for the Lord your God is God in heaven above and on earth below. Swear to me by the Lord that you will keep faith with my family, as I have kept faith with you. Give me a token of good faith; promise that you will spare the lives of my father and mother, my brothers and sisters, and all who belong to them, and preserve us from death.' The men replied, 'Our lives for yours, so long as you do not betray our business. When the Lord gives us the country, we shall deal loyally and faithfully by you.'

She then let them down through a window by a rope; for the house where she lived was on an angle of the wall. 'Make for the hills,' she said, 'or the pursuers will come upon you. Hide there for three days until they return; then go on your way.' The men warned her that, unless she did what they told her, they would be free from the oath she had made them take. 'When we invade the land,' they said, 'you must fasten this strand of scarlet cord in the window through which you have lowered us, and get everybody together here inside the house, your father and mother, your brothers, and all your family. Should anybody go out of doors into the street, his blood will be on his own head; we shall be free of the oath. But if a hand is laid on anyone who stays indoors with you, his blood be on our heads! Remember too that, if you betray our business, then we shall be free of the oath you have made us take.' 'It shall be as you say,' she replied,

152

and sent them on their way. When they had gone, she fastened the strand of scarlet cord in the window.

The men made their way into the hills and stayed there for three days until the pursuers returned. They had searched all along the road, but had not found them. The two men then came down from the hills and crossed the river. When they joined up with Joshua son of Nun, they reported all that had happened to them. 'The Lord has delivered the whole country into our hands,' they said; 'the inhabitants are all panic-stricken at our approach.'

ISRAEL CROSSES THE RIVER JORDAN
Joshua 3:1 – 4:20; 5:10–15

Early in the morning Joshua and all the Israelites set out from Shittim and came to the Jordan, where they encamped before crossing. At the end of three days the officers passed through the camp, giving the people these instructions: 'When you see the Ark of the Covenant of the Lord your God being carried forward by the levitical priests, then you too must leave your positions and set out. Follow it, but do not go close to it; keep some distance behind, about two thousand cubits. It will show you the route you are to follow, for you have not travelled this way before.' Joshua said to the people, 'Consecrate yourselves, for tomorrow the Lord will perform a great miracle among you.' To the priests he said, 'Lift the Ark of the Covenant and move ahead of the people.' So they lifted it up and went at the head of the people.

The Lord said to Joshua, 'Today I shall begin to exalt you in the eyes of all Israel, and they will know that I shall be with you as I was with Moses. Give this order to the priests who carry the Ark of the Covenant: When you come to the edge of the waters of the Jordan, you are to take your stand in the river.'

Joshua said to the Israelites, 'Draw near and listen to the words of the Lord your God.' He went on, 'By this you will know that the living God is among you and that he will without fail drive out before you the Canaanites, Hittites, Hivites, Perizzites, Girgashites, Amorites, and Jebusites: the Ark of the Covenant of the Lord of all the earth is to cross the Jordan at your head. Choose now twelve men from the tribes of Israel, one from each tribe. As soon as the priests carrying the Ark of the Lord, the Lord of all the earth, set foot in the waters of the Jordan, then the waters of the Jordan will be cut off; the water coming down from upstream will stand piled up like a bank.'

The people set out from their encampment to cross the Jordan, with the priests in front carrying the Ark of the Covenant. Now the Jordan is in full flood in all its reaches throughout the time of harvest, but as soon as the priests reached the Jordan and their feet touched the water at the edge,the water flowing down from upstream was brought to a standstill; it piled up like a bank for a long way back, as far as Adam, a town near Zarethan. The water coming down to the sea of the Arabah, the Dead Sea, was completely cut off, and the people crossed over opposite Jericho. The priests carrying the Ark of the Covenant of the Lord stood firmly on the dry bed in the middle of the river, and all Israel passed over on dry ground, until the whole nation had completed the crossing of the Jordan.

When the whole nation had completed the crossing of the Jordan, the Lord said to Joshua, 'Choose twelve men from the people, one from each tribe, and order them to take up twelve stones from this place in the middle of the Jordan, where the priests have taken their stand. They are to carry the stones across and place them in the camp where you spend the night.' Joshua summoned the twelve Israelites whom he had appointed, one man from each tribe, and said to them, 'Go over in front of the Ark of the Lord your God as far as the middle of the Jordan, and let each of you take up a stone on his shoulder, one for each of the tribes of Israel. These stones are to stand as a memorial among you: in days to come, when your children ask what these stones mean, you will tell them how the waters of the Jordan were cut off before the Ark of the Covenant of the Lord; when it crossed the Jordan the waters of the Jordan were cut off. These stones will always be a reminder to the Israelites.' The Israelites did as Joshua had commanded: they took up twelve stones from the middle of the Jordan, as the Lord had instructed Joshua, one for each of the tribes of Israel, carried them across to the camp, and placed them there. Joshua also erected twelve stones in the middle of the Jordan at the place where the priests who carried the Ark of the Covenant had stood; they are there to this day. The priests carrying the Ark remained standing in the middle of the Jordan until every command which the Lord had told Joshua to give the people was fulfilled. The people crossed hurriedly, and when they had all got across, then the Ark of the Lord crossed, and the priests with it to lead the people. At the head of the Israelites, there crossed over the Reubenites, the Gadites, and the half tribe of Manasseh, as a fighting force, as Moses had told them to do; about forty thousand strong, drafted for active service, they crossed over to the lowlands of Jericho in the presence of the Lord to do battle.

That day the Lord exalted Joshua in the eyes of all Israel, and the people revered him, as they had revered Moses all his life.

The Lord said to Joshua, 'Command the priests carrying the Ark of the Testimony to come up from the Jordan.' Joshua passed the command to the priests; and no sooner had the priests carrying the Ark of the Covenant of the Lord come up from the river bed, and set foot on dry land, than the waters of the Jordan returned to their course and filled up all its reaches as before.

On the tenth day of the first month the people went up from the Jordan and encamped in Gilgal in the district east of Jericho, and there Joshua set up these twelve stones they had taken from the Jordan...

While the Israelites were encamped in Gilgal, at sunset on the fourteenth day of the month they kept the Passover in the lowlands of Jericho. On the day after the Passover they ate of the produce of the country, roasted grain and loaves made without leaven. It was from that day, when they first ate the produce of the country, that the manna ceased. The Israelites got no more manna; that year they ate what had grown in the land of Canaan.

When Joshua was near Jericho he looked up and saw a man standing in front of him with a drawn sword in his hand. Joshua approached him and asked, 'Are you for us or for our enemies?' The man replied, 'Neither! I am here as captain of the army of the Lord.' Joshua prostrated himself in homage, and said, 'What have you to say to your servant, my lord?' The captain of the Lord's army answered, 'Remove your sandals, for the place where you are standing is holy'; and Joshua did so.

155

THE FALL OF JERICHO
Joshua 6

Jericho was bolted and barred against the Israelites; no one could go out or in. The Lord said to Joshua, 'See, I am delivering Jericho, its king, and his warriors into your hands. You are to march round the city with all your fighting men, making the circuit of it once a day for six days. Seven priests carrying seven trumpets made from rams' horns are to go ahead of the Ark. On the seventh day you are to march round the city seven times with the priests blowing their trumpets. At the blast of the rams' horns, when you hear the trumpet sound, the whole army must raise a great shout; the city wall will collapse and the army will advance, every man straight ahead.'

Joshua son of Nun summoned the priests and gave them instructions: 'Take up the Ark of the Covenant; let seven priests with seven trumpets of ram's horn go ahead of the Ark of the Lord.' Then he gave orders to the army: 'Move on, march round the city, and let the men who have been drafted go in front of the Ark of the Lord.'

After Joshua had issued this command to the army, the seven priests carrying the seven trumpets of ram's horn before the Lord moved on and blew the trumpets; the Ark of the Covenant of the Lord followed them. The drafted men marched in front of the priests who blew the trumpets, and the rearguard came behind the Ark, the trumpets sounding as they marched. But Joshua commanded the army not to shout, or to raise their voices or even utter a word, till the day when he would tell them to shout; then they were to give a mighty shout. Thus he made the Ark of the Lord go round the city, making the circuit of it once, and then they returned to the camp and spent the night there. Joshua rose early next morning, and the priests took up the Ark of the Lord. The seven priests carrying the seven trumpets of ram's horn marched in front of the Ark of the Lord, blowing the trumpets as they went, with the drafted men in front of them and the rearguard following the Ark, the trumpets sounding as they marched. They marched round the city once on the second day and returned to the camp; this they did for six days.

On the seventh day they rose at dawn and marched seven times round the city in the same way; that was the only day on which they marched round seven times. The seventh time, as the priests blew the trumpets, Joshua said to the army, 'Shout! The Lord has given you the city. The city is to be under solemn ban: everything in it belongs to the Lord. No one is to be spared except the prostitute Rahab and everyone who is with her in the house, because she hid the men we sent. And you must beware of coveting anything that is forbidden under the ban; you must take none of it for yourselves, or else you will put the Israelite camp itself under the ban and bring disaster on it. All silver and gold, all the vessels of copper and iron, are to be holy; they belong to the Lord and must go into his treasury.'

So the trumpets were blown, and when the army heard the trumpets sound, they raised a great shout, and the wall collapsed. The army advanced on the city, every man straight ahead, and they captured it. Under the ban they destroyed everything there; they put everyone to the sword, men and women, young and old, as well as the cattle, the sheep, and the donkeys.

The two men who had been sent out to reconnoitre the land were told by Joshua to go to the prostitute's house and bring out the woman and all who belonged to her, as they had sworn to do. The young men went and brought out Rahab, her father and mother, her brothers, and all who belonged to her; they brought the whole family and placed them outside the Israelite camp. The city and everything in it were then set on fire, except that the silver and gold and the vessels of copper and iron were deposited in the treasury of the Lord's house. Thus Joshua spared the lives of Rahab the prostitute, her household, and all who belonged to her, because she had hidden the men whom Joshua had sent to reconnoitre Jericho; she and her family settled permanently among the Israelites.

At that time Joshua pronounced this curse:

'May the Lord's curse light on anyone who comes forward
to rebuild this city of Jericho:
the laying of its foundations shall cost him his eldest son,
the setting up of its gates shall cost him his youngest.'

The Lord was with Joshua, and his fame spread throughout the country.

THE SIN OF ACHAN
Joshua 7

In a perfidious act, however, Israelites violated the ban: Achan son of Carmi, son of Zabdi, son of Zerah, of the tribe of Judah, took some of the forbidden things, and the Lord's anger blazed out against Israel.

Joshua sent men from Jericho with orders to go up to Ai, near Beth-aven, east of Bethel, and reconnoitre the land. The men went and explored Ai, and on their return reported to Joshua that there was no need for the whole army to move: 'Let some two or three thousand men advance to attack Ai. Do not have the whole army toil up there; the population is small.' About three thousand troops went up, but they were routed by the men of Ai, who killed some thirty-six of them; they chased the rest all the way from the gate to the Quarries and killed them on the pass. At this the courage of the people melted and flowed away like water.

Joshua and the elders of Israel tore their clothes and flung themselves face downwards to the ground; throwing dust on their heads, they lay in front of the Ark of the Lord till evening. Joshua cried, 'Alas, Lord God, why did you bring this people across the Jordan just to hand us over to the Amorites to be destroyed? If only we had been content to settle on the other side of the Jordan! I beseech you, Lord; what can I say, now that Israel has been routed by the enemy? When the Canaanites and all the other natives of the country hear of this, they will close in upon us and wipe us off the face of the earth. What will you do then for the honour of your great name?'

The Lord answered, 'Stand up; why lie prostrate on your face? Israel has sinned: they have violated the covenant which I laid upon them; they have taken things forbidden under the ban; they have stolen them; they have concealed them by putting them among their own possessions. That is why the Israelites cannot stand against their enemies: they are defeated because they have brought themselves under the ban. Unless you Israelites destroy every single thing among you that is forbidden under the ban, I shall be with you no longer.

'Get up and consecrate the people; tell them they must consecrate themselves for tomorrow. Say to them that these are the words of the Lord the God of Israel: You have among you forbidden things, Israel, and you will not be able to stand against your enemies until you have rid yourselves of these things. In the morning come forward tribe by tribe, and the tribe which the Lord takes must come forward clan by clan; the clan which the Lord takes must come forward family by family, and the family which the Lord takes must come forward man by man. The man who is taken as the harbourer of forbidden things must be burnt, he and all that is his, because he has violated the covenant of the Lord and committed an outrage in Israel.'

Early next morning Joshua rose and had Israel come forward tribe by tribe, and the tribe of Judah was taken; he brought forward the clans of Judah, and the clan of Zerah was taken; then the clan of Zerah family by family, and the family of Zabdi was taken. He had that family brought forward man by man, and Achan son of Carmi, son of Zabdi, son of Zerah, of the tribe of Judah, was taken.

Then Joshua said to Achan, 'My son, give honour to the Lord the God of Israel and make your confession to him. Tell me what you have done; hide nothing from me.' Achan answered, 'It is true; I have sinned against the Lord the God of Israel. This is what I did: among the booty I saw a fine mantle from Shinar, two hundred shekels of silver, and a bar of gold weighing fifty shekels; I coveted them and I took them. You will find them hidden in the ground inside my tent, with the silver underneath.' Joshua sent messengers, who went straight to the tent, and there it was hidden in the tent with the silver underneath. They took the things from the tent, brought them to Joshua and all the Israelites, and laid them out before the Lord.

Then Joshua and all Israel with him took Achan son of Zerah, with the silver, the mantle, and the bar of gold, together with his sons and daughters, his oxen, his donkeys, and his sheep, his tent, and everything he had, and they brought them up to the vale of Achor. Joshua said, 'What trouble you have brought on us! Now the Lord will bring trouble on you.' Then all the Israelites stoned him to death; and they raised over him a great cairn of stones which is there to this day. So the Lord's anger was abated. That is why to this day the place is called the vale of Achor.

THE FALL OF AI
Joshua 8:1–29

The Lord said to Joshua, 'Do not be afraid or discouraged; take the whole army with you and go and attack Ai. I am delivering the king of Ai into your hands, along with his people, his city, and his territory. Deal with Ai and its king as you dealt with Jericho and its king, except that you may keep for yourselves the cattle and any other spoil you take. Set an ambush for the city to the west of it.'

Joshua and the army prepared for the assault on Ai. He chose thirty thousand warriors and dispatched them by night, with these orders: 'Lie in ambush to the west of the city, not far distant from it, and hold yourselves in readiness, all of you. I myself will advance on the city with the rest of the army, and when the enemy come out to meet us as they did last time, we shall turn and flee before them. They will come in pursuit until we have drawn them away from the city, for they will think we are in flight as before. While we are retreating, rise from your ambush and occupy the city; the Lord your God will deliver it into your hands. When you have taken it, set it on fire. Thus you will do what the Lord commands; these are my orders to you.' After Joshua sent them off, they went to the place of ambush and lay in wait between Bethel and Ai to the west of Ai, while Joshua spent the night with the army.

Early in the morning Joshua mustered the army and, with Joshua himself and the elders of Israel at its head, they marched against Ai. All the armed forces with him marched on until they came within sight of the city, where they encamped north of Ai, with the valley between them and the city. Joshua took some five thousand men and set them in ambush between Bethel and Ai to the west of the city. When the king of Ai saw them, he and the citizens set off hurriedly and marched out to do battle against Israel, being unaware that an ambush had been prepared for him to the west of the city. Joshua and the Israelites made as if they were worsted by them and fled towards the wilderness, while all the people of the city were called out in pursuit. In pursuing Joshua they were drawn away from the city, until not a man was left in Ai; they had all gone out in pursuit of the Israelites and thus had left the place wide open.

The Lord then said to Joshua, 'Point towards Ai with the dagger you are holding, for I will deliver the city into your hands.' Joshua pointed with his dagger towards Ai and, at his signal, the men in ambush rose quickly from their position; dashing into the city, they captured it and at once set it on fire. The men of Ai looked back and saw the smoke from the city already going up to the sky; they were powerless to make their escape in any direction.

The Israelites who had feigned flight towards the wilderness now turned on their pursuers, for when Joshua and all the Israelites with him saw that the men in ambush had seized the city and that smoke from it was already going up, they faced about and attacked the men of Ai. Those who had come out to contend with the Israelites were now hemmed in by Israelites on both sides of them, and the Israelites cut them down until there was not a single survivor; no one escaped. Only the king of Ai was taken alive and brought to Joshua.

When the Israelites had slain all the inhabitants of Ai in the open country and the wilderness where they had pursued them, and the massacre was complete, they all went back to Ai and put it to the sword. The number who fell that day, men and women, was twelve thousand, the whole population of Ai. Joshua held out his dagger and did not draw back his hand until all who lived in Ai had been destroyed; but the Israelites kept for themselves the cattle and any other spoil that they took, following the Lord's instructions given to Joshua.

So Joshua burnt Ai to the ground, and left it the desolate ruined mound it remains to this day. He hanged the king of Ai on a gibbet and left him there till evening. At sunset they cut down the body on Joshua's orders and flung it on the ground at the entrance of the city gate. Over it they raised a great cairn of stones, which is there to this day.

THE TREATY WITH THE GIBEONITES
Joshua 9

News of these happenings reached all the kings west of the Jordan, in the hill-country, in the Shephelah, and in all the coast of the Great Sea running up to the Lebanon, and the kings of the Hittites, Amorites, Canaanites, Perizzites, Hivites, and Jebusites agreed to join forces and fight against Joshua and Israel.

When the inhabitants of Gibeon heard how Joshua had dealt with Jericho and Ai, they resorted to a ruse: they set out after disguising themselves, with old sacks on their donkeys, old wineskins split and mended, old and patched sandals for their feet, old clothing to wear, and by way of provisions nothing but dry and crumbling bread. They came to Joshua in the camp at Gilgal, where they said to him and the Israelites, 'We have come from a distant country to ask you now to grant us a treaty.' The Israelites said to these Hivites, 'But it may be that you live in our neighbourhood: if so, how can we grant you a treaty?' They said to Joshua, 'We are your slaves.'

Joshua asked them who they were and where they came from. 'Sir,' they replied, 'our country is very far away, and we have come because of the renown of the Lord your God. We have heard the report of all that he did to Egypt and to the two Amorite kings east of the Jordan, King Sihon of Heshbon and King Og of Bashan who lived at Ashtaroth. Our elders and all the people of our country told us to take provisions for the journey and come to meet you, and say, "We are your slaves; please grant us a treaty." Look at our bread; it was hot from the oven when we packed it at home on the day we came away. Now, as you see, it is dry and crumbling. Here are our wineskins; they were new when we filled them, and now they are all split; look at our clothes and our sandals, worn out by the very long journey.' Without seeking guidance from the Lord, the leaders of the community accepted some of their provisions. Joshua received them peaceably and granted them a treaty, promising to spare their lives, and the leaders ratified it on oath.

However, within three days of granting them the treaty the Israelites learnt that these people were in fact neighbours, living nearby. The Israelites then set out and on the third day they reached their towns, Gibeon, Kephirah, Beeroth, and Kiriath-jearim. The Israelites did not attack them, because of the oath which the chief men of the community had sworn to them by the Lord the God of Israel. When the whole community was indignant with the leaders, they all made this reply: 'We swore an oath to them by the Lord the

God of Israel; so now we cannot touch them. What we shall do is this: we shall spare their lives so that the oath which we swore to them may bring down no wrath on us. But though their lives must be spared, they will be set to cut wood and draw water for the community.' The people agreed to do as their chiefs had said.

Joshua summoned the Gibeonites and said to them, 'Why did you play this trick on us? You told us that you live a long way off, when in fact you are near neighbours. From now there is a curse on you: for all time you shall provide us with slaves, to cut wood and draw water for the house of my God.' They answered Joshua, 'We were told, sir, that the Lord your God had commanded his servant Moses to give you the whole country and to wipe out its inhabitants; so because of you we were in terror of our lives, and that is why we did this. We are in your hands: do with us whatever you think right and proper.' What he did was this: he saved them from death at the hands of the Israelites, and they did not kill them; but from that day he assigned them to cut wood and draw water for the community and for the altar of the Lord. And to this day they do so at the place which the Lord chose.

THE DAY THE SUN STOOD STILL
Joshua 10:1–27

When King Adoni-zedek of Jerusalem heard that Joshua had captured and destroyed Ai, dealing with Ai and its king as he had dealt with Jericho and its king, and also that the inhabitants of Gibeon had come to terms with Israel and were living among them, he was greatly alarmed; for Gibeon was a large place, like a royal city: it was larger than Ai, and its men were all good fighters. So King Adoni-zedek of Jerusalem sent this message to King Hoham of Hebron, King Piram of Jarmuth, King Japhia of Lachish, and King Debir of Eglon: 'Come up and assist me to attack Gibeon, because it has come to terms with Joshua and the Israelites.'

The five Amorite kings, the kings of Jerusalem, Hebron, Jarmuth, Lachish, and Eglon, advanced with their united forces to take up position for the attack on Gibeon. The Gibeonites sent word to Joshua in the camp at Gilgal: 'Do not abandon your slaves; come quickly to our relief. Come and help us, for all the Amorite kings in the hill-country have joined forces against us.' When Joshua went up from Gilgal followed by his whole force, all his warriors, the Lord said to him, 'Do not be afraid; I have delivered these kings into your hands, and not one of them will be able to withstand you.' After a night march from Gilgal, Joshua launched a surprise assault on the five kings, and the Lord threw them into confusion before the Israelites. Joshua utterly defeated them at Gibeon; he pursued them down the pass of Beth-horon and kept up the attack as far as Azekah and Makkedah. As they fled from Israel down the pass, the Lord hurled great hailstones at them out of the sky all the way to Azekah, and they perished: more died from the hailstones than were slain by the swords of the Israelites.

On that day when the Lord delivered up the Amorites into the hands of Israel, Joshua spoke with the Lord, and in the presence of Israel said:

'Stand still, you sun, at Gibeon;
you moon, at the vale of Aijalon.'

The sun stood still and the moon halted until the nation had taken vengeance on its enemies, as indeed is written in the Book of Jashar. The sun stayed in mid-heaven and made no haste to set for almost a whole day. Never before or since has there been such a day as that on which the Lord listened to the voice of a mortal. Surely the Lord fought for Israel! Then Joshua returned with all the Israelites to the camp at Gilgal.

The five kings fled and hid in a cave at Makkedah, and Joshua was told that they had been found hiding there. Joshua replied, 'Roll large stones against the mouth of the cave, and post men there to keep watch over the kings. But you yourselves must not stay. Keep up the pursuit, attack your enemies from the rear and do not let them reach their towns; the Lord your God has delivered them into your hands.'

When Joshua and the Israelites had completed the work of slaughter and everyone had been put to the sword – all except a few survivors who escaped into the fortified towns – the whole army returned safely to Joshua at Makkedah; not one of the Israelites suffered so much as a scratch.

Joshua gave the order: 'Open up the mouth of the cave, and bring out those five kings to me.' This was done; the five kings, the kings of Jerusalem, Hebron, Jarmuth, Lachish, and Eglon, were taken from the cave and brought to Joshua. When he had summoned all the Israelites he said to the commanders of the troops who had served with him, 'Come forward and put your feet on the necks of these kings.' They did so, and Joshua said to them, 'Do not be afraid or discouraged; be strong and resolute; for the Lord will do this to every enemy whom you fight.' He fell on the kings and slew them; then he hung their bodies on five gibbets, where they remained hanging till evening. At sunset they were taken down on Joshua's orders and thrown into the cave in which they had hidden; large stones were piled against its mouth, where they remain to this very day.

JOSHUA'S VICTORIES
Joshua 10:28 – 11:23

On that same day Joshua captured Makkedah and put both king and people to the sword, destroying under the ban both them and every living thing in the city. He left no survivor, and he dealt with the king of Makkedah as he had dealt with the king of Jericho. Then Joshua with all the Israelites marched on from Makkedah to Libnah and attacked it. The Lord delivered the city and its king to the Israelites, and they put its people and every living thing in it to the sword; they left no survivor there, and dealt with its king as they had dealt with the king of Jericho. From Libnah Joshua and all the Israelites marched on to Lachish, where they took up their positions against it and attacked it. The Lord delivered Lachish into their hands; they took it on the second day and put every living thing in it to the sword, as they had done at Libnah.

Meanwhile King Horam of Gezer had advanced to the relief of Lachish; but Joshua attacked him and his army until not a survivor was left to him. From Lachish Joshua and all the Israelites marched on to Eglon, took up their positions against it, and attacked it; that same day they captured it and put its inhabitants to the sword, destroying every living thing in it as they had done at Lachish. From Eglon Joshua and all the Israelites advanced to Hebron and attacked it. They captured it and put its king to the sword together with every living thing in it and in all its villages; as at Eglon, he left no survivor, destroying it and every living thing in it. Then Joshua and all the Israelites wheeled round towards Debir and attacked it. They captured the king, the city, and all its villages, put them to the sword, and destroyed every living thing; they left no survivor. They dealt with Debir and its king as they had dealt with Hebron and with Libnah and its king.

So Joshua conquered the whole region – the hill-country, the Negeb, the Shephelah, the watersheds – and all its kings. He left no survivor, destroying everything that drew breath, as the Lord the God of Israel had commanded. Joshua's conquests extended from Kadesh-barnea to Gaza, over the whole land of Goshen, and as far as Gibeon. All these kings he captured at the same time, and their country with them, for the Lord the God of Israel fought for Israel. Then Joshua returned with all the Israelites to the camp at Gilgal.

When King Jabin of Hazor heard of these events, he sent to King Jobab of Madon, to the kings of Shimron and Akshaph, to the northern kings in the hill-country, in the Arabah opposite Kinnereth, in the Shephelah, and in the district of Dor on the west, the Canaanites to the east and the west, the Amorites, Hittites, Perizzites, and Jebusites in the hill-country, and the Hivites below Hermon in the land of Mizpah. They took the field with all their forces, a great host countless as the grains of sand on the seashore, among them a very large number of horses and chariots. All these kings, making common cause, came and encamped at the waters of Merom to fight against Israel.

The Lord said to Joshua, 'Do not be afraid of them, for at this time tomorrow I shall deliver them to Israel all dead men; you are to hamstring their horses and burn their chariots.' Joshua with his whole army launched a surprise attack on them by the waters of Merom, and the Lord delivered them into the hands of Israel, who defeated them, cutting down the fugitives the whole way to Greater Sidon, Misrephoth on the west, and the vale of Mizpah on the east. They cut them down until they had left not a single survivor. Joshua dealt with them as the Lord had commanded: he hamstrung their horses and burnt their chariots.

At this point, Joshua turned his forces against Hazor, formerly the leader among all these kingdoms. He captured the city and put its king to death with the sword. They put under the ban and killed every living thing in it; they spared nothing that drew breath, and Hazor itself was destroyed by fire.

So Joshua captured these kings and their cities and put them to the sword, destroying them all, as Moses the servant of the Lord had commanded. The cities whose ruined mounds are still standing were not burnt by the Israelites; it was Hazor alone that Joshua burnt. The Israelites plundered all these cities and kept for themselves the cattle and any other spoil they took; but they put every living soul to the sword until they had destroyed everyone; they did not leave alive anyone that drew breath. The Lord had laid his commands on his servant Moses, and Moses laid these same commands on Joshua, and Joshua carried them out. Not one of the commands laid on Moses by the Lord was left unfulfilled.

Thus Joshua took the whole land, the hill-country, all the Negeb, all the land of Goshen, the Shephelah, the Arabah, and the Israelite hill-country with the adjoining lowlands. His conquests extended from the bare mountain which leads up to Seir as far as Baalgad in the vale of Lebanon under Mount Hermon. He captured all their kings, struck them down, and put them to death. It was a lengthy campaign he waged against all those kingdoms; except for the Hivites who lived in Gibeon, not one of their towns or cities came to terms with the Israelites; all had to be taken by storm. It was the Lord's purpose that they should offer stubborn resistance to the Israelites, and thus be annihilated and utterly destroyed without mercy, as the Lord had commanded Moses.

It was then that Joshua proceeded to wipe out the Anakim from the hill-country, from Hebron, Debir, Anab, all the hill-country of Judah, and all the hill-country of Israel, destroying both them and their towns. No Anakim were left in the land taken by the Israelites; they survived only in Gaza, Gath, and Ashdod.

Joshua took the whole land, fulfilling all the commands that the

Lord had laid on Moses; he assigned it to Israel, allotting to each tribe its share. Then the land was at peace.

THE LAST WORDS OF JOSHUA
Joshua 23:1–6; 24:2–5, 12–16, 24–28

Joshua was now very old. He summoned all Israel, their elders and heads of families, their judges and officers, and said to them, 'I am now an old man, far advanced in years. You have seen for yourselves everything the Lord your God has done to all these peoples for your sake; it was the Lord God himself who fought for you. I have allotted to you tribe by tribe your holdings, the land of all the peoples that I have wiped out and of all these that remain between the Jordan and the Great Sea which lies towards the setting sun. The Lord your God himself drove them out at your approach; he dispossessed them to make way for you, and you occupied their land, as the Lord your God had promised you.

'Be very resolute therefore to observe and perform everything written in the book of the law of Moses, without swerving either to the right or to the left.'...

Joshua said to all the people: 'This is the word of the Lord the God of Israel: Long ago your forefathers, including Terah the father of Abraham and Nahor, lived beyond the Euphrates and served other gods. I took your ancestor Abraham from beside the Euphrates and led him through the length and breadth of Canaan. I gave him many descendants: I gave him Isaac, and to Isaac I gave Jacob and Esau. I assigned the hill-country of Seir to Esau as his possession; Jacob and his sons went down to Egypt.

'Later I sent Moses and Aaron, and I struck the Egyptians with plagues – you know well what I did among them – and after that I brought you out...

'I spread panic before your advance, and it was this, not your sword or your bow, that drove out the two kings of the Amorites. I gave you land on which you had not laboured, towns which you had not built; you have settled in those towns and you eat the produce of vineyards and olive groves which you did not plant.

'Now hold the Lord in awe, and serve him in loyalty and truth. Put away the gods your fathers served beyond the Euphrates and in Egypt, and serve the Lord. But if it does not please you to serve the Lord, choose here and now whom you will serve: the gods whom your forefathers served beyond the Euphrates, or the gods of the Amorites in whose land you are living. But I and my family, we shall serve the Lord.'

The people answered, 'God forbid that we should forsake the Lord to serve other gods!...We shall serve the Lord our God and his voice we shall obey.'

So Joshua made a covenant for the people that day; he drew up a statute and an ordinance for them in Shechem and recorded its terms in the book of the law of God. He took a great stone and set it up there under the terebinth in the sanctuary of the Lord. He said to all the people, 'You see this stone – it will be a witness against us; for it has heard all the words which the Lord has spoken to us. If you renounce your God, it will be a witness against you.' Then Joshua dismissed the people, each man to his allotted holding.

THE DEATH OF JOSHUA
Joshua 24:29–31

After these events, Joshua son of Nun, the servant of the Lord, died at the age of a hundred and ten. They buried him within his own holding in Timnath-serah to the north of Mount Gaash in the hill-country of Ephraim. Israel served the Lord throughout the lifetime of Joshua and of the elders who outlived him and who knew all that the Lord had done for Israel.

Part Five

The Times of the Judges

THE ISRAELITES TURN AWAY FROM GOD
Judges 2:10–19

When that whole generation was gathered to its forefathers, and was succeeded by another generation, who did not acknowledge the Lord and did not know what he had done for Israel, then the Israelites did what was wrong in the eyes of the Lord by serving the baalim. They forsook the Lord, their fathers' God who had brought them out of Egypt, and went after other gods, the gods of the peoples among whom they lived; by bowing down before them they provoked the Lord to anger; they forsook the Lord and served the baalim and the ashtaroth. In his anger the Lord made them the prey of bands of raiders and plunderers; he sold them into the power of their enemies around them, so that they could no longer stand against them. Every time they went out to do battle the Lord brought disaster on them, as he had said when he gave them his solemn warning; and they were in dire straits.

Then the Lord raised up judges to rescue them from the marauding bands, yet even to their judges they did not listen. They prostituted themselves by worshipping other gods and bowed down before them; all too soon they abandoned the path of obedience to the Lord's commands which their forefathers had followed. They did not obey the Lord. Whenever the Lord set up a judge over them, he was with that judge, and kept them safe from their enemies so long as the judge lived. The Lord would relent when he heard them groaning under oppression and tyranny. But on the death of the judge they would relapse into corruption deeper than that of their predecessors and go after other gods; serving them and bowing before them, they would give up none of their evil practices and wilful ways.

EHUD DEFEATS THE MOABITES
Judges 3:12–30

Once again the Israelites did what was wrong in the eyes of the Lord, and because of this he roused King Eglon of Moab against Israel. Eglon mustered the Ammonites and the Amalekites, attacked Israel, and took possession of the city of palm trees. The Israelites were subject to King Eglon of Moab for eighteen years.

Then they cried to the Lord for help, and to deliver them he raised up Ehud son of Gera the Benjamite; he was left-handed. The Israelites sent him to hand over their tribute to King Eglon. Ehud had made himself a two-edged sword, about eighteen inches long, which he fastened on his right side under his clothes when he brought the tribute to King Eglon. Eglon was a very fat man. After Ehud had finished presenting the tribute, he sent on the men who had carried it, while he himself turned back from the Carved Stones at Gilgal. 'My lord king,' he said, 'I have a message for you in private.' Eglon called for silence and dismissed all his attendants. Ehud then approached him as he sat in the roof-chamber of his summer palace. He said, 'Your majesty, I have a message from God for you.' As Eglon rose from his seat, Ehud reached with his left hand, drew the sword from his right side, and drove it into Eglon's belly. The hilt went in after the blade and the fat closed over the blade, for he did not draw the sword out but left it protruding behind. Ehud then went out to the porch, where he shut the door on him and fastened it.

After he had gone, Eglon's servants came and, finding the doors fastened, they said, 'He must be relieving himself in the closet of his summer palace.' They waited until they became alarmed and, when he still did not open the door of the roof-chamber, they took the key and opened the door; and there was their master lying dead on the floor.

While they had been waiting, Ehud had made good his escape; he passed the Carved Stones and escaped to Seirah. Once there, he sounded the trumpet in the hill-country of Ephraim, and the Israelites went down from the hills with him at their head. He said to them, 'Follow me, for the Lord has delivered your enemies, the Moabites, into your hands.' They went down after him, and held the fords of the Jordan against the Moabites, allowing no one to cross. They killed at that time some ten thousand Moabites, all of them stalwart and valiant fighters; not one escaped. Moab became subject to Israel on that day, and the land was at peace for eighty years.

DEBORAH AND BARAK DEFEAT THE CANAANITES
Judges 4:1 – 5:13, 24–31

After Ehud's death the Israelites once again did what was wrong in the eyes of the Lord, and he sold them into the power of Jabin, the Canaanite king who ruled in Hazor. The commander of his forces was Sisera, who lived in Harosheth-of-the-Gentiles. The Israelites cried to the Lord for help, because Sisera with his nine hundred iron-clad chariots had oppressed Israel harshly for twenty years.

At that time Deborah wife of Lappidoth, a prophetess, was judge in Israel. It was her custom to sit under the Palm Tree of Deborah between Ramah and Bethel in the hill-country of Ephraim, and Israelites seeking a judgment went up to her. She sent for Barak son of Abinoam from Kedesh in Naphtali and said to him, 'This is the command of the Lord the God of Israel: Go and lead out ten thousand men from Naphtali and Zebulun and bring them with you to Mount Tabor. I shall draw out to you at the wadi Kishon Jabin's commander Sisera, along with his chariots and troops, and deliver him into your power.' Barak answered, 'If you go with me, I shall go, but if you will not go, neither shall I.' 'Certainly I shall go with you,' she said, 'but this venture will bring you no glory, because the Lord will leave Sisera to fall into the hands of a woman.' Deborah set off with Barak and went to Kedesh. Barak mustered Zebulun and Naphtali to Kedesh and marched up with ten thousand followers; Deborah went up with him.

Now Heber the Kenite had parted company with the Kenites, the descendants of Hobab, Moses' brother-in-law, and he had pitched his tent at Elon-bezaanannim near Kedesh.

When it was reported to Sisera that Barak son of Abinoam had gone up to Mount Tabor, he mustered all nine hundred of his iron-clad chariots, along with all the troops he had, and marched from Harosheth-of-the-Gentiles to the wadi Kishon. Deborah said to Barak,

172

'Up! This day the Lord is to give Sisera into your hands. See, the Lord has marched out at your head!' Barak came down from Mount Tabor with ten thousand men at his back, and the Lord threw Sisera and all his chariots and army into panic-stricken rout before Barak's onslaught; Sisera himself dismounted from his chariot and fled on foot. Barak pursued the chariots and the troops as far as Harosheth, and the whole army was put to the sword; not a man was left alive.

Meanwhile Sisera fled on foot to the tent of Jael wife of Heber the Kenite, because King Jabin of Hazor and the household of Heber the Kenite were on friendly terms. Jael came out to greet Sisera and said, 'Come in, my lord, come in here; do not be afraid.' He went into the tent, and she covered him with a rug. He said to her, 'Give me some water to drink, for I am thirsty.' She opened a skin of milk, gave him a drink, and covered him again. He said to her, 'Stand at the tent door, and if anyone comes and asks if there is a man here, say "No."' But as Sisera lay fast asleep through exhaustion Jael took a tent-peg, picked up a mallet, and, creeping up to him, drove the peg into his temple, so that it went down into the ground, and Sisera died. When Barak came by in pursuit of Sisera, Jael went out to meet him. 'Come,' she said, 'I shall show you the man you are looking for.' He went in with her, and there was Sisera lying dead with the tent-peg in his temple. That day God gave victory to the Israelites over King Jabin of Canaan, and they pressed home their attacks upon him until he was destroyed.

On that day Deborah and Barak son of Abinoam sang this song:

'For the leaders, the leaders in Israel,
for the people who answered the call,
bless the Lord.
Hear, you kings; princes, give ear!
I shall sing, I shall sing to the Lord,
making music to the Lord, the God of Israel.

'Lord, when you set forth from Seir,
when you marched from the land of Edom,
earth trembled; heaven quaked;
the clouds streamed down in torrents.

173

Mountains shook in fear before the Lord, the Lord of Sinai,
before the Lord, the God of Israel.

'In the days of Shamgar son of Anath,
in the days of Jael, caravans plied no longer;
travellers who had followed the high roads
went round by devious paths.
Champions there were none,
none left in Israel,
until you, Deborah, arose,
arose as a mother in Israel.
They chose new gods,
they consorted with demons.
Not a shield was to be seen, not a lance
among forty thousand Israelites.

'My heart goes out to you, the marshals of Israel;
you among the people that answered the call,
bless the Lord.
You that sit on saddle-cloths
riding your tawny she-donkeys,
and you that take the road on foot,
ponder on this.
Hark, the sound of the merrymakers
at the places where they draw water!
There they commemorate the victories of the Lord,
his triumphs as the champion of Israel.

'Down to the gates came the Lord's people:
"Rouse yourself, rouse yourself, Deborah,
rouse yourself, break into song.
Up, Barak! Take prisoners in plenty,
you son of Abinoam."

'Then down marched the column and its chieftains,
the people of the Lord marching down like warriors...

'Blest above women be Jael
wife of Heber the Kenite;
blest above all women in the tents.
He asked for water: she gave him milk,
she offered him curds in a bowl fit for a chieftain.
She reached out her hand for the tent-peg,
her right hand for the workman's hammer.
With the hammer she struck Sisera, crushing his head;
with a shattering blow she pierced his temple.
At her feet he sank, he fell, he lay prone;
at her feet he sank down and fell.
Where he sank down, there he fell, done to death.

'The mother of Sisera peered through the lattice,
through the window she peered and cried,
"Why is his chariot so long in coming?
Why is the clatter of his chariots so delayed?"
The wisest of her ladies answered her,
yes, she found her own answer:
"They must be finding spoil, taking their shares,
a damsel for each man, two damsels,
booty of dyed stuffs for Sisera,
booty of dyed stuffs,
dyed stuff and brocade, two lengths of brocade
to grace the victor's neck."

'So perish all your enemies, Lord;
but let those who love you be like the sun rising in strength.'

The land was at peace for forty years.

GIDEON DEFEATS THE MIDIANITES
Judges 6:1 – 8:35

The Israelites did what was wrong in the eyes of the Lord and he
delivered them into the hands of Midian for seven years. The

Midianites were too strong for the Israelites, who were forced to find themselves hollow places in the mountains, in caves and fastnesses. If the Israelites had sown seed, the Midianites and the Amalekites and other eastern tribes would come up and attack Israel, pitching their camps in the country and destroying the crops as far as the outskirts of Gaza. They left nothing to support life in Israel, neither sheep nor ox nor donkey. They came up with their herds and their tents, swarming like locusts; they and their camels were past counting. They would come into the land and lay it waste. The Israelites, brought to destitution by the Midianites, cried to the Lord for help.

When the Israelites cried to the Lord because of what they were suffering from the Midianites, he sent them a prophet who said to them, 'These are the words of the Lord the God of Israel: I brought you up from Egypt, that land of slavery. I rescued you from the Egyptians and from all your oppressors, whom I drove out before you to give you their lands. I said to you, "I am the Lord your God: do not worship the gods of the Amorites in whose country you are settling." But you did not listen to me.'

The angel of the Lord came to Ophrah and sat under the terebinth which belonged to Joash the Abiezrite. While Gideon son of Joash was threshing wheat in the winepress, so that he might keep it out of sight of the Midianites, the angel of the Lord appeared to him and said, 'You are a brave man, and the Lord is with you.' 'Pray, my lord,' said Gideon, 'if the Lord really is with us, why has all this happened to us? What has become of all those wonderful deeds of his, of which we have heard from our forefathers, when they told us how the Lord brought us up from Egypt? But now the Lord has cast us off and delivered us into the power of the Midianites.'

The Lord turned to him and said, 'Go and use this strength of yours to free Israel from the Midianites. It is I who send you.' Gideon said, 'Pray, my lord, how can I save Israel? Look at my clan: it is the weakest in Manasseh, and I am the least in my father's family.' The Lord answered, 'I shall be with you, and you will lay low all Midian as one man.' He replied, 'If I stand so well with you, give me a sign that it is you who speak to me. Do not leave this place, I beg you, until I come with my gift and lay it before you.' He answered, 'I shall stay until you return.'

So Gideon went in, and prepared a young goat and made an ephah of flour into unleavened bread. He put the meat in a basket, poured the broth into a pot, and brought it out to the angel under the terebinth. As he approached, the angel of God said to him, 'Take the meat and the bread, and put them here on the rock and pour out the broth.' When he did so, the angel of the Lord reached out the staff in his hand and touched the meat and bread with the tip of it. Fire sprang up from the rock and consumed the meat and the bread. Then the angel of the Lord vanished from his sight. Gideon realized it was the angel of the Lord and said, 'Alas, Lord God! Then it is true: I have seen the angel of the Lord face to face.' But the Lord said to him, 'Peace be with you! Do not be afraid; you shall not die.' Gideon built an altar there to the Lord and named it The Lord is Peace. It stands to this day at Ophrah-of-the-Abiezrites.

That night the Lord said to Gideon, 'Take a young bull of your father's, the yearling bull; tear down the altar of Baal belonging to your father, and cut down the sacred pole which stands beside it. Then build an altar of the proper pattern to the Lord your God on the top of this earthwork; take the yearling bull and offer it as a whole-offering with the wood of the sacred pole that you cut down.' Gideon took ten of his servants and did as the Lord had told him; but because he was afraid of his father's family and the people of the town, he did it by night and not by day. When the people rose early next morning, they found the altar of Baal overturned, the sacred pole which had stood beside it cut down, and the yearling bull offered up as a whole-offering on an altar which had been built. They asked among themselves who had done it, and, after searching enquiries, they declared it was Gideon son of Joash. The townspeople said to Joash, 'Bring out your son. He has overturned the altar of Baal and cut down the sacred pole beside it; he must die.' But as they crowded round him Joash retorted, 'Are you pleading Baal's cause then? Do you think it is for you to save him? Whoever pleads his cause shall be put to death at dawn. If Baal is a god, and someone has torn down his altar, let him take up his own cause.' That day Joash named Gideon Jerubbaal, saying, 'Let Baal plead his own cause against this man, for he has torn down his altar.'

When all the Midianites, the Amalekites, and the eastern tribes

177

joined forces, crossed the river, and encamped in the valley of Jezreel, the spirit of the Lord took possession of Gideon. He sounded the trumpet to call out the Abiezrites to follow him, and sent messengers all through Manasseh; and they too rallied to him. He sent messengers to Asher, Zebulun, and Naphtali, and they advanced to meet the others.

Gideon said to God, 'If indeed you are going to deliver Israel through me as you promised, I shall put a fleece of wool on the threshing-floor, and if there is dew on the fleece while all the ground is dry, then I shall be sure that it is through me you will deliver Israel as you promised.' And that is what happened. When he rose early next day and wrung out the fleece, he squeezed enough dew from it to fill a bowl with water. Gideon then said to God, 'Do not be angry with me, but give me leave to speak once again. Allow me, I pray, to make one more test with the fleece. This time let the fleece be dry, and all the ground be covered with dew.' God let it be so that night: the fleece alone was dry, and all over the ground there was dew.

Early next morning Jerubbaal, that is Gideon, with all his troops pitched camp at En-harod; the Midianite encampment was in the valley to the north of his by the hill at Moreh. The Lord said to Gideon, 'Those with you are more than I need to deliver Midian into their hands: Israel might claim the glory for themselves and say that it is their own strength that has given them the victory. Make a proclamation now to the army to say that anyone who is afraid or anxious is to leave Mount Galud at once and go home.' Twenty-two thousand of them went, and ten thousand remained.

'There are still too many,' said the Lord to Gideon. 'Bring them down to the water, and I shall separate them for you there. If I say to you, "This man shall go with you," he shall go; and if I say, "This man shall not go," he shall not go.' When Gideon brought the men down to the water, the Lord said to him, 'Make every man who laps the water with his tongue like a dog stand on one side, and on the other every man who kneels down and drinks.' The number of those who lapped, putting their hands to their mouths, was three hundred; all the rest had gone down on their knees to drink. The Lord said, 'By means of the three hundred men who lapped I shall save you and give Midian into your power; the rest may go home.' Gideon sent all these

Israelites home, but he kept the three hundred, and they took with them the jars and the trumpets which the people had.

The Midianite camp was below him in the valley, and that night the Lord said to Gideon, 'Go down at once and attack the camp, for I have delivered it into your hands. If you are afraid to do so, then go down first with your servant Purah, and when you hear what they are saying, that will give you courage to attack the camp.' So he and his servant Purah went down to the outposts of the camp where the fighting men were stationed. The Midianites, the Amalekites, and all the eastern tribes were so many that they lay there in the valley like a swarm of locusts; there was no counting their camels, which in number were like grains of sand on the seashore. As Gideon came close, there was a man telling his comrades about a dream. He said, 'I dreamt that I saw a barley loaf rolling over and over through the Midianite camp; it came to a tent, struck it, and the tent collapsed and turned upside down.' The other answered, 'This can be none other than the sword of Gideon son of Joash the Israelite. God has delivered Midian and the whole army into his hands.'

When Gideon heard the account of the dream and its interpretation, he bowed down in worship. Then going back to the Israelite camp he said, 'Let us go! The Lord has delivered the camp of the Midianites into our hands.' He divided the three hundred men into three companies, and furnished every man with a trumpet and an empty jar, with a torch inside each jar. 'Watch me,' he said to them. 'When I come to the edge of the camp, do exactly as I do. When I and those with me blow our trumpets, you too all round the camp blow your trumpets and shout, "For the Lord and for Gideon!"'

Gideon and the hundred men who were with him reached the outskirts of the camp at the beginning of the middle watch, just after the posting of the sentries. They blew the trumpets and smashed the jars they were holding. All three companies blew their trumpets and smashed their jars; then, grasping the torches in their left hands and the trumpets in their right, they shouted, 'A sword for the Lord and for Gideon!' Every man stood where he was, all round the camp, and the whole camp leapt up in a panic and took flight. When the three hundred blew their trumpets, the Lord set all the men in the camp fighting against each other. They fled as far as Beth-shittah in the direction of Zererah, as far as the ridge of Abel-meholah near Tabbath.

The Israelites from Naphtali and Asher and all Manasseh were called out to pursue the Midianites. Gideon also sent messengers throughout the hill-country of Ephraim to say: 'Come down and cut off the Midianites. Hold the fords of the Jordan against them as far as Beth-barah.' So all the Ephraimites when called out held the fords of the Jordan as far as Beth-barah. They captured the two Midianite princes, Oreb and Zeeb. Oreb they killed at the Rock of Oreb, and Zeeb by the Winepress of Zeeb, and they kept up the pursuit of the Midianites; afterwards they brought the heads of Oreb and Zeeb to Gideon on the other side of Jordan.

The men of Ephraim said to Gideon, 'Why have you treated us like this? Why did you not summon us when you went to fight Midian?' and they upbraided him fiercely. But he replied, 'What have I now accomplished compared with you? Are not Ephraim's gleanings better than the whole grape harvest of Abiezer? God delivered Oreb and Zeeb, the princes of Midian, into your hands. What have I been able to accomplish compared with you?' At that their anger against him died down.

Gideon came to the Jordan, and he and his three hundred men crossed over to continue the pursuit, exhausted though they were. He said to the people of Succoth, 'Will you give my followers some bread? They are exhausted, and I am pursuing Zebah and Zalmunna, the kings of Midian.' But the chief men of Succoth replied, 'Are Zebah and Zalmunna already in your hands, that we should give bread to your troops?' Gideon said, 'For that, when the Lord delivers Zebah and Zalmunna into my hands, I shall thresh your bodies with desert thorns and briars.' He went on from there to Penuel and made the same request; the people of Penuel gave the same answer as had the people of Succoth. He said to them, 'When I return victorious, I shall pull down your tower.'

Zebah and Zalmunna were at Karkor with an army of about fifteen thousand men. Those were all that remained of the entire host of the eastern tribes, a hundred and twenty thousand warriors having fallen in battle. Gideon advanced along the track used by the tent-dwellers east of Nobah and Jogbehah, and his attack caught the enemy off guard. Zebah and Zalmunna fled; but he went in pursuit of the Midianite kings and captured them both; and their whole army melted away.

As Gideon son of Joash was returning from battle by the ascent of Heres, he caught a young man from Succoth. When questioned the young man listed for him the names of the rulers of Succoth and its elders, seventy-seven in all. Gideon then came to the people of Succoth and said, 'Here are Zebah and Zalmunna, about whom you taunted me. "Are Zebah and Zalmunna already in your hands," you said, "that we should give your exhausted men bread?"' Then he took the elders of Succoth and inflicted punishment on them with desert thorns and briars. He also pulled down the tower of Penuel and put the men of the town to death.

He said to Zebah and Zalmunna, 'What sort of men did you kill in Tabor?' They answered, 'They were like you; every one had the look of a king's son.' 'They were my brothers,' he said, 'my mother's sons. I swear by the Lord, if you had let them live I would not have killed you.' Then he said to his eldest son Jether, 'Stand up and kill them.' But he was still only a lad, and did not draw his sword, because he was afraid. Zebah and Zalmunna said, 'Rise up yourself and dispatch us, for you have a man's strength.' So Gideon got up and killed them both, and he took the crescents from the necks of their camels.

The Israelites said to Gideon, 'You have saved us from the Midianites; now you be our ruler, you and your son and your grandson.' But Gideon replied, 'I shall not rule over you, nor will my son; the Lord will rule over you.' He went on, 'I have a request to make: will every one of you give me an ear-ring from his booty?' – for the enemy, being Ishmaelites, wore gold ear-rings. They said, 'Of course we shall give them.' So a cloak was spread out and every man threw on to it a gold ear-ring from his booty. The ear-rings he asked for weighed seventeen hundred shekels of gold; this was in addition to the crescents and pendants and the purple robes worn by the Midianite kings, and not counting the chains on the necks of their camels. Gideon made the gold into an ephod which he set up in his own town of Ophrah. All the Israelites went astray by worshipping it, and it became a snare for Gideon and his household.

Thus the Midianites were subdued by the Israelites; they could no longer hold up their heads. For forty years the land was at peace, all the lifetime of Gideon, that is Jerubbaal son of Joash; and he retired to his own home. Gideon had seventy sons, his own offspring, for he had many wives. He had a concubine who lived in Shechem, and she also bore him a son, whom he named Abimelech. Gideon son of Joash died at a ripe old age and was buried in his father's grave at Ophrah-of-the-Abiezrites.

After Gideon's death the Israelites again went astray: they worshipped the baalim and made Baal-berith their god. They were unmindful of the Lord their God who had delivered them from all their enemies around them, nor did they show to the family of Jerubbaal, that is Gideon, the loyalty that was due to them for all the good he had done Israel.

ABIMELECH THE KING
Judges 9

Abimelech son of Jerubbaal went to Shechem to his mother's brothers, and spoke with them and with the rest of the clan of his mother's family. 'I beg you,' he said, 'whisper a word in the ears of all the people of Shechem. Ask them which is better for them: that seventy men, all the sons of Jerubbaal, should rule over them, or one man. Tell them to remember that I am their own flesh and blood.' When his mother's kinsfolk repeated all this to every Shechemite on his behalf, they were moved to come over to Abimelech's side, because, as they said, he was their kinsman. They gave him seventy pieces of silver from the temple of Baal-berith, and with these he hired good-for-nothing, reckless fellows as his followers. He went to his father's house in Ophrah and butchered his seventy brothers, the sons of Jerubbaal, on a single stone block, all but Jotham, the youngest, who survived because he had gone into hiding. Then all the inhabitants of Shechem and all Beth-millo came together and made Abimelech king beside the propped-up terebinth at Shechem.

When this was reported to Jotham, he climbed to the summit of Mount Gerizim, and standing there he cried at the top of his voice: 'Listen to me, you people of Shechem, and may God listen to you.

'Once upon a time the trees set out to anoint a king over them. They said to the olive tree: "Be king over us." But the olive tree answered: "What, leave my rich oil by which gods and men are honoured, to go and hold sway over the trees?"

'So the trees said to the fig tree: "Then will you come and be king over us?"

But the fig tree answered: "What, leave my good fruit and all its sweetness, to go and hold sway over the trees?"

'So the trees said to the vine: "Then will you come and be king over us?"

But the vine answered: "What, leave my new wine which gladdens gods and men, to go and hold sway over the trees?"

'Then all the trees said to the thorn bush: "Will you come and be king over us?" The thorn answered: "If you really mean to anoint me as your king, then come under the protection of my shadow; if not, fire will come out of the thorn and burn up the cedars of Lebanon."'

Jotham said, 'Now have you acted fairly and honourably in making Abimelech king? Have you done the right thing by Jerubbaal and his household? Have you given my father his proper due – who fought for you, and risked his life to deliver you from the Midianites? Today you have risen against my father's family, butchered his sons, seventy on a single stone block, and made Abimelech, the son of his slave-girl, king over the inhabitants of Shechem just because he is your kinsman. In this day's work have you acted fairly and honourably by Jerubbaal and his family? If so, I wish you joy in Abimelech and wish him joy in you! If not, may fire come out of Abimelech and devour the inhabitants of Shechem and all Beth-millo; may fire also come out from the inhabitants of Shechem and Beth-millo to devour Abimelech.' Jotham then slipped away and made his escape; he came to Be-er, and there he settled, to be out of reach of his brother Abimelech.

After Abimelech had been prince over Israel for three years, God sent an evil spirit to create a breach between Abimelech and the inhabitants of Shechem, and they broke faith with him. This was done in order that the violent murder of the seventy sons of Jerubbaal might recoil on their brother Abimelech who did the murder, and on the people of Shechem who encouraged him to do it. The people of Shechem set men to lie in wait for him on the hilltops, and they robbed all who passed that way. But Abimelech had word of it.

Gaal son of Ebed came with his kinsmen to Shechem, and the

people of Shechem gave him their allegiance. They went out into the countryside, picked the early grapes in their vineyards, trod them in the winepress, and made merry. They went into the temple of their god, where they ate and drank and reviled Abimelech. 'Who is Abimelech,' said Gaal son of Ebed, 'and who are the Shechemites, that we should be his subjects? Have not this son of Jerubbaal and his lieutenant Zebul been subjects of the men of Hamor the father of Shechem? Why indeed should we be subject to him? If only this people were in my charge I should know how to get rid of Abimelech! I should say to him, "Muster your force and come out."'

When Zebul the governor of the city heard what Gaal son of Ebed said, he was furious. He resorted to a ruse and sent messengers to report to Abimelech, 'Gaal son of Ebed and his kinsmen have come to Shechem and are turning the city against you. Set off by night, you and the people with you, and lie in wait out in the country. Then in the morning start at sunrise, and advance with all speed on the city. When he and his people come out to you, do to him what the situation demands.'

So Abimelech and all the troops with him set out under cover of night, and lay in wait in four companies to attack Shechem. Gaal son of Ebed came out and stood in the entrance of the city gate. When Abimelech and his men rose from their hiding-place, and Gaal saw them, he said to Zebul, 'There are people coming down from the tops of the hills,' but Zebul replied, 'What you see that looks like men is the shadow of the hills.' Once more Gaal said, 'There are people coming down from the central ridge, and another group is advancing along the road of the Soothsayers' Terebinth.' Then Zebul said to him, 'Where are your brave words now? You said, "Who is Abimelech that we should be subject to him?" Are not these the people you despised? Go out and fight him.' Gaal led out the men of Shechem and attacked Abimelech, but Abimelech routed him and he fled. The ground was strewn with corpses all the way to the entrance of the gate. Abimelech established himself in Arumah, and Zebul drove out Gaal and his kinsmen and allowed them no place in Shechem.

Next day the people came out into the open country, and this was reported to Abimelech. He took his supporters, divided them into three companies, and lay in wait in the open country; when he saw the people coming out of the city, he rose and attacked them.

Abimelech and the company with him advanced rapidly and took up position at the entrance of the city gate, while the other two companies made a dash against all those who were in the open and struck them down. Abimelech kept up the attack on the city all that day and, when he captured it, he slaughtered the people inside, razed the city to the ground, and sowed it with salt.

When news of this reached the occupants of the tower of Shechem, they took refuge in the crypt of the temple of Elberith. It was reported to Abimelech that all the occupants of the tower of Shechem had flocked together, and he and all his men went up Mount Zalmon, where with an axe he cut brushwood. He took it and, hoisting it on his shoulder, he said to his men, 'You see what I am doing; quick, do the same.' Each man cut brushwood and then following Abimelech they laid the brushwood on the crypt. They burnt it over the heads of the occupants of the tower, and they all died, about a thousand men and women.

Abimelech proceeded to Thebez, which he besieged and captured. There was a strong tower in the middle of the town, and all the townspeople, men and women, took refuge there. They shut themselves in and went up on the roof. Abimelech came up to the tower and attacked it, and as he approached the entrance to set fire to it, a woman threw a millstone down on his head and fractured his skull. He called hurriedly to his armour-bearer and said, 'Draw your sword and dispatch me, or it will be said of me: A woman killed him.' So the young man ran him through, and he died. When the Israelites saw that Abimelech was dead, they all went back to their homes. In this way God repaid the crime which Abimelech had committed against his father by the murder of his seventy brothers, and brought all the wickedness of the men of Shechem on their own heads. The curse of Jotham son of Jerubbaal overtook them.

JEPHTHAH DEFEATS THE AMMONITES
Judges 11:1–16, 22 – 12:7

Jephthah the Gileadite was an intrepid warrior; he was the son of Gilead by a prostitute. Gilead's wife also bore him sons, and when they grew up they drove Jephthah away, saying to him, 'You have no inheritance in our father's house; you are another woman's son.' To escape his brothers, Jephthah fled and settled in the land of Tob, and a number of good-for-nothing fellows rallied to him and became his followers.

The time came when the Ammonites launched an offensive against Israel and, when the fighting began, the elders of Gilead went to fetch Jephthah from the land of Tob. 'Come and be our commander so that we can fight the Ammonites,' they said to him. But Jephthah answered, 'You drove me from my father's house in hatred. Why come to me now when you are in trouble?' 'It is because of that', they replied, 'that we have turned to you now. Come with us, fight the Ammonites, and become head over all the inhabitants of Gilead.' Jephthah said to them, 'If you ask me back to fight the Ammonites and if the Lord delivers them into my hands, then I must become your head.' The Gilead elders said to him, 'We swear by the Lord, who will be witness between us, that we will do what you say.' Jephthah then went with the elders of Gilead, and the people made him their head and commander. And at Mizpah, in the presence of the Lord, Jephthah repeated the terms he had laid down.

Jephthah sent a mission to the king of Ammon to ask what quarrel he had with them that made him invade their country. The king replied to the messengers: 'When the Israelites came up from Egypt, they seized our land all the way from the Arnon to the Jabbok and the Jordan. Now return these lands peaceably.' Jephthah sent a second mission to the king of Ammon to say, 'This is Jephthah's answer: Israel took neither Moabite nor Ammonite territory. When they came up from Egypt, the Israelites passed through the wilderness to the Red Sea, and on to Kadesh...

'They took possession of the entire Amorite country from the Arnon to the Jabbok and from the wilderness to the Jordan. The Lord the God of Israel drove out the Amorites for the benefit of his people Israel. And do you now propose to take their place? It is for you to possess whatever Kemosh your god gives you; and all that the Lord our God gave us as we advanced is ours.

'For that matter, are you any better than Balak son of Zippor, king of Moab? Did he ever pick a quarrel with Israel or attack them?

For three hundred years Israelites have lived in Heshbon and its dependent villages, in Aroer and its villages, and in all the towns by the Arnon. Why did you not retake them during all that time? We have done you no wrong; it is you who are doing us wrong by attacking us. The Lord who is judge will decide this day between the Israelites and the Ammonites.' But the king of the Ammonites would not listen to the message Jephthah sent him.

Then the spirit of the Lord came upon Jephthah, who passed through Gilead and Manasseh, by Mizpeh of Gilead, and from Mizpeh over to the Ammonites. Jephthah made this vow to the Lord: 'If you will deliver the Ammonites into my hands, then the first creature that comes out of the door of my house to meet me when I return from them safely shall be the Lord's; I shall offer that as a whole-offering.'

So Jephthah crossed over to attack the Ammonites, and the Lord delivered them into his hands. He routed them with very great slaughter all the way from Aroer to near Minnith, taking twenty towns, and as far as Abel-keramim. Thus Ammon was subdued by Israel.

When Jephthah arrived home in Mizpah, it was his daughter who came out to meet him with tambourines and dancing. She was his only child; apart from her he had neither son nor daughter. At the sight of her, he tore his clothes and said, 'Oh, my daughter, you have broken my heart! Such calamity you have brought on me! I have made a vow to the Lord and I cannot go back on it.'

She replied, 'Father, since you have made a vow to the Lord, do to me as your vow demands, now that the Lord has avenged you on the Ammonites, your enemies. But, father, grant me this one favour: spare me for two months, that I may roam the hills with my companions and mourn that I must die a virgin.' 'Go,' he said, and he let her depart for two months. She went with her companions and mourned her virginity on the hills. At the end of two months she came back to her father, and he fulfilled the vow he had made; she died a virgin. It became a tradition that the daughters of Israel should go year by year and commemorate for four days the daughter of Jephthah the Gileadite.

The Ephraimites mustered their forces and, crossing over to Zaphon, said to Jephthah, 'Why did you march against the Ammonites and not summon us to go with you? We shall burn your house over your head.' Jephthah answered, 'I and my people had a grave feud with the Ammonites, and had I appealed to you for help, you would not have saved us from them. When I saw that we were not to look for help from you, I took my life in my hands and marched against the Ammonites, and the Lord delivered them into my power. So why do you now attack me?' Jephthah then mustered all the men of Gilead and fought Ephraim, and the Gileadites defeated them. The Gileadites seized the fords of the Jordan and held them against Ephraim. When any Ephraimite who had escaped wished to cross, the men of Gilead would ask, 'Are you an Ephraimite?' and if he said, 'No,' they would retort, 'Say "Shibboleth."' He would say 'Sibboleth,' and because he could not pronounce the word properly, they seized him and killed him at the fords. At that time forty-two thousand men of Ephraim lost their lives.

Jephthah was judge over Israel for six years; when he died he was buried in his own town in Gilead.

SAMSON AND THE PHILISTINES
Judges 13:1 – 16:31

Once more the Israelites did what was wrong in the eyes of the Lord, and he delivered them into the hands of the Philistines for forty years.

There was a certain man from Zorah of the tribe of Dan whose name was Manoah and whose wife was barren; she had no child. The angel of the Lord appeared to her and said, 'Though you are barren and have no child, you will conceive and give birth to a son. Now be careful to drink no wine or strong drink, and to eat no forbidden food. You will conceive and give birth to a son, and no razor must touch his head, for the boy is to be a Nazirite, consecrated to God from birth. He will strike the first blow for Israel's freedom from the power of the Philistines.'

The woman went and told her husband. 'A man of God came to me,' she said to him; 'his appearance was that of an angel of God, most terrible to see. I did not ask him where he came from, nor did he tell me his name, but he said to me, "You are going to conceive and give birth to a son. From now on drink no wine or strong drink and eat no forbidden food, for the boy is to be a Nazirite, consecrated to God from his birth to the day of his death."'

Manoah prayed to the Lord, 'If it is pleasing to you, Lord, let the man of God whom you sent come again to tell us what we are to do for the boy that is to be born.' God heard Manoah's prayer, and the angel of God came again to the woman, as she was sitting in the field. Her husband not being with her, the woman ran quickly and said to him, 'The man who came to me the other day has appeared to me again.' Manoah went with her at once and approached the man and said, 'Are you the man who talked with my wife?' 'Yes,' he replied, 'I am.' 'Now when your words come true,' Manoah said, 'what kind of boy will he be and what will he do?' The angel of the Lord answered, 'Your wife must be careful to do all that I told her: she must not taste anything that comes from the vine; she must drink no wine or strong drink, and she must eat no forbidden food. She must do whatever I say.'

Manoah said to the angel of the Lord, 'May we urge you to stay? Let us prepare a young goat for you.' The angel replied, 'Though you urge me to stay, I shall not eat your food; but prepare a whole-offering if you will, and offer that to the Lord.' Manoah did not know that he was the angel of the Lord, and said to him, 'What is your name? For we shall want to honour you when your words come true.' The angel of the Lord said to him, 'How can you ask my name? It is a name of wonder.' Manoah took a young goat with the proper grain-offering, and offered it on the rock to the Lord, to him whose works are full of wonder. While Manoah and his wife were watching, the flame went up from the altar towards heaven, and the angel of the Lord ascended in the flame. Seeing this, Manoah and his wife fell face downward to the ground.

The angel of the Lord did not appear again to Manoah and his wife. When Manoah realized that it had been the angel of the Lord, he said to his wife, 'We are doomed to die, for we have seen God.' But she replied, 'If the Lord had wanted to kill us, he would not have accepted a whole-offering and a grain-offering at our hands; he would not now have let us see and hear all this.'

The woman gave birth to a son and named him Samson. The boy grew up in Mahaneh-dan between Zorah and Eshtaol, and the Lord blessed him, and the spirit of the Lord began to move him.

Samson went down to Timnah, and there a woman, one of the Philistines, caught his notice. On his return he told his father and mother that he had seen this Philistine woman in Timnah and asked them to get her for him as his wife. His parents protested, 'Is there no woman among your cousins or in all our own people? Must you go to the uncircumcised Philistines to find a wife?' But Samson said to his father, 'Get her for me, because she pleases me.' Neither his father nor his mother knew that the Lord was at work in this, seeking an opportunity against the Philistines, who at that time held Israel in subjection.

Samson went down to Timnah and, when he reached the vineyards there, a young lion came at him growling. The spirit of the Lord suddenly seized him and, without any weapon in his hand, Samson tore the lion to pieces as if it were a kid. He did not tell his parents what he had done. Then he went down and spoke to the woman, and she pleased him.

When, after a time, he went down again to make her his wife, he turned aside to look at the carcass of the lion, and saw there was a swarm of bees in it, and honey. He scraped the honey into his hands and went on, eating as he went. When he came to his father and mother, he gave them some and they ate it; but he did not tell them that he had scraped the honey out of the lion's carcass.

His father went down to see the woman, and Samson gave a feast there as the custom of young men was. When the people saw him, they picked thirty companions to escort him. Samson said to them, 'Let me ask you a riddle. If you can solve it during the seven days of the feast, I shall give you thirty lengths of linen and thirty changes of clothing; but if you cannot guess the answer, then you will give me thirty lengths of linen and thirty changes of clothing.' 'Tell us your riddle,' they said; 'let us hear it.' So he said to them:

'Out of the eater came something to eat;
out of the strong came something sweet.'

At the end of three days they had failed to guess the answer. On the fourth day they said to Samson's wife, 'Coax your husband and make him explain the riddle to you, or we shall burn you and your father's house. Did you invite us here to beggar us?' So Samson's wife wept

190

on his shoulder and said, 'You only hate me, you do not love me. You have asked my kinsfolk a riddle and you have not told it to me.' He said to her, 'I have not told it even to my father and mother; and am I to tell it to you?' But she wept on his shoulder every day until the seven feast days were ended, and on the seventh day, because she pestered him so, he told her, and she told the riddle to her kinsfolk. So on the seventh day the men of the city said to Samson just before he entered the bridal chamber:

'What is sweeter than honey?
What is stronger than a lion?'

He replied, 'If you had not ploughed with my heifer, you would not have solved my riddle.' Then the spirit of the Lord suddenly seized him, and he went down to Ashkelon, where he killed thirty men, took their belts, and gave their clothes to the men who had answered his riddle; then in a furious temper he went off to his father's house. Samson's wife was given in marriage to the one who had been his groomsman.

After a while, during the time of wheat harvest, Samson went to visit his wife, taking a young goat as a present for her. He said, 'I am going to my wife in our bridal chamber,' but her father would not let him in. He said, 'I was sure that you were really hostile to her, so I gave her in marriage to your groomsman. Her young sister is better than she is – take her instead.' Samson said, 'This time I shall settle my score with the Philistines; I shall do them some real harm.' He went and caught three hundred jackals and got some torches; he tied the jackals tail to tail and fastened a torch between each pair of tails. He then lit the torches and turned the jackals loose in the standing grain of the Philistines, setting fire to standing grain and sheaves, as well as to vineyards and olive groves.

'Who has done this?' the Philistines demanded, and when they were told that it was Samson, because the Timnite, his father-in-law, had taken his wife and given her to his groomsman, they came and burnt her and her father to death. Samson said to them, 'If you do things like that, I swear I will be revenged on you before I have done.' He smote them hip and thigh, causing great slaughter; and after that he went down to live in a cave in the Rock of Etam.

The Philistines came up and pitched camp in Judah, and overran Lehi. The Judahites said, 'Why have you attacked us?' They answered, 'We have come to take Samson prisoner, and do to him as he did to us.' Then three thousand men from Judah went down to the cave in the Rock of Etam, where they said to Samson, 'Surely you know that the Philistines are our masters? Now look what you have done to us.' He answered, 'I only did to them as they had done to me.' They told him, 'We have come down to bind you and hand you over to the Philistines.' 'Swear to me that you will not set upon me yourselves,' he said. 'No, we shall not kill you,' they answered; 'we shall only bind you and hand you over to them.' They bound him with two new ropes and brought him up from the cave in the Rock.

When Samson came to Lehi, the Philistines met him with shouts of triumph; but the spirit of the Lord suddenly seized him, the ropes on his arms became like burnt tow, and his bonds melted away. He came on the fresh jaw-bone of a donkey, and seizing it he slew a thousand men. He made up this saying:

'With the jaw-bone of a donkey
    I have flayed them like donkeys;
with the jaw-bone of a donkey
    I have slain a thousand men.'

Having said this he threw away the jaw-bone; and he called that place Ramath-lehi.

He began to feel very thirsty and cried aloud to the Lord, 'You have let me, your servant, win this great victory, and must I now die of thirst and fall into the hands of the uncircumcised?' God split open the Hollow of Lehi and water came out of it. Samson drank, his strength returned, and he revived. This is why to this day the spring in Lehi is called En-hakkore.

Samson was judge over Israel for twenty years in the days of the Philistines.

Samson went to Gaza, and seeing a prostitute there he lay with her. The people of Gaza heard that Samson had come, and they gathered round and lay in wait for him all night at the city gate. During the night, however, they took no action, saying to themselves, 'When dawn comes we shall kill him.' Samson stayed in bed till midnight; but then he rose, took hold of the doors of the city gate and the two gateposts, and pulled them out, bar and all; he hoisted them on his shoulders, and carried them to the top of the hill east of Hebron.

Afterwards Samson fell in love with a woman named Delilah, who lived by the wadi of Sorek. The lords of the Philistines went up to her and said, 'Cajole him and find out what gives him his great strength, and how we can overpower and bind him and render him helpless. We shall each give you eleven hundred pieces of silver.'

Delilah said to Samson, 'Tell me, what gives you your great strength? How could you be bound and made helpless?' 'If I were bound with seven fresh bowstrings not yet dry,' replied Samson, 'then I should become no stronger than any other man.' The lords of the Philistines brought her seven fresh bowstrings not yet dry, and she bound him with them. She had men concealed in the inner room, and she cried, 'Samson, the Philistines are upon you!' Thereupon he snapped the bowstrings as a strand of tow snaps at the touch of fire, and his strength was not impaired.

Delilah said to Samson, 'You have made a fool of me and lied to me. Now tell me this time how you can be bound.' He said to her, 'If I were tightly bound with new ropes that have never been used, then I should become no stronger than any other man.' Delilah took new ropes and bound him with them. Then, with men concealed in the inner room, she cried, 'Samson, the Philistines are upon you!' But he snapped the ropes off his arms like thread.

Delilah said to him, 'You are still making a fool of me, still lying to me. Tell me: how can you be bound?' He said, 'Take the seven loose locks of my hair, weave them into the warp, and drive them tight with the beater; then I shall become no stronger than any other man.' So she lulled him to sleep, wove the seven loose locks of his hair into the warp, drove them tight with the beater, and cried, 'Samson, the Philistines are upon you!' He woke from sleep and pulled away the warp and the loom with it.

She said to him, 'How can you say you love me when you do not confide in me? This is the third time you have made a fool of me and have not told me what gives you your great strength.' She so pestered him with these words day after day, pressing him hard and wearying him to death, that he told her the whole secret. 'No razor has touched my head,' he said, 'because I am a Nazirite, consecrated to God from the day of my birth. If my head were shaved, then my strength would leave me, and I should become no stronger than any other man.'

Delilah realized that he had told her his secret, and she sent word to the lords of the Philistines: 'Come up at once,' she said; 'he has told me his secret.' The lords of the Philistines came, bringing the money with them. She lulled Samson to sleep on her lap, and then summoned a man to shave the seven locks of his hair. She was now making him helpless. When his strength had left him, she cried, 'Samson, the Philistines are upon you!' He woke from his sleep and thought, 'I will go out as usual and shake myself'; he did not know that the Lord had left him. Then the Philistines seized him, gouged out his eyes, and brought him down to Gaza. There they bound him with bronze fetters, and he was set to grinding grain in the prison. But his hair, after it had been shaved, began to grow again.

The lords of the Philistines assembled to offer a great sacrifice to their god Dagon, and to rejoice and say,

'Our god has delivered into our hands
Samson our enemy.'

The people, when they saw him, praised their god, chanting:

'Our god has delivered our enemy into our hands,
the scourge of our land who piled it with our dead.'

When they grew merry, they said, 'Call Samson, and let him entertain us.' When Samson was summoned from prison, he was a source of entertainment to them. They then stood him between the pillars, and Samson said to the boy who led him by the hand, 'Put me where I can feel the pillars which support the temple, so that I may lean against them.' The temple was full of men and women, and all the lords of the Philistines were there, and there were about three thousand men and women on the roof watching the entertainment.

Samson cried to the Lord and said, 'Remember me, Lord God, remember me: for this one occasion, God, give me strength, and let me at one stroke be avenged on the Philistines for my two eyes.' He put his arms round the two central pillars which supported the temple, his right arm round one and his left round the other and, bracing himself, he said, 'Let me die with the Philistines.' Then Samson leaned forward with all his might, and the temple crashed down on the lords and all the people who were in it. So the dead whom he killed at his death were more than those he had killed in his life.

His brothers and all his father's family came down, carried him up to the grave of his father Manoah between Zorah and Eshtaol, and buried him there. He had been judge over Israel for twenty years.

MICAH AND THE CARVED IMAGE
Judges 17:1 – 18:31

Once there was a man named Micah from the hill-country of Ephraim who said to his mother, 'You remember the eleven hundred pieces of silver which were stolen from you, and how in my hearing you called down a curse on the thief? I have the money; I took it, and now I give it back to you.' His mother said, 'May the Lord bless you, my son!' He gave back the eleven hundred pieces of silver to his mother, and she said, 'I now solemnly dedicate this silver to the Lord for the benefit of my son, to make a carved image and a cast idol.' When he returned the money to his mother, she handed two hundred of the pieces of silver to a silversmith, who made them into an image and an idol, which were placed in Micah's house. This man Micah had a shrine, and he made an ephod and teraphim and installed one of his sons to be his priest. In those days there was no king in Israel and everyone did what was right in his own eyes.

There was a young man from Bethlehem in Judah, from the clan of Judah, a Levite named Ben-gershom. He had left the city of Bethlehem to go and find somewhere to live. On his way he came to Micah's house in the hill-country of Ephraim. Micah asked him, 'Where have you come from?' and he replied, 'I am a Levite from Bethlehem in Judah, and I am looking for somewhere to live.' 'Stay with me and be a father and priest to me,' Micah said. 'I shall give you ten pieces of silver a year, and provide you with food and clothes.' The

Levite agreed to stay with the man, who treated him as one of his own family. Micah installed the Levite, and the young man became his priest and a member of his household. Micah said, 'Now I know that the Lord will make me prosper, because I have a Levite as my priest.'

In those days when Israel had no king, the tribe of Dan was looking for territory to occupy, because they had not so far come into possession of the territory allotted to them among the tribes of Israel. The Danites therefore sent out five of their valiant fighters from Zorah and Eshtaol, instructing them to reconnoitre and explore the land. As they followed their instructions, they came to Micah's house in the hill-country of Ephraim and spent the night there. While at the house, they recognized the speech of the young Levite, and turning they said, 'Who brought you here, and what are you doing? What is your business here?' He explained, 'Micah did such and such: he hired me and I have become his priest.' They said to him, 'Then enquire of God on our behalf whether our mission will be successful.' The priest replied, 'Go and prosper. The Lord looks favourably on the mission you have undertaken.'

The five men went on their way and came to Laish. There they found the inhabitants living free of care in the same way as the Sidonians, quiet and carefree with nothing lacking in the country. They were a long way from the Sidonians, and had no contact with the Aramaeans.

On their return to Zorah and Eshtaol, the five men were asked by their kinsmen for their report, and they replied, 'Go and attack them at once. The land that we saw was very good. Why hang back? Do not hesitate to go there and take possession. When you get there, you will find a people living a carefree life in a wide expanse of open country. It is a place where nothing on earth is lacking, and God has delivered it into your hands.'

Six hundred fully armed men from the Danite clan set out from Zorah and Eshtaol, and went up country, where they encamped in Kiriath-jearim in Judah, which is why that place is called Mahaneh-dan to this day; it lies west of Kiriath-jearim. From there they passed on to the hill-country of Ephraim until they came to Micah's house. The five men who had been sent to reconnoitre the country round Laish addressed their kinsmen. 'Do you know', they said, 'that in one of these houses there are an ephod and teraphim, an image and an idol? Now consider what you had best do.'

They turned aside to Micah's house and greeted him. As the six hundred armed Danites took their stand at the entrance of the gate, the five men who had gone to explore the country went indoors to take the image and the idol, the ephod and the teraphim; the priest meanwhile was standing at the entrance with the six hundred armed men. When the five men entered Micah's house and laid hands on the image and the idol, the ephod and the teraphim, the priest asked them what they were doing. They said to him, 'Be quiet; not a word. Come with us and be to us a father and priest. Which is better, to be priest in the household of one man or to be priest to a tribe and clan in Israel?' This pleased the priest, and carrying off the ephod and the teraphim, the image and the idol, he went with the people. They set out on their way, putting their dependants, herds, and possessions in front.

The Danites had gone some distance from Micah's house, when his neighbours were called out in pursuit. As they caught up with them, they shouted, and the Danites turned round and said to Micah, 'What is the matter with you that you have called out your men?' 'You have taken the gods which I made for myself and have taken the priest,' he answered; 'you have gone off and left me nothing. How can you ask, "What is the matter with you?"' The Danites said to him, 'Not another word from you! We are desperate men and if we set about you it will be the death of you and your family.' With that the Danites went on their way, and Micah, seeing that they were too strong for him, turned and went home.

Carrying off the things which Micah had made for himself along with his priest, the Danites then attacked Laish, whose people were quiet and carefree. They put the people to the sword and set fire to their town. There was no one to save them, for it was a long way from Sidon and they had no contact with the Aramaeans; the town was in the valley near Beth-rehob. They rebuilt the town and settled in it, naming it Dan after their forefather Dan, a son of Israel; its original name was Laish. The Danites set up the image, and Jonathan son of Gershom, son of Moses, and his sons were priests to the tribe of Dan until the exile. They set up for themselves the image which Micah had made, and it was there as long as the house of God was at Shiloh.

197

A LEVITE AND HIS CONCUBINE
Judges 19:1 – 21:25

In those days when Israel had no king, a Levite residing in the heart of the hill-country of Ephraim had taken himself a concubine from Bethlehem in Judah. In a fit of anger she had left him and gone to her father's house in Bethlehem in Judah. When she had been there four months, her husband set out after her, with his servant and two donkeys, to appeal to her and bring her back. She brought him into the house of her father, who was delighted to see him and made him welcome. Being pressed by his father-in-law, the girl's father, he stayed there three days, and they were regaled with food and drink during their visit. On the fourth day, they rose early in the morning, and the Levite prepared to leave, but the father said to his son-in-law, 'Have a bite of something to sustain you before you go,' and the two of them sat down and ate and drank together. The girl's father said to the man, 'Why not spend the night and enjoy yourself?' The man, however, rose to go, but his father-in-law urged him to stay, and again he stayed for the night. He rose early in the morning on the fifth day to depart, but the girl's father said, 'Have something to eat first.' So they lingered till late afternoon, eating and drinking together. Then the man stood up to go with his concubine and his servant, but his father-in-law said, 'Look, the day is wearing on towards sunset. Spend the night here and enjoy yourself, and tomorrow rise early and set out for home.' But the man would not stay the night; he set off on his journey.

He reached a point opposite Jebus, that is Jerusalem, with his two laden donkeys and his concubine. Since they were close to Jebus and the day was nearly gone, the servant said to his master, 'Do let us turn into this Jebusite town for the night.' His master replied, 'No, not into a strange town where the people are not Israelites; let us go on to Gibeah. Come, we will go and find some other place, Gibeah or Ramah, to spend the night.' So they went on until sunset overtook them; they were then near Gibeah which belongs to Benjamin. They turned in there to spend the night, and went and sat down in the open square of the town; but nobody took them into his house for the night.

At nightfall an old man was coming home from his work in the fields. He was from the hill-country of Ephraim, though he lived in Gibeah, where the people were Benjamites. When his eye lighted on the traveller in the town square, he asked him where he was going and where he came from. He answered, 'We are travelling from Bethlehem in Judah to the heart of the hill-country of Ephraim. I come from there; I have been to Bethlehem in Judah and I am going home, but nobody has taken me into his house. I have straw and provender for our donkeys, food and wine for myself, the girl, and the young man; we have all we need.' The old man said, 'You are welcome. I shall supply all your wants; you must not spend the night in the open.' He took him inside, where he provided fodder for the donkeys. Then, having bathed their feet, they all ate and drank.

While they were enjoying themselves, some of the most depraved scoundrels in the town surrounded the house, beating the door violently and shouting to the old man whose house it was, 'Bring out the man who has come to your house, for us to have intercourse with him.' The owner of the house went outside to them and said, 'No, my friends, do nothing so wicked. This man is my guest; do not commit this outrage. Here are my daughter, who is a virgin, and the man's concubine; let me bring them out to you. Abuse them and do what you please; but you must not commit such an outrage against this man.' When the men refused to listen to him, the Levite took his concubine and thrust her outside for them. They raped and abused her all night till the morning; only when dawn broke did they let her go. The woman came at daybreak and collapsed at the entrance of the man's house where her husband was, and lay there until it was light.

Her husband rose in the morning and opened the door of the house to be on his way, and there was his concubine lying at the door with her hands on the threshold. He said to her, 'Get up and let us be off'; but there was no answer. So he lifted her on to his donkey and set off for home.

When he arrived there, he picked up a knife, took hold of his concubine, and cut her limb by limb into twelve pieces, which he then sent through the length and breadth of Israel. He told the men he sent with them to say to every Israelite, 'Has the like of this happened or been seen from the time the Israelites came up from

Egypt till today? Consider among yourselves and speak your minds.'
Everyone who saw them said, 'Since that time no such thing has ever
happened or been seen.'

All the Israelites, the whole community from Dan to Beersheba
and also from Gilead, left their homes and as one man assembled
before the Lord at Mizpah. The leaders of the people and all the tribes
of Israel presented themselves in the assembly of God's people, four
hundred thousand foot-soldiers armed with swords. That the
Israelites had gone up to Mizpah became known to the Benjamites.

The Israelites asked how this wicked crime happened, and the
Levite, to whom the murdered woman belonged, answered, 'I and my
concubine arrived at Gibeah in Benjamin to spend the night. The
townsmen of Gibeah rose against me that night and surrounded the
house where I was, intending to kill me; and they raped my concubine
so that she died. I took her and cut her in pieces, and sent the pieces
through the length and breadth of Israel, because of the abominable
outrage they had committed in Israel. It is for you, the whole of Israel,
to come to a decision as to what action should be taken.'

As one man all the people stood up and declared, 'Not one of
us will go back to his tent, not one will return home. But this is what
we shall do to Gibeah: we shall draw lots for the attack, and in all the
tribes of Israel we shall take ten men out of every hundred, a hundred
out of every thousand, and a thousand out of every ten thousand, and
they will collect provisions for the army, for those who have taken the
field against Gibeah in Benjamin to avenge the outrage committed in
Israel.' Thus all the Israelites, united to a man, were massed against
the town.

The tribes of Israel sent messengers throughout the tribe of
Benjamin saying, 'What crime is this that has taken place among you?
Hand over to us now those scoundrels in Gibeah; we shall put them
to death and purge Israel of this wickedness.' The Benjamites,
however, refused to listen to their fellow-Israelites. They flocked from
their towns to Gibeah to do battle with the Israelites, and that day
they mustered out of their towns twenty-six thousand men armed
with swords. There were also seven hundred picked men from
Gibeah, left-handed men, who could sling a stone and not miss by a
hair's breadth. The Israelites, without the Benjamites, numbered four

hundred thousand men armed with swords, every one a warrior. The Israelites at once moved on to Bethel and there sought an oracle from God. 'Which of us is to lead the attack on the Benjamites?' they enquired, and the Lord's answer was, 'Judah is to lead the attack.'

The Israelites set out at dawn and encamped opposite Gibeah. They advanced to do battle with the Benjamites and drew up their forces before the town. The Benjamites sallied out from Gibeah and laid low twenty-two thousand of Israel on the field that day.

The Israelites went up to Bethel, where they lamented before the Lord until evening, and enquired whether they should again attack their kinsmen the Benjamites. The Lord said, 'Go up to the attack.' The Israelite army took fresh courage and formed up again on the same ground as the first day. So on the second day they advanced against the Benjamites, who sallied out from Gibeah to meet them and laid low on the field another eighteen thousand armed men.

The Israelites, the whole army, went back to Bethel, where they sat before the Lord lamenting and fasting until evening, and they offered whole-offerings and shared-offerings before the Lord. In those days the Ark of the Covenant of God was there, and Phinehas son of Eleazar, son of Aaron, served before the Lord. The Israelites enquired of the Lord, 'Shall we again march out to battle against Benjamin our kin, or shall we desist?' The Lord answered, 'Attack! Tomorrow I shall deliver him into your hands.'

The Israelites posted men in ambush all round Gibeah, and on the third day they advanced against the Benjamites and drew up their forces at Gibeah as before. The Benjamites sallied out to meet them, and were drawn away from the town. They began the attack as before by killing a few Israelites, about thirty, on the highways which led across open country, one to Bethel and the other to Gibeon. They thought that once again they were inflicting a defeat, but the Israelites had planned a retreat to draw them out on the highways away from the town. Meanwhile the main body of Israelites left their positions and re-formed at Baal-tamar, while those in ambush, ten thousand picked men all told, burst out from their position in the neighbourhood of Gibeah and came in on the east of the town. There was soon heavy fighting; yet the Benjamites did not suspect the disaster threatening them. So the Lord put Benjamin to flight before

Israel, and on that day the Israelites killed twenty-five thousand one hundred Benjamites, all armed with swords.

The men of Benjamin now saw that they had suffered a defeat, for all that the Israelites, trusting in the ambush which they had set by Gibeah, had given ground before them. The men in ambush made a sudden dash on Gibeah, fell on the town from all sides, and put all the inhabitants to the sword. The agreed signal between the Israelites and those in ambush was to be a column of smoke sent up from the town, and the Israelites would then face about in the battle. Benjamin began to cut down the Israelites, killing about thirty of them, in the belief that they were defeating the enemy as they had done in the first encounter. But as the column of smoke began to go up from the town, the Benjamites looked back and thought the whole town was in flames. Then the Israelites faced about, and the Benjamites saw that disaster had overtaken them. They were seized with panic, and turned in flight before the Israelites in the direction of the wilderness; but the fighting caught up with them, and soon those from the town were among them, cutting them down. They hemmed in the Benjamites, pursuing them without respite, and overtook them at a point to the east of Gibeah. Eighteen thousand of the Benjamites fell, all of them valiant warriors. The survivors turned and fled into the wilderness towards the Rock of Rimmon. The Israelites picked off the stragglers on the roads, five thousand of them, and continued the pursuit until they had cut down two thousand more. Twenty-five thousand armed men of Benjamin fell in battle that day, all valiant warriors. The six hundred who survived made off into the wilderness as far as the Rock of Rimmon, and there they remained for four months. The Israelites then turned back to deal with the other Benjamites, and put to the sword the people in the towns and the cattle, every creature that they found; they also set fire to every town within their reach.

The Israelites had taken an oath at Mizpah that none of them would give his daughter in marriage to a Benjamite. The people now came to Bethel and remained there in God's presence till sunset, raising their voices in bitter lamentation. 'Lord God of Israel,' they cried, 'why has it happened among us that one tribe should this day be lost to Israel?' Early next morning the people built an altar there and offered whole-offerings and shared-offerings. At that the Israelites asked themselves whether among all the tribes of Israel there was any who did not go up to the assembly before the Lord; for under the terms of the weighty oath they had sworn, anyone who had not gone up to the Lord at Mizpah was to be put to death. The Israelites felt remorse over their kinsmen the Benjamites, because, as they said, 'This day one whole tribe has been lopped off Israel.'

They asked, 'What shall we do to provide wives for those who are left, as we ourselves have sworn to the Lord not to give any of our daughters to them in marriage? Is there anyone in all the tribes of Israel who did not go up to the Lord at Mizpah?' Now it happened that no one from Jabesh-gilead had come to the camp for the assembly; so when they held a roll-call of the people, they found that none of the inhabitants of Jabesh-gilead was present. The community therefore sent off twelve thousand valiant fighting men with orders to go and put the inhabitants of Jabesh-gilead to the sword, men, women, and dependants. 'This is what you are to do,' they said: 'put to death every male person, and every woman who has had intercourse with a man, but spare any who are virgins.' This they did. Among the inhabitants of Jabesh-gilead they found four hundred young women who were virgins and had not had intercourse with a man, and they brought them to the camp at Shiloh in Canaan. The whole community sent messengers to the Benjamites at the Rock of Rimmon to parley with them, and peace was proclaimed. The Benjamites came back then, and were given those of the women of Jabesh-gilead who had been spared; but these were not enough.

The people were still full of remorse over Benjamin because the Lord had made this gap in the tribes of Israel. The elders of the community said, 'What can we do for wives for those who are left, as all the women in Benjamin have been wiped out?' They said, 'Heirs there must be for the surviving Benjamites! Then Israel will not see one of its tribes destroyed. Yet we cannot give them our own daughters in marriage, because we have sworn that there shall be a curse on the man who gives a wife to a Benjamite.'

They bethought themselves of the pilgrimage in honour of the Lord, made every year to Shiloh, the place which lies to the north of Bethel, on the east side of the highway from Bethel to Shechem and to the south of Lebonah. They told the Benjamites to go and hide in the vineyards. 'Keep watch,' they said, 'and when the girls of Shiloh come out to take part in the dance, come from the vineyards, and each of you seize one of them for his wife; then be off to the territory of Benjamin. If their fathers or brothers come and complain to us, we shall say to them, "Let them keep them with your approval, for none of us has captured a wife in battle. Had you yourselves given them the women, you would now have incurred guilt."'

The Benjamites did this; they carried off as many wives as they needed, snatching them from the dance; then they went their way back to their own territory, where they rebuilt their towns and settled in them. The Israelites also dispersed by tribes and families, and every man returned to his own holding.

In those days there was no king in Israel; everyone did what was right in his own eyes.

Part Six
The Story of Ruth

RUTH AND NAOMI
Ruth 1:1–22

Once, in the time of the Judges when there was a famine in the land, a man from Bethlehem in Judah went with his wife and two sons to live in Moabite territory. The man's name was Elimelech, his wife was Naomi, and his sons were Mahlon and Chilion; they were Ephrathites from Bethlehem in Judah. They came to Moab and settled there.

Elimelech died, and Naomi was left a widow with her two sons. The sons married Moabite women, one of whom was called Orpah and the other Ruth. They had lived there about ten years when both Mahlon and Chilion died. Then Naomi, bereaved of her two sons as well as of her husband, got ready to return to her own country with her daughters-in-law, because she heard in Moab that the Lord had shown his care for his people by giving them food. Accompanied by her two daughters-in-law she left the place where she had been living, and they took the road leading back to Judah.

Naomi said to her daughters-in-law, 'Go back, both of you, home to your own mothers. May the Lord keep faith with you, as you have kept faith with the dead and with me; and may he grant each of you the security of a home with a new husband.' And she kissed them goodbye. They wept aloud and said, 'No, we shall return with you to your people.' But Naomi insisted, 'Go back, my daughters. Why should you come with me? Am I likely to bear any more sons to be husbands for you? Go back, my daughters, go; for I am too old to marry again. But if I could say that I had hope of a child, even if I were to be married tonight and were to bear sons, would you, then, wait until they grew up? Would you on their account remain unmarried? No, my daughters! For your sakes I feel bitter that the Lord has inflicted such misfortune on me.' At this they wept still more. Then

Orpah kissed her mother-in-law and took her leave, but Ruth clung to her.

'Look,' said Naomi, 'your sister-in-law has gone back to her people and her god. Go, follow her.' Ruth answered, 'Do not urge me to go back and desert you. Where you go, I shall go, and where you stay, I shall stay. Your people will be my people, and your God my God. Where you die, I shall die, and there be buried. I solemnly declare before the Lord that nothing but death will part me from you.' When Naomi saw that Ruth was determined to go with her, she said no more.

The two of them went on until they came to Bethlehem, where their arrival set the whole town buzzing with excitement. The women cried, 'Can this be Naomi?' 'Do not call me Naomi,' she said; 'call me Mara, for the Almighty has made my life very bitter. I went away full, and the Lord has brought me back empty. Why call me Naomi? The Lord has pronounced against me, the Almighty has brought me misfortune.'

That was how Naomi's daughter-in-law, Ruth the Moabite, returned with her from Moab; they arrived in Bethlehem just as the barley harvest was beginning.

RUTH AND BOAZ
Ruth 2:1 – 4:16

Naomi had a relative on her husband's side, a prominent and well-to-do member of Elimelech's family; his name was Boaz. One day Ruth the Moabite asked Naomi, 'May I go to the harvest fields and glean behind anyone who will allow me?' 'Yes, go, my daughter,' she replied. So Ruth went gleaning in the fields behind the reapers. As it happened, she was in that strip of the fields which belonged to Boaz of Elimelech's family, and there was Boaz himself coming out from Bethlehem. He greeted the reapers, 'The Lord be with you!' and they responded, 'The Lord bless you!' 'Whose girl is this?' he asked the servant in charge of the reapers. The servant answered, 'She is a Moabite girl who has come back with Naomi from Moab. She asked if she might glean, gathering among the sheaves behind the reapers.

She came and has been on her feet from morning till now; she has hardly had a moment's rest in the shelter.'

Boaz said to Ruth, 'Listen, my daughter: do not go to glean in any other field. Do not look any farther, but stay close to my servant-girls. Watch where the men reap, and follow the gleaners; I have told the men not to molest you. Any time you are thirsty, go and drink from the jars they have filled.' She bowed to the ground and said, 'Why are you so kind as to take notice of me, when I am just a foreigner?' Boaz answered, 'I have been told the whole story of what you have done for your mother-in-law since the death of your husband, how you left father and mother and homeland and came among a people you did not know before. The Lord reward you for what you have done; may you be richly repaid by the Lord the God of Israel, under whose wings you have come for refuge.' She said: 'I hope you will continue to be pleased with me, sir, for you have eased my mind by speaking kindly to me, though I am not one of your slave-girls.'

When mealtime came round, Boaz said to Ruth, 'Come over here and have something to eat. Dip your piece of bread in the vinegar.' She sat down beside the reapers, and he passed her some roasted grain. She ate all she wanted and still had some left. When she got up to glean, Boaz instructed the men to allow her to glean right among the sheaves. 'Do not find fault with her,' he added; 'you may even pull out some ears of grain from the handfuls as you cut, and leave them for her to glean; do not check her.'

Ruth gleaned in the field until sunset, and when she beat out what she had gathered it came to about a bushel of barley. She carried it into the town and showed her mother-in-law how much she had got; she also brought out and handed her what she had left over from the meal. Her mother-in-law asked, 'Where did you glean today? Which way did you go? Blessings on the man who took notice of you!' She told her mother-in-law in whose field she had been working. 'The owner of the field where I worked today', she said, 'is a man called Boaz.' Naomi exclaimed, 'Blessings on him from the Lord, who has kept faith with the living and the dead! This man', she explained, 'is related to us; he is one of our very near kinsmen.' 'And what is more,' Ruth said, 'he told me to stay close to his workers until they had finished all his harvest.' Naomi said, 'My daughter, it would be as well for you to go with his girls; in another field you might come to harm.' So Ruth kept close to them, gleaning with them till the end of both barley and wheat harvests; but she lived with her mother-in-law.

One day Naomi, Ruth's mother-in-law, said to her, 'My daughter, I want to see you settled happily. Now there is our kinsman Boaz, whose girls you have been with. Tonight he will be winnowing barley at the threshing-floor. Bathe and anoint yourself with perfumed oil, then get dressed and go down to the threshing-floor; but do not make yourself known to the man until he has finished eating and drinking. When he lies down make sure you know the place where he is. Then go in, turn back the covering at his feet and lie down. He will tell you what to do.' 'I will do everything you say,' replied Ruth.

She went down to the threshing-floor and did exactly as her mother-in-law had told her. When Boaz had eaten and drunk, he felt at peace with the world and went and lay down to sleep at the far end of the heap of grain. Ruth came quietly, turned back the covering at his feet and lay down. About midnight the man woke with a start; he turned over, and there, lying at his feet, was a woman! 'Who are you?' he said. 'Sir, it is I, Ruth,' she replied. 'Spread the skirt of your cloak over me, for you are my next-of-kin.' Boaz said, 'The Lord bless you, my daughter! You are proving yourself more devoted to the family than ever by not running after any young man, whether rich or poor. Set your mind at rest, my daughter: I shall do all you ask, for the whole town knows what a fine woman you are. Yes, it is true that I am a near kinsman; but there is one even closer than I am. Stay tonight, and then in the morning, if he is willing to act as your next-of-kin, well and good; but if he is not, then as sure as the Lord lives, I shall do so. Now lie down till morning.'

She lay at his feet till next morning, but rose before it was light enough for one man to recognize another; Boaz had it in mind that no one should know that the woman had been to the threshing-floor. He said to her, 'Take the cloak you are wearing, and hold it out.' When she did so, he poured in six measures of barley and lifted it for her to carry, and she went off to the town.

When she came to her mother-in-law, Naomi asked, 'How did things go with you, my daughter?' Ruth related all that the man had done for her, and she added, 'He gave me these six measures of barley; he would not let me come home to my mother-in-law empty-handed.' Naomi said, 'Wait, my daughter, until you see what will come of it; he will not rest till he has settled the matter this very day.'

Boaz meanwhile had gone up to the town gate and was sitting there when the next-of-kin of whom he had spoken came past. Calling him by name, Boaz cried, 'Come over here and sit down.' He went over and sat down. Boaz also stopped ten of the town's elders and asked them to sit there. When they were seated, he addressed the next-of-kin: 'You will remember the strip of field that belonged to our kinsman Elimelech. Naomi is selling it, now that she has returned from Moab. I promised to open the matter with you, to ask you to acquire it in the presence of those sitting here and in the presence of the elders of my people. If you are going to do your duty as next-of-kin, then do so; but if not, someone must do it. So tell me, and then I shall know, for I come after you as next-of-kin.' He answered, 'I shall act as next-of-kin.' Boaz continued: 'On the day you take over the field from Naomi, I take over the widow, Ruth the Moabite, so as to perpetuate the name of the dead man on his holding.' 'Then I cannot act,' said the next-of-kin, 'lest it should be detrimental to my own holding; and as I cannot act, you yourself must take over my duty as next-of-kin.'

Now it used to be the custom when ratifying any transaction by which property was redeemed or transferred for a man to take off his sandal and give it to the other party; this was the form of attestation in Israel. Accordingly when the next-of-kin said to Boaz, 'You must take it over,' he drew off his sandal and handed it over. Then Boaz addressed the elders and all the other people there: 'You are witnesses this day that I have taken over from Naomi all that belonged to Elimelech and all that belonged to Chilion and Mahlon; and, further, that I have taken over Mahlon's widow, Ruth the Moabite, to be my wife, in order to keep alive the dead man's name on his holding, so that his name may not be missing among his kindred and at the gate of his native town. You are witnesses this day.' All who were at the gate, including the elders, replied, 'We are witnesses. May the Lord make this woman, who is about to come into your home, to be like Rachel and Leah, the two who built up the family of Israel. May you do a worthy deed in Ephrathah by keeping this name alive in Bethlehem. Through the offspring the Lord gives you by this young woman may your family be like the family of Perez, whom Tamar bore to Judah.'

So Boaz took Ruth and she became his wife. When they had come together the Lord caused her to conceive, and she gave birth to a son. The women said to Naomi, 'Blessed be the Lord, who has not left you this day without next-of-kin. May the name of your dead son be kept alive in Israel! The child will give you renewed life and be your support and stay in your old age, for your devoted daughter-in-law, who has proved better to you than seven sons, has borne him.' Naomi took the child and laid him in her own lap, and she became his foster-mother.

Part Seven

Samuel the Prophet

DEDICATED TO THE LORD
1 Samuel 1:1 – 2:11, 19–21

There was a certain man from Ramathaim, a Zuphite from the hill-country of Ephraim, named Elkanah son of Jeroham, son of Elihu, son of Tohu, son of Zuph an Ephraimite. He had two wives, Hannah and Peninnah; Peninnah had children, but Hannah was childless. Every year this man went up from his town to worship and offer sacrifice to the Lord of Hosts at Shiloh, where Eli's two sons, Hophni and Phinehas, were priests of the Lord.

When Elkanah sacrificed, he gave several shares of the meat to his wife Peninnah with all her sons and daughters; but to Hannah he gave only one share; the Lord had not granted her children, yet it was Hannah whom Elkanah loved. Hannah's rival also used to torment and humiliate her because she had no children. This happened year after year when they went up to the house of the Lord; her rival used to torment her, until she was in tears and would not eat. Her husband Elkanah said to her, 'Hannah, why are you crying and eating nothing? Why are you so miserable? Am I not more to you than ten sons?'

After they had finished eating and drinking at the sacrifice at Shiloh, Hannah rose in deep distress, and weeping bitterly stood before the Lord and prayed to him. Meanwhile Eli the priest was sitting on his seat beside the door of the temple of the Lord. Hannah made this vow: 'Lord of Hosts, if you will only take notice of my trouble and remember me, if you will not forget me but grant me offspring, then I shall give the child to the Lord for the whole of his life, and no razor shall ever touch his head.'

For a long time she went on praying before the Lord, while Eli watched her lips. Hannah was praying silently; her lips were moving although her voice could not be heard, and Eli took her for a drunken woman. 'Enough of this drunken behaviour!' he said to her. 'Leave off until the effect of the wine has gone.' 'Oh, sir!' she answered, 'I am a heart-broken woman; I have drunk neither wine nor strong drink, but I have been pouring out my feelings before the Lord. Do not think me so devoid of shame, sir; all this time I have been speaking out of the depths of my grief and misery.' Eli said, 'Go in peace, and may the God of Israel grant what you have asked of him.' Hannah replied, 'May I be worthy of your kindness.' And no longer downcast she went away and had something to eat.

Next morning they were up early and, after prostrating themselves before the Lord, returned to their home at Ramah. Elkanah had intercourse with his wife Hannah, and the Lord remembered her; she conceived, and in due time bore a son, whom she named Samuel, 'because', she said, 'I asked the Lord for him'.

Elkanah with his whole household went up to make the annual sacrifice to the Lord and to keep his vow. Hannah did not go; she said to her husband, 'After the child is weaned I shall come up with him to present him before the Lord; then he is to stay there always.' Her husband Elkanah said to her, 'Do what you think best; stay at home until you have weaned him. Only, may the Lord indeed see your vow fulfilled.' So the woman stayed behind and nursed her son until she had weaned him.

When she had weaned him, she took him up with her. She took also a bull three years old, an ephah of flour, and a skin of wine, and she brought him, child as he was, into the house of the Lord at Shiloh. When the bull had been slaughtered, Hannah brought the boy to Eli and said, 'Sir, as sure as you live, I am the woman who stood here beside you praying to the Lord. It was this boy that I prayed for and the Lord has granted what I asked. Now I make him over to the Lord; for his whole life he is lent to the Lord.' And they prostrated themselves there before the Lord.

Then Hannah offered this prayer:

'My heart exults in the Lord,
in the Lord I now hold my head high;
I gloat over my enemies;
I rejoice because you have saved me.
There is none but you,

none so holy as the Lord,
none so righteous as our God.

'Cease your proud boasting,
let no word of arrogance pass your lips,
for the Lord is a God who knows;
he governs what mortals do.
Strong men stand in mute dismay,
but those who faltered put on new strength.
Those who had plenty sell themselves for a crust,
and the hungry grow strong again.
The barren woman bears seven children,
and the mother of many sons is left to languish.

'The Lord metes out both death and life:
he sends down to Sheol, he can bring the dead up again.
Poverty and riches both come from the Lord;
he brings low and he raises up.
He lifts the weak out of the dust
and raises the poor from the refuse heap
to give them a place among the great,
to assign them seats of honour.

'The foundations of the earth are the Lord's,
and he has set the world upon them.
He will guard the footsteps of his loyal servants,
while the wicked will be silenced in darkness;
for it is not by strength that a mortal prevails.

'Those who oppose the Lord will be terrified
when from the heavens he thunders against them.
The Lord is judge even to the ends of the earth;
he will endow his king with strength
and raise high the head of his anointed one.'

Then Elkanah went home to Ramah, but the boy remained behind in
the service of the Lord under Eli the priest...

Every year his mother made him a little cloak and took it to him when she went up with her husband to offer the annual sacrifice. Eli would give his blessing to Elkanah and his wife and say, 'The Lord grant you children by this woman in place of the one whom you made over to the Lord.' Then they would return home.

The Lord showed his care for Hannah, and she conceived and gave birth to three sons and two daughters; meanwhile the boy Samuel grew up in the presence of the Lord.

GOD'S JUDGMENT ON THE HOUSE OF ELI
1 Samuel 2:22–24, 27, 31, 33–34; 3:1–13, 15 – 4:22

When Eli, now a very old man, heard a detailed account of how his sons were treating all the Israelites, and how they lay with the women who were serving at the entrance to the Tent of Meeting, he said to them, 'Why do you do such things? I hear from every quarter how wickedly you behave. Do stop it, my sons; for this is not a good report that I hear spreading among the Lord's people...

A man of God came to Eli and said, 'This is the word of the Lord:... The time is coming when I shall lop off every limb of your own and of your father's family, so that no one in your house will attain old age... If I allow any to survive to serve my altar, his eyes will grow dim, his appetite fail, and his issue will be weaklings and die off. The fate of your two sons will be a proof to you; Hophni and Phinehas will both die on the same day...

The boy Samuel was in the Lord's service under Eli. In those days the word of the Lord was rarely heard, and there was no outpouring of vision. One night Eli, whose eyes were dim and his sight failing, was lying down in his usual place, while Samuel slept in the temple of the Lord where the Ark of God was. Before the lamp of God had gone out, the Lord called him, and Samuel answered, 'Here I am!' and ran to Eli saying, 'You called me: here I am.' 'No, I did not call you,' said Eli; 'lie down again.' So he went and lay down. The Lord called Samuel again, and he got up and went to Eli. 'Here I am!' he said. 'Surely you called me.' 'I did not call, my son,' he answered; 'lie down again.' Samuel had not yet come to know the Lord, and the word of the Lord had not been disclosed to him. When the Lord called him for the third time, he again went to Eli and said, 'Here I am! You did call me.' Then Eli understood that it was the Lord calling the boy; he told Samuel to go and lie down and said, 'If someone calls once more, say, "Speak, Lord; your servant is listening."' So Samuel went and lay down in his place.

Then the Lord came, and standing there called, 'Samuel, Samuel!' as before. Samuel answered, 'Speak, your servant is listening.' The Lord said, 'Soon I shall do something in Israel which will ring in the ears of all who hear it. When that day comes I shall make good every word from beginning to end that I have spoken against Eli and his family. You are to tell him that my judgment on his house will stand for ever because he knew of his sons' blasphemies against God and did not restrain them...

Samuel lay down till morning, when he opened the doors of the house of the Lord; but he was afraid to tell Eli about the vision. Eli called Samuel: 'Samuel, my son!' he said; and Samuel answered, 'Here I am!' Eli asked, 'What did the Lord say to you? Do not hide it from me. God's curse upon you if you conceal from me one word of all that he said to you.' Then Samuel told him everything, concealing nothing. Eli said, 'The Lord must do what is good in his eyes.'

As Samuel grew up, the Lord was with him, and none of his words went unfulfilled. From Dan to Beersheba, all Israel recognized that Samuel was attested as a prophet of the Lord. So the Lord continued to appear in Shiloh, because he had revealed himself there to Samuel. Samuel's word had authority throughout Israel.

The time came when the Philistines mustered for battle against Israel, and the Israelites, marching out to meet them, encamped near Eben-ezer, while the Philistines' camp was at Aphek. The Philistines drew up their lines facing the Israelites, and when battle was joined the Israelites were defeated by the Philistines, who killed about four thousand men on the field. When their army got back to camp, the Israelite elders asked, 'Why did the Lord let us be defeated today by the Philistines? Let us fetch the Ark of the Covenant of the Lord from Shiloh to go with us and deliver us from the power of our enemies.' The army sent to Shiloh and fetched the Ark of the Covenant of the Lord of Hosts, who is enthroned upon the cherubim; Eli's two sons, Hophni and Phinehas, were there with the Ark.

When the Ark came into the camp it was greeted with such a great shout by all the Israelites that the earth rang. The Philistines, hearing the noise, asked, 'What is this great shouting in the camp of the Hebrews?' When they learned that the Ark of the Lord had come into the camp, they were alarmed. 'A god has come into the camp,' they cried. 'We are lost! No such thing has ever happened before. We are utterly lost! Who can deliver us from the power of this mighty god? This is the god who broke the Egyptians and crushed them in the wilderness. Courage, act like men, you Philistines, or you will become slaves to the Hebrews as they were to you. Be men, and fight!' The Philistines then gave battle, and the Israelites were defeated and fled to their homes. It was a great defeat, and thirty thousand Israelite foot-soldiers fell. The Ark of God was captured, and Eli's two sons, Hophni and Phinehas, perished.

A Benjamite ran from the battlefield and reached Shiloh on the same day, his clothes torn and dust on his head. When he arrived Eli was sitting on a seat by the road to Mizpah, for he was deeply troubled about the Ark of God. The man entered the town with his news, and all the people cried out in horror. When Eli heard the uproar, he asked, 'What does it mean?' The man hurried to Eli and told him. Eli was ninety-eight years old and sat staring with sightless eyes. The man said to him, 'I am the one who has just come from the battle. I fled from the field this very day.' Eli asked, 'What is the news, my son?' The runner answered, 'The Israelites have fled before the Philistines; the army has suffered severe losses; your two sons, Hophni and Phinehas, are dead; and the Ark of God is taken.' At the mention of the Ark of God, Eli fell backwards from his seat by the gate and broke his neck, for he was an old man and heavy. So he died; he had been judge over Israel for forty years.

His daughter-in-law, the wife of Phinehas, was pregnant and near her time, and when she heard of the capture of the Ark and the deaths of her father-in-law and her husband, she went into labour and she crouched down and was delivered. As she lay dying, the women who attended her said, 'Do not be afraid; you have a son.' But she did not answer or heed what they said. She named the boy Ichabod, saying, 'Glory has departed from Israel,' referring to the capture of the Ark of God and the deaths of her father-in-law and her husband;

'Glory has departed from Israel,' she said, 'because the Ark of God is taken.'

THE PHILISTINES RETURN THE
ARK OF THE COVENANT
1 Samuel 5:1 – 7:1

After the Philistines had captured the Ark of God, they brought it from Eben-ezer to Ashdod, where they carried it into the temple of Dagon and set it beside the god. When the people of Ashdod rose next morning, there was Dagon fallen face downwards on the ground before the Ark of the Lord. They lifted him up and put him back in his place. But next morning when they rose, Dagon had again fallen face downwards on the ground before the Ark of the Lord, with his head and his two hands lying broken off beside his platform; only Dagon's body remained on it. That is why to this day the priests of Dagon and all who enter the temple of Dagon at Ashdod do not set foot on Dagon's platform.

The Lord's hand oppressed the people of Ashdod. He threw them into despair; he plagued them with tumours, and their territory swarmed with rats. There was death and destruction all through the city. Seeing this, the men of Ashdod decided, 'The Ark of the God of Israel must not stay here, for his hand is pressing on us and on Dagon our god.' When they called together all the Philistine lords to ask what should be done with the Ark, they were told, 'Let the Ark of the God of Israel be taken across to Gath.' They moved it there, and after its removal there the Lord caused great havoc in that city; he plagued everybody, high and low alike, with the tumours which broke out. So the Ark of God was sent on to Ekron, and when it arrived there, the people cried, 'They have moved the Ark of the God of Israel over to us, to kill us and our families.' Summoning all the Philistine lords they said, 'Send the Ark of the God of Israel away; let it go back to its own place, or it will be the death of us all.' There was death and destruction all through the city; for the hand of God lay heavy upon it. Those who did not die were plagued with tumours, and the cry of the city ascended to heaven.

When the Ark of the Lord had been in their territory for seven months, the Philistines summoned the priests and soothsayers and asked, 'What shall we do with the Ark of the Lord? Tell us how we ought to send it back to its own place.' Their answer was, 'If you send the Ark of the God of Israel back, do not let it go empty, but send it back with an offering by way of compensation; if you are then healed you will know why his hand had not been lifted from you.' When they were asked, 'What should we send to him?' they answered, 'Send five tumours modelled in gold and five gold rats, one for each of the Philistine lords, for the same plague afflicted all of you and your lords. Make models of your tumours and of the rats which are ravaging the land, and give honour to the God of Israel; perhaps he will relax the pressure of his hand on you, your god, and your land. Why be stubborn like Pharaoh and the Egyptians? Remember how this God made sport of them until they let Israel go.

'Now make ready a new wagon with two milch cows which have never been yoked; harness the cows to the wagon, but take their calves away and keep them in their stall. Fetch the Ark of the Lord and put it on the wagon, place beside it in a casket the gold offerings that you are sending to him, and let it go where it will. Watch: if it goes up towards its own territory to Beth-shemesh, then it was the Lord who has inflicted this great injury on us; but if not, then we shall know that it was not his hand that struck us, but that we have been the victims of chance.'

They did this: they took two milch cows and harnessed them to a wagon, meanwhile shutting up their calves in the stall; they placed the Ark of the Lord on the wagon together with the casket containing the gold rats, and the models of their tumours. The cows went straight in the direction of Beth-shemesh; they kept to the road, lowing as they went and turning neither right nor left, while the Philistine lords followed them as far as the territory of Beth-shemesh.

The people of Beth-shemesh, busy harvesting their wheat in the valley, looked up and saw the Ark, and they rejoiced at the sight. The wagon came to the field of Joshua of Beth-shemesh and halted there, close by a great stone. The people chopped up the wood of the wagon and offered the cows as a whole-offering to the Lord. The Levites who lifted down the Ark of the Lord and the casket containing the gold offerings laid them on the great stone; and the men of Beth-shemesh offered whole-offerings and shared-offerings that day to the Lord. The five lords of the Philistines watched all this, and returned to Ekron the same day.

These golden tumours which the Philistines sent back as an offering to the Lord were for Ashdod, Gaza, Ashkelon, Gath, and Ekron, one for each city. The gold rats were for all the towns of the Philistines governed by the five lords, both fortified towns and open settlements. The great stone where they deposited the Ark of the Lord stands witness on the farm of Joshua of Beth-shemesh to this day.

But the sons of Jeconiah did not rejoice with the rest of the men of Beth-shemesh when they welcomed the Ark of the Lord, and he struck down seventy of them. The people mourned because the Lord had struck them so heavy a blow, and the men of Beth-shemesh said, 'No one is safe in the presence of the Lord, this holy God. To whom can we send the Ark, to be rid of him?' So they sent this message to the inhabitants of Kiriath-jearim: 'The Philistines have returned the Ark of the Lord; come down and take charge of it.' The men of Kiriath-jearim came and took the Ark of the Lord away; they brought it into the house of Abinadab on the hill and consecrated his son Eleazar as its custodian.

SAMUEL JUDGES ISRAEL
1 Samuel 7:2–17

For a long while, some twenty years in all, the Ark was housed in Kiriath-jearim. Then there was a movement throughout Israel to follow the Lord, and Samuel addressed these words to the whole nation: 'If your return to the Lord is whole-hearted, banish the foreign gods and the ashtaroth from your shrines; turn to the Lord with heart and mind, and worship him alone, and he will deliver you from the Philistines.' So the Israelites banished the baalim and the ashtaroth, and worshipped the Lord alone.

Samuel summoned all Israel to an assembly at Mizpah, so that he might intercede with the Lord for them. When they had assembled, they drew water and poured it out before the Lord and fasted all day, confessing that they had sinned against the Lord. It was at Mizpah that Samuel acted as judge over Israel.

When the Philistines heard that the Israelites had assembled at Mizpah, their lords marched against them. The Israelites heard that the Philistines were advancing, and they were afraid and begged Samuel, 'Do not cease to pray for us to the Lord our God to save us from the power of the Philistines.' Samuel took a sucking-lamb, offered it up complete as a whole-offering, and prayed aloud to the Lord on behalf of Israel, and the Lord answered his prayer. As Samuel was offering the sacrifice and the Philistines were advancing to the attack, the Lord with mighty thunder threw the Philistines into confusion. They fled in panic before the Israelites, who set out from Mizpah in pursuit and kept up the slaughter of the Philistines till they reached a point below Beth-car.

There Samuel took a stone and set it up as a monument between Mizpah and Jeshanah, naming it Eben-ezer. 'This is a witness', he said, 'that the Lord has helped us.' Thus the Philistines were subdued and no longer encroached on the territory of Israel; as long as Samuel lived, the hand of the Lord was against them. The towns they had captured were restored to Israel, and from Ekron to Gath the borderland was freed from Philistine control. Between Israel and the Amorites also peace was maintained.

Samuel acted as judge in Israel as long as he lived, and every year went on circuit to Bethel, Gilgal, and Mizpah; he dispensed justice at all these places. But always he went back to Ramah; that was his home and the place from which he governed Israel, and there he built an altar to the Lord.

THE PEOPLE DEMAND A KING
1 Samuel 8:1–22

When Samuel grew old, he appointed his sons to be judges in Israel. The eldest son was called Joel and the second Abiah; they acted as judges in Beersheba. His sons did not follow their father's ways but were intent on their own profit, taking bribes and perverting the course of justice. So all the elders of Israel met, and came to Samuel at Ramah. They said to him, 'You are now old and your sons do not follow your ways; appoint us a king to rule us, like all the other nations.' But their request for a king displeased Samuel. He prayed to the Lord, and the Lord told him, 'Listen to the people and all that they are saying; they have not rejected you, it is I whom they have rejected, I whom they will not have to be their king. They are now doing to you just what they have done to me since I brought them up from Egypt: they have forsaken me and worshipped other gods. Hear what they have to say now, but give them a solemn warning and tell them what sort of king will rule them.'

Samuel reported to the people who were asking him for a king all that the Lord had said to him. 'This will be the sort of king who will bear rule over you,' he said. 'He will take your sons and make them serve in his chariots and with his cavalry, and they will run before his chariot. Some he will appoint officers over units of a thousand and units of fifty. Others will plough his fields and reap his harvest; others again will make weapons of war and equipment for the chariots. He will take your daughters for perfumers, cooks, and bakers. He will seize the best of your fields, vineyards, and olive groves, and give them to his courtiers. He will take a tenth of your grain and your vintage to give to his eunuchs and courtiers. Your slaves, both men and women, and the best of your cattle and your donkeys he will take for his own use. He will take a tenth of your flocks, and you yourselves will become his slaves. There will come a day when you will cry out against the king whom you have chosen; but the Lord will not answer you on that day.'

The people, however, refused to listen to Samuel. 'No,' they said, 'we must have a king over us; then we shall be like other nations, with a king to rule us, to lead us out to war and fight our battles.' When Samuel heard what the people had decided, he told the Lord, who said, 'Take them at their word and appoint them a king.' Samuel then dismissed all the Israelites to their homes.

SAUL SEARCHES FOR HIS FATHER'S DONKEYS
1 Samuel 9:1 – 10:11, 13–16

There was a man from the territory of Benjamin, whose name was Kish son of Abiel, son of Zeror, son of Bechorath, son of Aphiah a

Benjamite. He was a man of substance, and had a son named Saul, a young man in his prime; there was no better man among the Israelites than he. He stood a head taller than any of the people.

One day some donkeys belonging to Saul's father Kish had strayed, so he said to his son Saul, 'Take one of the servants with you, and go and look for the donkeys.' They crossed the hill-country of Ephraim and went through the district of Shalisha but did not find them; they passed through the district of Shaalim but they were not there; they passed through the district of Benjamin but again did not find them. When they reached the district of Zuph, Saul said to the servant who was with him, 'Come, we ought to turn back, or my father will stop thinking about the donkeys and begin to worry about us.' The servant answered, 'There is a man of God in this town who has a great reputation, because everything he says comes true. Suppose we go there; he may tell us which way to take.' Saul said, 'If we go, what shall we offer him? There is no food left in our packs and we have no present to give the man of God, nothing at all.' The servant answered him again, 'Wait! I have here a quarter-shekel of silver. I can give that to the man, to tell us the way.' Saul said, 'Good! Let us go to him.' So they went to the town where the man of God lived. (In Israel in days gone by, when someone wished to consult God, he would say, 'Let us go to the seer.' For what is nowadays called a prophet used to be called a seer.)

As they were going up the ascent to the town they met some girls coming out to draw water and asked them, 'Shall we find the seer there?' 'Yes,' they answered, 'he is ahead of you; hurry now, for he has just arrived in the town because there is a feast at the shrine today. As you enter the town you will meet him before he goes up to the shrine to eat; the people will not start until he comes, for he has to bless the sacrifice before the invited company can eat. Go up now, and you will find him at once.' So they went up to the town and, just as they were going in, there was Samuel coming towards them on his way up to the shrine.

The day before Saul's arrival there, the Lord had disclosed his intention to Samuel: 'At this time tomorrow', he said, 'I shall send you a man from the territory of Benjamin, and you are to anoint him prince over my people Israel. He will deliver my people from the

Philistines; for I have seen the sufferings of my people, and their cry has reached my ears.' The moment Saul appeared the Lord said to Samuel, 'Here is the man of whom I spoke to you. This man will govern my people.' Saul came up to Samuel in the gateway and said, 'Tell me, please, where the seer lives.' Samuel replied, 'I am the seer. Go on ahead of me to the shrine and eat with me today; in the morning I shall set you on your way, after telling you what you have on your mind. Trouble yourself no more about the donkeys lost three days ago; they have been found. To whom does the tribute of all Israel belong? It belongs to you and to your whole ancestral house.' 'But I am a Benjamite,' said Saul, 'from the smallest of the tribes of Israel, and my family is the least important of all the families of the tribe of Benjamin. Why do you say this to me?'

Samuel brought Saul and his servant into the dining-hall and gave them a place at the head of the invited company, about thirty in number. He said to the cook, 'Bring the portion that I gave you and told you to put on one side.' The cook took up the whole haunch and leg and put it before Saul; and Samuel said, 'Here is the portion of meat kept for you. Eat it: it has been reserved for you at this feast to which I have invited the people.'

Saul dined with Samuel that day, and when they came down from the shrine to the town a bed was spread on the roof for Saul, and he stayed there that night. At dawn Samuel called to Saul on the roof, 'Get up, and I shall set you on your way.' When Saul rose, he and Samuel went outside together, and as they came to the edge of the town, Samuel said to Saul, 'Tell the boy to go on ahead.' He did so; then Samuel said, 'Stay here a moment, and I shall tell you what God has said.'

Samuel took a flask of oil and poured it over Saul's head; he kissed him and said, 'The Lord anoints you prince over his people Israel. You are to rule the people of the Lord and deliver them from the enemies round about. You will receive a sign that the Lord has anointed you prince to govern his possession: when you leave me today, you will meet two men by Rachel's tomb at Zelzah in the territory of Benjamin. They will tell you that the donkeys you set out to look for have been found and that your father is concerned for them no longer; he is anxious about you and keeps saying, "What shall I do about my son?" From there go across country as far as the terebinth of Tabor, where three men going up to Bethel to worship God will meet you. One of them will be carrying three young goats, the second three loaves, and the third a skin of wine. They will greet you and offer you two loaves, which you will accept. Then when you reach the hill of God, where the Philistine governor resides, you will meet a company of prophets coming down from the shrine, led by lute, drum, fife, and lyre, and filled with prophetic rapture. The spirit of the Lord will suddenly take possession of you, and you too will be rapt like a prophet and become another man. When these signs happen, do whatever the occasion demands; God will be with you. You are to go down to Gilgal ahead of me, and I shall come to you to sacrifice whole-offerings and shared-offerings. Wait seven days until I join you; then I shall tell you what to do.'

As Saul turned to leave Samuel, God made him a different person. On that same day all these signs happened. When they reached the hill there was a company of prophets coming to meet him, and the spirit of God suddenly took possession of him, so that he too was filled with prophetic rapture. When people who had known him previously saw that he was rapt like the prophets, they said to one another, 'What can have happened to the son of Kish? Is Saul also among the prophets?...' When the prophetic rapture had passed, he went home. Saul's uncle said to him and the boy, 'Where have you been?' Saul answered, 'To look for the donkeys, and when we could not find them, we went to Samuel.' His uncle said, 'Tell me what Samuel said.' 'He told us that the donkeys had been found,' replied Saul; but he did not repeat what Samuel had said about his being king.

SAUL BECOMES KING
1 Samuel 10:17 – 12:1, 14–15, 23–25

Samuel summoned the Israelites to the Lord at Mizpah and said to them, 'This is the word of the Lord the God of Israel: I brought Israel up from Egypt; I delivered you from the Egyptians and from all the kingdoms that oppressed you. But today you have rejected your God who saved you from all your misery and distress; you have said, "No, set a king over us." Therefore take up your positions now before the Lord tribe by tribe and clan by clan.'

Samuel presented all the tribes of Israel, and Benjamin was picked by lot. Then he presented the tribe of Benjamin, family by family, and the family of Matri was picked. He presented the family of Matri, man by man, and Saul son of Kish was picked; but when search was made he was not to be found. They went on to ask the Lord, 'Will the man be coming?' The Lord answered, 'There he is, hiding among the baggage.' So some ran and fetched him out, and as he took his stand among the people, he was a head taller than anyone else. Samuel said to the people, 'Look at the man whom the Lord has chosen; there is no one like him in this whole nation.' They all acclaimed him, shouting, 'Long live the king!'

Samuel explained to the people the nature of a king, and made a written record of it on a scroll which he deposited before the Lord. He then dismissed them to their homes. Saul too went home to Gibeah, and with him went some fighting men whose hearts God had moved. But there were scoundrels who said, 'How can this fellow deliver us?' They thought nothing of him and brought him no gifts.

About a month later Nahash the Ammonite attacked and besieged Jabesh-gilead. The men of Jabesh said to Nahash, 'Grant us terms and we will be your subjects.' Nahash answered, 'On one condition only shall I grant you terms: that I gouge out the right eye of every one of you and bring disgrace on all Israel.' The elders of Jabesh-gilead said, 'Give us seven days' respite to send messengers throughout Israel and then, if no one relieves us, we shall surrender to you.' The messengers came to Gibeah, where Saul lived, and delivered their message, and all the people broke into lamentation and weeping. Saul was just coming from the field, driving in the oxen, and asked why the people were lamenting; and they told him what the men of Jabesh had said. When Saul heard this, the spirit of God suddenly seized him; in anger he took a pair of oxen, cut them in pieces, and sent messengers with the pieces all through Israel to proclaim that the same would be done to the oxen of any man who did not follow Saul and Samuel to battle. The fear of the Lord fell upon the people and they came out to a man. Saul mustered them in

Bezek, three hundred thousand men from Israel and thirty thousand from Judah. He said to the messengers, 'Tell the men of Jabesh-gilead, "Victory will be yours tomorrow by the time the sun is hot."'

When they received this message, the men of Jabesh took heart; but they said to Nahash, 'Tomorrow we shall surrender to you, and then you may deal with us as you think fit.' Next day Saul with his men in three columns forced a way right into the enemy camp during the morning watch and massacred the Ammonites until the day grew hot; those who survived were scattered until no two of them were left together.

The people said to Samuel, 'Who said that Saul should not reign over us? Hand the men over to us to be put to death.' But Saul said, 'No man is to be put to death on a day when the Lord has won such a victory in Israel.' Samuel said to the people, 'Let us now go to Gilgal and there establish the kingship anew.' So they all went to Gilgal and invested Saul there as king in the presence of the Lord. They sacrificed shared-offerings before the Lord, and Saul and all the Israelites celebrated with great joy.

Samuel thus addressed the assembled Israelites: 'I have listened to your request and installed a king to rule over you...

'If you will revere the Lord and give true and loyal service, if you do not rebel against his commands, and if you and the king who reigns over you are faithful to the Lord your God, well and good; but if you do not obey the Lord, and if you rebel against his commands, then his hand will be against you and against your king...

'As for me, God forbid that I should sin against the Lord by ceasing to pray for you. I shall show you what is right and good: to revere the Lord and worship him faithfully with all your heart; for consider what great things he has done for you. But if you persist in wickedness, both you and your king will be swept away.'

JONATHAN WINS A VICTORY OVER THE PHILISTINES
1 Samuel 13:1 – 14:46

Saul was thirty years old when he became king, and he reigned over Israel for twenty-two years.

Saul picked three thousand men from Israel, two thousand to be with him in Michmash and the hill-country of Bethel and a thousand to be with Jonathan in Gibeah of Benjamin; the rest of the army he dismissed to their homes.

Jonathan defeated the Philistine garrison in Geba, and the news spread among the Philistines that the Hebrews were in revolt. Saul sounded the trumpet all through the land; and when the Israelites heard that Saul had defeated a Philistine garrison and that the very name of Israel was offensive among the Philistines, they answered the call to arms and rallied to Saul at Gilgal.

The Philistines mustered to attack Israel; they had thirty thousand chariots and six thousand horse, with infantry as countless as sand on the seashore. They went up and camped at Michmash, to the east of Beth-aven. The Israelites found themselves in sore straits, for the army was hard pressed, so they hid themselves in caves and holes and among the rocks, in pits and cisterns. Some of them crossed the Jordan into the district of Gad and Gilead, but Saul remained at Gilgal, and all his followers were in a state of alarm. He waited seven days for his meeting with Samuel, but Samuel failed to appear, and when the people began to drift away, Saul said, 'Bring me the whole-offering and the shared-offerings,' and he offered up the whole-offering. Saul had just finished the sacrifice, when Samuel arrived, and he went out to greet him. Samuel said, 'What have you done?' Saul answered, 'I saw that the people were drifting away from me, and you yourself had not come at the time fixed, and the Philistines were mustering at Michmash; and I thought, "The Philistines will now fall on me at Gilgal, and I have not ensured the Lord's favour"; so I felt compelled to make the whole-offering myself.' Samuel said to Saul, 'You have acted foolishly! You have not kept the command laid on you by the Lord your God; if you had, he would have established your dynasty over Israel for all time. But now your line will not endure; the Lord will seek out a man after his own heart, and appoint him prince over his people, because you have not kept the Lord's command.

Without more ado Samuel left Gilgal and went on his way. The rest of the people followed Saul, as he moved from Gilgal towards the enemy. At Gibeah of Benjamin he mustered his followers; they were about six hundred men. Saul, his son Jonathan, and their men took up their quarters in Gibeah of Benjamin, while the Philistines were encamped in Michmash. Raiding parties went out from the Philistine camp in three directions. One party headed towards Ophrah in the district of Shual, another towards Beth-horon, and the third towards the range of hills overlooking the valley of Zeboim and the wilderness beyond.

No blacksmith was to be found in the whole of Israel, for the Philistines were determined to prevent the Hebrews from making swords and spears. The Israelites had all to go down to the Philistines for their ploughshares, mattocks, axes, and sickles to be sharpened. The charge was two thirds of a shekel for ploughshares and mattocks, and one third of a shekel for sharpening the axes and pointing the goads. So when war broke out the followers of Saul and Jonathan had neither sword nor spear; only Saul and Jonathan carried arms.

The Philistines had posted a company of troops to hold the pass of Michmash, and one day Saul's son Jonathan said to his armour-bearer, 'Come, let us go over to the Philistine outpost across there.' He did not tell his father, who at the time had his tent under the pomegranate tree at Migron on the outskirts of Gibeah; with him were about six hundred men. The ephod was carried by Ahijah son of Ahitub, Ichabod's brother, son of Phinehas son of Eli, the priest of the Lord at Shiloh. Nobody knew that Jonathan had gone. On either side of the pass through which Jonathan sought to make his way to the Philistine post stood two sharp columns of rock, called Bozez and Seneh; one of them was on the north towards Michmash, and the other on the south towards Geba. Jonathan said to his armour-bearer, 'Let us go and pay a visit to the post of the uncircumcised yonder. Perhaps the Lord will do something for us. Nothing can stop him from winning a victory, by many or by few.' The armour-bearer answered, 'Do what you will, go ahead; I am with you whatever you do.' Jonathan said, 'We shall cross over and let the men see us. If they say, "Stay there till we come to you," then we shall stay where we are and not go up to them. But if they say, "Come up to us," we shall go up; that will be the proof that the Lord has given them into our power.' The two showed themselves to the Philistine outpost. 'Look!' said the Philistines. 'Hebrews coming out of the holes where they have been hiding!' And they called across to Jonathan and his armour-bearer, 'Come up to us; we shall show you something.' Jonathan said to the armour-bearer, 'Come on, the Lord has put them into Israel's power.' Jonathan climbed up on hands and feet, and the armour-bearer followed him. The Philistines fell before Jonathan, and the armour-bearer, coming behind, dispatched them. In that first attack Jonathan and his armour-bearer killed about twenty of them, like men cutting a furrow across a half-acre field. Terror spread throughout the army in the camp and in the field; the men at the post and the raiding parties were terrified. The very ground quaked, and there was great panic.

Saul's men on the watch in Gibeah of Benjamin saw the mob of Philistines surging to and fro in confusion. Saul ordered his forces to call the roll to find out who was missing and, when it was called, they found that Jonathan and his armour-bearer were absent. Saul said to Ahijah, 'Bring forward the ephod,' for it was he who at that time carried the ephod before Israel. While Saul was speaking, the confusion in the Philistine camp kept increasing, and he said to the priest, 'Hold your hand.' Then Saul and all his men made a concerted rush for the battlefield, where they found the enemy in complete disorder, every man's sword against his fellow. Those Hebrews who up to now had been under the Philistines, and had been with them in camp, changed sides and joined the Israelites under Saul and Jonathan. When all the Israelites in hiding in the hill-country of Ephraim heard that the Philistines were in flight, they also joined in and set off in close pursuit. That day the Lord delivered Israel, and the fighting passed on beyond Beth-aven.

The Israelites had been driven to exhaustion on that day. Saul had issued this warning to the troops: 'A curse on any man who takes food before nightfall and before I have taken vengeance on my enemies.' So no one tasted any food. There was honeycomb in the countryside; but when his men came upon it, dripping with honey though it was, not one of them put his hand to his mouth for fear of the curse. Jonathan, however, had not heard his father's interdict to the army, and he stretched out the stick that was in his hand, dipped the end of it in the honeycomb, put it to his mouth, and was refreshed. One of the people said to him, 'Your father strictly forbade this, saying, "A curse on the man who eats food today!" And the men are faint.' Jonathan said, 'My father has done the people great harm; see how I am refreshed by this mere taste of honey. How much better if the army had eaten today whatever they took from their enemies by way of spoil! Then there would indeed have been a great slaughter of Philistines.'

Israel defeated the Philistines that day, and pursued them from Michmash to Aijalon. But the troops were so faint with hunger that they turned to plunder and seized sheep, cattle, and calves; they slaughtered them on the bare ground, and ate the meat with the blood in it. Someone told Saul that the people were sinning against the Lord by eating meat with the blood in it. 'This is treacherous behaviour!' cried Saul. 'Roll a great stone here at once.' He then said, 'Go about among the troops and tell them to bring their oxen and sheep, and to slaughter and eat them here; and so they will not sin against the Lord by eating meat with the blood in it.' So as night fell each man came, driving his own ox, and slaughtered it there. Thus Saul came to erect an altar to the Lord, and this was the first altar to the Lord that he erected.

Saul said, 'Let us go down and make a night attack on the Philistines and harry them till daylight; we will not spare a single one of them.' His men answered, 'Do what you think best,' but the priest said, 'Let us first consult God.' Saul enquired of God, 'Shall I pursue the Philistines? Will you put them into Israel's power?' But this time he received no answer. So he said, 'Let all the leaders of the people come forward and let us find out where the sin lies this day. As the Lord, the deliverer of Israel, lives, even if the sin lies in my son Jonathan, he shall die.' Not a soul answered him. Then he said to the Israelites, 'All of you stand on one side, and I and my son Jonathan will stand on the other.' His men answered, 'Do what you think best.' Saul said to the Lord the God of Israel, 'Why have you not answered your servant today? Lord God of Israel, if this guilt lies in me or in my son Jonathan, let the lot be Urim; if it lies in your people Israel, let it be Thummim.' Jonathan and Saul were taken, and the people were cleared. Then Saul said, 'Cast lots between me and my son Jonathan'; and Jonathan was taken.

Saul said to Jonathan, 'Tell me what you have done.' Jonathan told him, 'True, I did taste a little honey on the tip of my stick. Here

I am; I am ready to die.' Then Saul swore a solemn oath that Jonathan should die. But his men said to Saul, 'Shall Jonathan die, Jonathan who has won this great victory in Israel? God forbid! As the Lord lives, not a hair of his head shall fall to the ground, for he has been at work with God today.' So the army delivered Jonathan and he did not die. Saul broke off the pursuit of the Philistines, who then made their way home.

SAUL IS REJECTED AS KING
1 Samuel 15

Samuel said to Saul, 'The Lord sent me to anoint you king over his people Israel. Now listen to the voice of the Lord: this is the very word of the Lord of Hosts: I shall punish the Amalekites for what they did to Israel, when they opposed them on their way up from Egypt. Go now, fall upon the Amalekites, destroy them, and put their property under ban. Spare no one; put them all to death, men and women, children and babes in arms, herds and flocks, camels and donkeys.'

Saul called out the levy and reviewed them at Telaim: there were two hundred thousand foot-soldiers and another ten thousand from Judah. When he reached the city of Amalek, he halted for a time in the valley. Meanwhile he sent word to the Kenites to leave the Amalekites and come down, 'or', he said, 'I shall destroy you as well as them; but you were friendly to Israel as they came up from Egypt'. So the Kenites left the Amalekites.

Saul inflicted defeat on the Amalekites all the way from Havilah to Shur on the borders of Egypt. Agag king of the Amalekites he took alive, but he destroyed all the people, putting them to the sword. Saul and his army spared Agag and the best of the sheep and cattle, the fat beasts and the lambs, and everything worth keeping; these they were unwilling to destroy, but anything that was useless and of no value they destroyed.

The word of the Lord came to Samuel: 'I repent of having made Saul king, for he has turned away from me and has not obeyed my instructions.' Samuel was angry; all night long he cried aloud to the Lord. Early next morning he went to meet Saul, but was told that he had gone to Carmel, for he had set up a monument to himself there, and then had turned and gone on down to Gilgal. There Samuel found him, and Saul greeted him with the words, 'The Lord's blessing on you! I have carried out the Lord's instructions.' 'What then is this bleating of sheep in my ears?' demanded Samuel. 'How do I come to hear the lowing of cattle?' Saul answered, 'The troops have taken them from the Amalekites. These are what they spared, the best of the sheep and cattle, to sacrifice to the Lord your God; the rest we completely destroyed.' Samuel said to Saul, 'Be quiet! Let me tell you what the Lord said to me last night.' 'Tell me,' said Saul. So Samuel went on, 'Once you thought little of yourself, but now you are head of the tribes of Israel. The Lord, who anointed you king over Israel, charged you with the destruction of that wicked nation, the Amalekites; you were to go and wage war against them until you had wiped them out. Why then did you not obey the Lord? Why did you swoop on the spoil, so doing what was wrong in the eyes of the Lord?' Saul answered, 'But I did obey the Lord; I went where the Lord sent me, and I have brought back Agag king of the Amalekites. The rest of them I destroyed. Out of the spoil the troops took sheep and oxen, the choicest of the animals laid under ban, to sacrifice to the Lord your God at Gilgal.' Samuel then said:

> 'Does the Lord desire whole-offerings and sacrifices
> as he desires obedience?
> To obey is better than sacrifice,
> and to listen to him better than the fat of rams.
> Rebellion is as sinful as witchcraft,
> arrogance as evil as idolatry.
> Because you have rejected the word of the Lord,
> he has rejected you as king.'

Saul said to Samuel, 'I have sinned. I have not complied with the Lord's command or with your instructions: I was afraid of the troops and gave in to them. But now forgive my sin, I implore you, and come back with me, and I shall bow in worship before the Lord.' Samuel answered, 'I shall not come back with you; you have rejected the word of the Lord and therefore the Lord has rejected you as king over Israel.' As he turned to go, Saul caught the corner of his cloak and it tore. And Samuel said to him, 'The Lord has torn the kingdom of Israel from your hand today and will give it to another, a better man than you. God who is the Splendour of Israel does not deceive, nor does he change his mind, as a mortal might do.' Saul pleaded, 'I have sinned; but honour me this once before the elders of my people and before Israel and come back with me, and I will bow in worship before the Lord your God.' Samuel went back with Saul, and Saul worshipped the Lord.

Samuel said, 'Bring Agag king of the Amalekites.' So Agag came to him with faltering step and said, 'Surely the bitterness of death has passed.' Samuel said,

'As your sword has made women childless,
so your mother will be childless among women.'

Then Samuel hewed Agag in pieces before the Lord at Gilgal.

Saul went to his own home at Gibeah, and Samuel went to Ramah; and he never saw Saul again to his dying day, but he grieved for him, because the Lord had repented of having made him king over Israel.

Index of Primary Sources